SASKATCHEWAN
BIRDS

LONE
PINE

Alan Smith
with contributions from
Eloise Pulos,
Andy Bezener and Chris Fisher

© 2001 by Lone Pine Publishing
First printed in 2001   10 9 8 7 6 5
Printed in China

The Publisher: Lone Pine Publishing
10145 – 81 Avenue
Edmonton, AB   T6E 1W9
Canada

Website: http://www.lonepinepublishing.com

National Library of Canada Cataloguing in Publication Data

Smith, Alan R.
    Saskatchewan birds

    Includes bibliographical references.
    ISBN-13: 978-1-55105-304-2
    ISBN-10: 1-55105-304-7

    1. Birds—Saskatchewan—Identification. 2. Bird watching—Saskatchewan. I. Pulos, Eloise. II. Title.
    QL685.5.S2S64 2001   598'.097124   C2001-910143-0

Editorial Director: Nancy Foulds
Project Editor: Genevieve Boyer
Editorial: Genevieve Boyer, Eloise Pulos, Roland Lines
Production Manager: Jody Reekie
Layout & Production: Monica Triska
Book Design: Robert Weidemann
Cover Design: Robert Weidemann
Cover Illustration: Great Blue Heron, by Gary Ross
Illustrations: Gary Ross, Ted Nordhagen, Ewa Pluciennik
Maps: Robert Weidemann, Arlana Anderson-Hale, Ian Dawe, Elliot Engley
Separations & Film: Elite Lithographers Co., Edmonton, Alberta

We acknowledge the financial support of the Government of Canada through the Book Publishing Industry Development Program (BPIDP) for our publishing activities.

PC: P13

CONTENTS

ACKNOWLEDGEMENTS

Many thanks go to Gary Ross and Ted Nordhagen, whose skilled illustrations have brought each page to life. John Acorn and Chris Fisher provided much of the initial text for this book by way of their book, *Birds of Alberta*. Eloise Pulos and Andy Bezener also added their own magic to the text. Thanks are extended to the growing family of ornithologists and dedicated birders who have offered their inspiration and expertise to help build Lone Pine's expanding library of field guides. Finally, thanks go to Randi Edmonds, Nick and Lila Pulos and Jay Gedir for their support.

DIVING BIRDS

Common Loon
size 80 cm • p. 20

Pied-billed Grebe
size 34 cm • p. 21

Horned Grebe
size 35 cm • p. 22

Red-necked Grebe
size 50 cm • p. 23

American White Pelican
size 160 cm • p. 24

Double-crested Cormorant
size 74 cm • p. 25

HERON-LIKE BIRDS

American Bittern
size 64 cm • p. 26

Great Blue Heron
size 135 cm • p. 27

Black-crowned
Night-Heron
size 62 cm • p. 28

Turkey Vulture
size 74 cm • p. 29

WATERFOWL

Snow Goose
size 78 cm • p. 30

Canada Goose
size 89 cm • p. 31

Tundra Swan
size 135 cm • p. 32

Gadwall
size 51 cm • p. 33

American Wigeon
size 52 cm • p. 34

Mallard
size 60 cm • p. 35

Blue-winged Teal
size 38 cm • p. 36

Northern Shoveler
size 49 cm • p. 37

Northern Pintail
size 62 cm • p. 38

Canvasback
size 54 cm • p. 39

Lesser Scaup
size 42 cm • p. 40

Bufflehead
size 37 cm • p. 41

Common Goldeneye
size 46 cm • p. 42

Common Merganser
size 63 cm • p. 43

Ruddy Duck
size 40 cm • p. 44

BIRDS OF PREY

Osprey
size 60 cm • p. 45

Bald Eagle
size 98 cm • p. 46

Northern Harrier
size 51 cm • p. 47

Sharp-shinned Hawk
size 31 cm • p. 48

Northern Goshawk
size 58 cm • p. 49

Swainson's Hawk
size 50 cm • p. 50

Red-tailed Hawk
size 55 cm • p. 51

Ferruginous Hawk
size 63 cm • p. 52

American Kestrel
size 27 cm • p. 53

Merlin
size 28 cm • p. 54

Peregrine Falcon
size 43 cm • p. 55

GROUSE-LIKE BIRDS

Gray Partridge
size 32 cm • p. 56

Ruffed Grouse
size 43 cm • p. 57

Spruce Grouse
size 41 cm • p. 58

Sharp-tailed Grouse
size 45 cm • p. 59

RAILS, COOTS & CRANES

Sora
size 23 cm • p. 60

American Coot
size 37 cm • p. 61

Sandhill Crane
size 103 cm • p. 62

Whooping Crane
size 140 cm • p. 63

SHOREBIRDS

Black-bellied Plover
size 30 cm • p. 64

Piping Plover
size 18 cm • p. 65

Killdeer
size 25 cm • p. 66

American Avocet
size 45 cm • p. 67

Lesser Yellowlegs
size 26 cm • p. 68

Willet
size 34 cm • p. 69

Spotted Sandpiper
size 19 cm • p. 70

Long-billed Curlew
size 59 cm • p. 71

SHOREBIRDS

Marbled Godwit
size 46 cm • p. 72

Semipalmated Sandpiper
size 16 cm • p. 73

Common Snipe
size 28 cm • p. 74

Wilson's Phalarope
size 23 cm • p. 75

GULLS & ALLIES

Franklin's Gull
size 36 cm • p. 76

Ring-billed Gull
size 48 cm • p. 77

Common Tern
size 37 cm • p. 78

Black Tern
size 24 cm • p. 79

DOVES & CUCKOOS

Rock Dove
size 35 cm • p. 80

Mourning Dove
size 31 cm • p. 81

Black-billed Cuckoo
size 30 cm • p. 82

OWLS

Great Horned Owl
size 55 cm • p. 83

Snowy Owl
size 60 cm • p. 84

Burrowing Owl
size 26 cm • p. 85

NIGHTJARS, HUMMINGBIRDS & KINGFISHERS

Short-eared Owl
size 38 cm • p. 86

Common Nighthawk
size 24 cm • p. 87

Ruby-throated Hummingbird
size 9 cm • p. 88

WOODPECKERS

Belted Kingfisher
size 32 cm • p. 89

Yellow-bellied Sapsucker
size 22 cm • p. 90

Downy Woodpecker
size 17 cm • p. 91

Three-toed Woodpecker
size 23 cm • p. 92

Northern Flicker
size 33 cm • p. 93

Pileated Woodpecker
size 45 cm • p. 94

FLYCATCHERS

Least Flycatcher
size 14 cm • p. 95

Eastern Phoebe
size 18 cm • p. 96

Western Kingbird
size 22 cm • p. 97

Eastern Kingbird
size 22 cm • p. 98

SHRIKES & VIREOS

Loggerhead Shrike
size 23 cm • p. 99

Red-eyed Vireo
size 15 cm • p. 100

Gray Jay
size 29 cm • p. 101

Blue Jay
size 30 cm • p. 102

JAYS & CROWS

Black-billed Magpie
size 51 cm • p. 103

American Crow
size 48 cm • p. 104

Common Raven
size 61 cm • p. 105

LARKS & SWALLOWS

Horned Lark
size 18 cm • p. 106

Purple Martin
size 19 cm • p. 107

Tree Swallow
size 14 cm • p. 108

Bank Swallow
size 13 cm • p. 109

Barn Swallow
size 18 cm • p. 110

Black-capped Chickadee
size 14 cm • p. 111

Red-breasted Nuthatch
size 11 cm • p. 112

Brown Creeper
size 13 cm • p. 113

CHICKADEES, NUTHATCHES & WRENS

House Wren
size 12 cm • p. 114

Marsh Wren
size 13 cm • p. 115

Ruby-crowned Kinglet
size 10 cm • p. 116

KINGLETS, BLUEBIRDS & THRUSHES

Mountain Bluebird
size 18 cm • p. 117

Swainson's Thrush
size 18 cm • p. 118

American Robin
size 25 cm • p. 119

Gray Catbird
size 22 cm • p. 120

Brown Thrasher
size 29 cm • p. 121

European Starling
size 22 cm • p. 122

Sprague's Pipit
size 17 cm • p. 123

Bohemian Waxwing
size 18 cm • p. 124

Tennessee Warbler
size 12 cm • p. 125

Orange-crowned Warbler
size 13 cm • p. 126

Yellow Warbler
size 13 cm • p. 127

Magnolia Warbler
size 13 cm • p. 128

Yellow-rumped Warbler
size 14 cm • p. 129

Palm Warbler
size 13 cm • p. 130

Blackpoll Warbler
size 14 cm • p. 131

American Redstart
size 13 cm • p. 132

Ovenbird
size 15 cm • p. 133

Northern Waterthrush
size 14 cm • p. 134

Mourning Warbler
size 14 cm • p. 135

Common Yellowthroat
size 13 cm • p. 136

Western Tanager
size 18 cm • p. 137

Spotted Towhee
size 20 cm • p. 138

Chipping Sparrow
size 14 cm • p. 139

Clay-colored Sparrow
size 14 cm • p. 140

Vesper Sparrow
size 16 cm • p. 141

Lark Bunting
size 18 cm • p. 142

Savannah Sparrow
size 14 cm • p. 143

Song Sparrow
size 16 cm • p. 144

White-throated Sparrow
size 18 cm • p. 145

SPARROWS, GROSBEAKS & BUNTINGS

Dark-eyed Junco
size 16 cm • p. 146

Lapland Longspur
size 16 cm • p. 147

Snow Bunting
size 17 cm • p. 148

Rose-breasted Grosbeak
size 20 cm • p. 149

BLACKBIRDS & ORIOLES

Red-winged Blackbird
size 21 cm • p. 150

Western Meadowlark
size 24 cm • p. 151

Yellow-headed Blackbird
size 24 cm • p. 152

Brewer's Blackbird
size 23 cm • p. 153

Common Grackle
size 31 cm • p. 154

Brown-headed Cowbird
size 17 cm • p. 155

Baltimore Oriole
size 19 cm • p. 156

FINCH-LIKE BIRDS

Pine Grosbeak
size 23 cm • p. 157

Purple Finch
size 14 cm • p. 158

White-winged Crossbill
size 16 cm • p. 159

Common Redpoll
size 13 cm • p. 160

Pine Siskin
size 12 cm • p. 161

American Goldfinch
size 13 cm • p. 162

Evening Grosbeak
size 20 cm • p. 163

House Sparrow
size 16 cm • p. 164

INTRODUCTION

In recent decades, birding has evolved from an eccentric pursuit practised by a few dedicated individuals to a continent-wide phenomenon that boasts millions of professional and amateur participants. There are many reasons why birding has become such a popular activity. Many find it simple and relaxing, while others enjoy the outdoor exercise it affords. Some see it as a rewarding learning experience, an opportunity to socialize with like-minded people or a way to monitor the health of the local environment.

Whether you are just beginning to take an interest in birds or have already learned to identify many species, this field guide has something for you. We've selected 145 of the province's most abundant or noteworthy birds. Some live in specialized habitats, but most are common species that you have a good chance of encountering on most outings or in your back yard.

Tree Swallow

BIRDING IN SASKATCHEWAN

Whether you are looking out your back window or walking a secluded trail, you will find that there are always birds close by. Some species, such as jays, chickadees and finches, are year-round neighbours. Many others visit Saskatchewan only in spring and summer when they take advantage of the abundance of food to raise their young. Included in this category are many waterbirds and songbirds. Other birds pass through Saskatchewan only briefly each spring and autumn on their way north to nesting grounds or south to wintering locales. Many of our shorebirds fall into this group. It is difficult to believe that Saskatchewan's sometimes harsh winters would be inviting to any bird, but a few species, such as the Snowy Owl, are visitors to our province only in winter.

Some of the birds featured in this book are so common and familiar that you will probably encounter them on a regular basis. Others are more shy and secretive or are restricted to certain habitats, so seeing them may be a noteworthy event. Likewise, some species are easily identified. If, for example, you see a Blue Jay, you are not likely to confuse it with any other bird. Sandpipers, on the other hand, and many songbirds and raptors, can be more challenging to properly identify.

Saskatchewan has a long tradition of friendly, recreational birding. In general, Saskatchewan birders are willing to help beginners, share their knowledge and involve novices in their projects. Christmas bird counts, Project Feeder Watch, the Breeding Bird Survey, the Prairie Nest Records Scheme, nest box programs, migration monitoring studies, and birding lectures and workshops all provide an opportunity for birders of all levels to interact and share their appreciation for birds. So, whatever your level of knowledge, there is ample opportunity for you to learn more and get involved.

Whooping Crane

For further information about participation in these and other projects, contact the Canadian Wildlife Service by phone at (306) 975-4087 or by mail at 115 Perimeter Road, Saskatoon, SK S7N 0X4.

SASKATCHEWAN'S TOP BIRDING SITES

Saskatchewan is as diverse as it is large, from the relatively untouched, subarctic forests with a dense network of lakes and rivers, to the lusher central boreal forests with rich flora and fauna to the arid southern prairie with scattered saline wetlands. Because of this diversity, it has a lot to offer bird species (and humans!). In fact, the boreal plain ecoregion of Saskatchewan, Alberta and Manitoba has the distinction of having Canada's most extensive assemblage of breeding birds.

There are hundreds of good birding areas throughout the province. The following areas have been selected to represent a broad range of bird communities and habitats, with an emphasis on diversity and accessibility.

Northern Pintail

Boreal Shield
1. Lac La Ronge PP

Boreal Plain
2. Besnard Lake
3. Candle Lake PP
4. Clarence-Steepbank Lakes PP
5. Duck Mountain PP
6. Greenwater Lake PP
7. Hudson Bay
8. Makwa Lake PP
9. Meadow Lake PP
10. Narrow Hills PP
11. Nisbet PF
12. Prince Albert NP
13. Tobin Lake

Prairie
14. Blackstrap Reservoir/PP
15. Buffalo Pound PP and Nicolle Flats
16. Buffer Lake
17. Chaplin Lake/Marsh
18. Crooked Lake PP
19. Cypress Hills PP
20. Danielson PP and Gardiner Dam
21. Douglas PP
22. Eastend
23. Echo Valley PP
24. Estevan
25. Foam Lake Marsh
26. Good Spirit Lake PP
27. Grasslands NP
28. Katepwa Point PP
29. Kindersley
30. Last Mountain Lake NWA
31. Leader
32. Luck Lake
33. Maple Creek
34. Moose Mountain PP
35. Pike Lake PP
36. Ponass Lake
37. Quill Lakes
38. Radisson Lake
39. Redberry Lake
40. Regina Beach
41. Saskatchewan Landing PP

NWA = National Wildlife Area
NP = National Park
PF = Provincial Forest
PP = Provincial Park

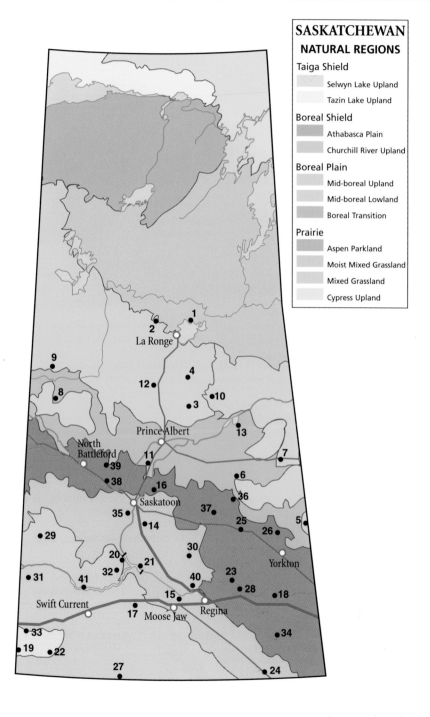

SASTATCHEWAN
NATURAL REGIONS

Taiga Shield
- Selwyn Lake Upland
- Tazin Lake Upland

Boreal Shield
- Athabasca Plain
- Churchill River Upland

Boreal Plain
- Mid-boreal Upland
- Mid-boreal Lowland
- Boreal Transition

Prairie
- Aspen Parkland
- Moist Mixed Grassland
- Mixed Grassland
- Cypress Upland

13

INTERESTING INTERPRETIVE CENTRES AND SANCTUARIES

Here are just a few of the interpretive centres and wildlife sanctuaries in Saskatchewan that can offer valuable insight into the lives of birds. A number are open year-round and many, but not all, offer free admission—we suggest you call in advance to check.

Beaver Creek Conservation Area (Saskatoon): interpretive centre; self-guided trails. Ph: (306) 374-2474.

Burrowing Owl Interpretive Centre (Moose Jaw Exhibition Park): offers insight into the ecology of one of Saskatchewan's endangered species. Ph: (306) 692-1765 or (306) 692-2723.

Chaplin Interpretive Centre (Chaplin): supports over 30 species of shorebirds; viewing towers; tourist information. Ph: 1-800-720-0060 or (306) 395-2223.

Greville Jones Wildlife Sanctuary (Tisdale): self-guided nature trails; bird and waterfowl observation site. Ph: (306) 873-5836.

Burrowing Owl

Last Mountain Interpretive Centre (Last Mountain National Wildife Area): interpretive kiosk; self guided auto tour and nature trails; observation tower. Ph: (306) 836-2022.

Last Mountain Bird Observatory (Last Mountain Regional Park): the only bird observatory in Saskatchewan; good birding site; bird-banding; visitors and volunteers welcome. Ph: (306) 975-4091.

Nicolle Flats Interpretive Area (Buffalo Pound Provincial Park): boardwalk through marsh; walking trails; interpretive services. Ph: (306) 693-2678 or (306) 694-3659.

Quill Lakes Interpretive Centre (Wynyard): interpretive services; ecotour referral service. Ph: (306) 554-3661.

Royal Saskatchewan Museum (Regina): Life Sciences Gallery features an extensive collection of Saskatchewan species. Ph: (306) 787-2815 or (306) 787-2810.

Silver Lake Viewing Site (near Maidstone): Ducks Unlimited site; viewing tower and walking trail. Ph: (306) 893-2831.

Wadena Wildlife Wetlands (Quill lakes area): hosts the "Shorebirds and Friends Festival" the last weekend in May; supports breeding American White Pelicans and endangered Piping Plovers in summer; hiking trails; observation towers; interpretive signs. Ph: (306) 338-3677.

American White Pelican

Wascana Waterfowl Park (Regina): waterfowl ponds with species identification displays. Ph: (306) 522-3661.

SASKATCHEWAN'S ECOLOGICAL REGIONS

Each bird species has special conditions under which it thrives, and it is under these conditions, and thus in these habitats, that you are most likely to find it. The more you get to know Saskatchewan's birds, the better you will understand why you can expect to find a certain species in one part of the province and not another. You will notice that some species, like the Sprague's Pipit, are quite "picky" and have very specific habitat requirements— such species are known as "habitat specialists." Other species, such as the Black-billed Magpie, are known as "habitat generalists" because they are more adaptable and can be found in a wide range of habitats.

Black-billed Magpie

Whatever the bird, you will find that a general knowl- edge of Saskatchewan's natural habitat types is invaluable when it comes to birding. Canada has been classified into sev- eral ecozones based on habitat types. According to this classification system, Saskatchewan is composed of four ecozones: taiga shield, boreal shield, boreal plain and prairie. These ecozones are subdivided into ecoregions, which can be divided further into ecodistricts, but only the ecozones are discussed in detail here. If you are interested in learning more about the natural regions of our province, Acton *et al* 1998 goes into greater detail.

Lesser Yellowlegs

Taiga Shield Ecozone

This ecozone represents the transi- tion between arctic tundra and boreal forest. If you ever get the opportunity to fly over this part of the province, you will notice that it is densely dotted with lakes that run parallel along a northeast to southwest axis—a product of the glaciation of Saskatchewan. Vegetation is limited to species that can tolerate harsh winter temperatures and a short growing season. The predominant forest type is classified as "lichen woodland" and is typified by open- canopy black spruce stands carpeted with lichen. Bogs and fens are found in lowland areas.

Only 0.1% of Saskatchewan's population is found in this ecozone, and mining is the only major economic activity. As a result, wildife habitat is less fragmented in this ecozone than in other areas of Saskatchewan, but there are no parks or other protected areas.

As a consequence of the low diversity of vegetation and the difficult living conditions, the diversity of wildlife in this ecozone is low. Approximately 120 bird species have been recorded in this part of Saskatchewan. Bohemian Waxwings, Dark-eyed Juncos and Lesser Yellowlegs are a few of the birds that come here to nest. Other birds, such as the Gray Jay and Common Redpoll, are year-round residents.

Common Redpoll

Boreal Shield Ecozone

The boreal shield ecozone covers approximately one third of Saskatchewan and is associated with the Precambrian Shield. It is composed of broad, rolling, rough-surfaced uplands and lowlands. Like in the taiga shield ecozone, the dominant tree species is black spruce, but forests in this ecozone are often closed (with the crowns of the trees touching) and the ground is usually carpeted with feather mosses. Upland forests often include fire-adapted jack pine, while moister, lowland forests include tamarack. Lakes and rivers are common and, as in the taiga shield ecozone, are arranged along a northeast to southwest axis. More diverse forest stands may be found around these waterbodies. Wetland areas are also common, usually in the form of bogs or, less frequently, fens. This ecozone also includes the Athabasca sand dunes on the southern shore of Lake Athabasca, which contains plant species that cannot be found anywhere else in the world.

Northern Goshawk

Less than 1% of Saskatchewan's population lives here but only 3% of the land in this ecozone is protected in parks, such as Lac La Ronge Provincial Park. The main economic activities are mining and forestry.

The diversity of bird species in this ecozone is considered moderately low, with around 220 species reported to occur. Some permanent residents include the Three-toed Woodpecker, Common Raven, White-winged Crossbill and Northern Goshawk. The greatest diversity of bird species occurs in the summer, when the forest is alive with the sounds of Swainson's Thrushes, Palm Warblers, Northern Waterthrushes, Pine Siskins and other birds. Wetlands are also productive areas and are home to many nesting waterbirds, such as Common Loons, Mallards and Common Terns.

Pine Siskin

Boreal Plain Ecozone

Occupying approximately one quarter of the province, the boreal plain ecozone lies between the southern edge of the Precambrian Shield and the aspen parkland ecoregion of the prairie ecozone. The vegetation in this part of Saskatchewan is diverse, owing to a relatively warm and humid climate. Closed-crown coniferous and mixed forests are characteristic, with the predominant coniferous species being white and black spruce, jack pine and tamarack, and the predominant deciduous species being aspen, white birch and balsam poplar. Lakes and rivers are common, but they do not necessarily run in a northeast to southwest orientation as they do in more northern parts of the province. Wetlands are primarily in the form of fens, although bogs are present as well.

Yellow-bellied Sapsucker

This ecozone supports 15% of the Saskatchewan population and the main economic activities are forestry, agriculture, mining and oil and gas exploration. Protected areas and parks, such as Prince Albert National Park and Duck Mountain Provincial Park, make up 8% of the ecozone.

The boreal plain ecozone supports a high diversity of bird species—approximately 300 species have been recorded here. Many warbler species are present in the woodlands in summer, as are Ruby-throated Hummingbirds, Yellow-bellied Sapsuckers, Western Tanagers and several hawk species. Wetland areas support Sandhill Cranes, Common Loons, Ospreys, American White Pelicans and Double-crested Cormorants. Year-round residents include Ruffed Grouse, Blue Jays, Common Ravens and a several species of owls.

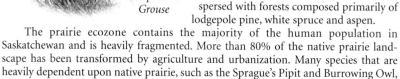

Western Tanager

Prairie Ecozone

The prairie ecozone covers the southern third of Saskatchewan. The aspen parkland ecoregion, a mosaic of fescue prairie and aspen forest, forms a belt across the northern portion of the prairie ecozone and represents the transition between boreal forest and grasslands habitats. Much of the rest of the prairie ecozone is made up of mixed grass prairie including blue gramma grass, wheatgrasses and other grasses, sedges, and herbs. In more humid parts of the grasslands, wetlands are primarily fresh water, are more permanent and are bordered with willows and aspen. In the drier, southern parts, wetlands are impermanent and saline, resulting in shorelines with salt rings and little or no vegetation. The Cypress upland ecoregion, in the southwest corner of the province, rises high above the plains. It is the only part of the province that escaped glaciation and is characterized by fescue prairie interspersed with forests composed primarily of lodgepole pine, white spruce and aspen.

Sharp-tailed Grouse

The prairie ecozone contains the majority of the human population in Saskatchewan and is heavily fragmented. More than 80% of the native prairie landscape has been transformed by agriculture and urbanization. Many species that are heavily dependent upon native prairie, such as the Sprague's Pipit and Burrowing Owl, are threatened or endangered. Parks and protected areas, including Grasslands National Park and Cypress Hills Provincial Park make up 9% of the ecozone.

Birds characteristic of grasslands in summer include Western Meadowlarks, Horned Larks and Loggerhead Shrikes. Wetlands of the prairie ecozone abound with waterfowl and shorebirds during the breeding season, and Ferruginous and Swainson's hawks survey the landscape for meals to bring home to their growing families. Year-round residents include the Sharp-tailed Grouse, Gray Partridge and Short-eared Owl. A number of birds that breed further north also seek refuge on the prairies in winter, including the Snowy Owl, Snow Bunting and Bohemian Waxwing.

Snowy Owl

ABOUT THE SPECIES ACCOUNTS

This book gives detailed accounts of 145 common and noteworthy bird species found in Saskatchewan. As well as discussing the identifying features of the birds, each species account also attempts to bring the birds to life by describing their various character traits. Personifying a bird helps us to relate to it, but the characterizations presented should not be mistaken for explanations of behaviour. Our limited understanding of non-human creatures, our interpretations and our assumptions most likely fall short of truly defining birds. Nevertheless, we hope that a lively, engaging text will communicate our scientific knowledge as smoothly and effectively as possible.

One of the challenges of birding is that many species look different in spring and summer than they do in autumn and winter. Many birds have what are generally called breeding and non-breeding plumages, and immature birds often look different from their parents. This book does not try to describe or illustrate all the different plumages of a species; instead, it focuses on the forms that are most likely to be seen in our area. Most of the illustrations are of adult birds. The order of the birds and their common and scientific names follow the American Ornithologists' Union's *Check-list of North American Birds* (7th edition, July 1998 and its supplements).

ID: It is difficult to try to describe the features of a bird without being able to visualize it, so this section is best used in combination with the illustrations. Where appropriate, the description is subdivided to highlight the differences between male and female birds, breeding and non-breeding birds and immature and adult birds. The descriptions use as few technical terms as possible, and favour easily understood language. Birds may not have "jaw lines," "moustaches," or "chins," but these and other terms are easily understood by all readers, in spite of their scientific inaccuracy. Some of the most common features of birds are labelled in the glossary illustration.

Size: The size measurement, an average length of the bird's body from bill to tail, is an approximate measure of the bird as it is seen in nature. The size of larger birds is often given as a range, because there is variation between individuals. In addition, wingspans are given for some of the larger birds that are often seen in flight. Please note that birds with long tails often have large measurements that do not necessarily reflect "body" size.

Status: A general comment, such as "common," "uncommon," or "rare," is usually sufficient to describe the relative abundance of a species. Situations are bound to differ somewhat since migratory pulses, seasonal changes and centres of activity tend to concentrate or disperse birds. Some birds are more abundant in some parts of the province than others. Therefore, some of the status comments include a reference to specific regions of the province, followed by the time of year that they are usually present.

Habitat: The habitats we have listed describe where each species is most commonly found. In most cases, it is a generalized description, but if a bird is restricted to a specific habitat, the habitat is described precisely. Because of the freedom flight gives them, birds can turn up in almost any type of habitat, but usually they will be found in environments that provide the specific food, water, cover and, in some cases, nesting habitat that they need to survive.

Nesting: The reproductive strategies used by different bird species vary: in each species account, nest location and structure, clutch size, incubation period and parental duties are discussed. Remember that birding ethics discourage the disturbance of active bird nests. If you disturb a nest, you may drive off the parents during a critical period or expose defenseless young to predators.

Feeding: Birds spend a great deal of time foraging for food. If you know what a bird eats and where the food is found, you will have a good chance of meeting the bird you are looking for. Birds are frequently encountered while they are foraging; we hope that our description of their feeding styles and diets provides important identifying characteristics, as well as interesting dietary facts.

Voice: You will hear many birds, particularly songbirds, that may remain hidden from view. With practice, you will be able to identify most birds without having to see them. Memorable paraphrases of distinctive sounds (songs and various call notes) will aid you in identifying species by ear. The paraphases we have provided often only loosely resemble the call, song or sound produced by each bird. Should one of our paraphrases not work for you, feel free to make up your own—this creative exercise will reinforce your memory of the bird's sound.

Similar Species: Easily confused species are discussed briefly. Subtle differences in colour, shape or behaviour are often all that separates one bird from another. As you learn, you might find it useful to consult this section before finalizing your identification. By concentrating on the most relevant field marks, it is usually fairly easy to distinguish similar-looking species. Keep in mind that even experienced birders can make errors in identification, and eliminating similar species lessens your chances of mistaking a bird's identity.

Best Sites: If you are looking for a particular bird in Saskatchewan, you will have more luck in some places than in others, even within the range shown on the range map. We have listed places that, besides providing a good chance of seeing a species, are easily accessible. As a result, many conservation areas and provincial and national parks are mentioned.

Range Maps: The range map for each species represents the overall distribution of the species in Saskatchewan in an average year. Most birds will confine their annual movements to this range, although each year some birds wander beyond their traditional boundaries. These maps do not show differences in abundance within the range—areas with good habitat will support denser populations than areas with poorer habitat. These maps are also too small to show small pockets within the range where the species may actually be absent, or how the range may change over time. Some rare or occasional occurrences may be indicated as such under "status," but these by their very nature cannot be shown on range maps. Unlike most other field guides, we have attempted to show migratory pathways—areas of the province where birds may appear while en route between their nesting and wintering ranges. Many of these migratory routes are "best guesses," which will no doubt be refined as new discoveries are made. In addition, representations of these pathways do not distinguish high-use migration corridors from areas that are seldom used. Although large waterbodies within each bird's range have been coloured over, only waterbirds will normally be found on these waterbodies.

Range Map Symbols

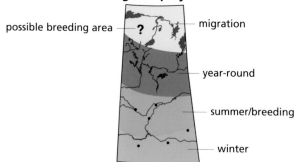

possible breeding area — ? — migration

year-round

summer/breeding

winter

COMMON LOON

Gavia immer

To many Canadians, the Common Loon is the quintessential symbol of northern wilderness. In summer, its plaintive cries are heard on our larger lakes, most often in locales well removed from human influence. • Most birds have hollow bones and have their legs placed below their centre of gravity so they can stand comfortably on land. However, these proficient divers have nearly solid bones that reduce their buoyancy when diving and rear-set legs that make walking on land awkward but help them propel themselves underwater. Common Loons rarely venture on land and locate their nests as close to water as possible. • Most loons, with the exception of the Red-throated Loon, are not able to take flight directly from land and require a lengthy sprint before they become airborne. Once in the air, loons fly quickly and directly, their long wings beating constantly. • One of the largest breeding concentrations of Common Loons in Canada can be found in Saskatchewan at Anglin Lake. Most of the loons that we encounter in our province are seen singly or in pairs.

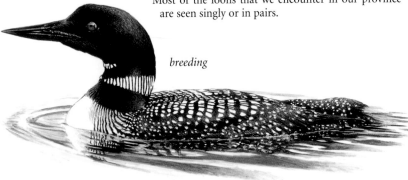

breeding

ID: *Breeding:* green-black head; stout, thick, black bill; white "necklace"; white breast and underparts; black-and-white checkerboard upperparts; red eyes. *Non-breeding:* bill stout and sharp; light band partway across mid-neck; mottled grey-brown upperparts; white underparts. *In flight:* long wings beat constantly; head held low gives hunchbacked appearance; legs trail behind tail.
Size: *L* 71–89 cm; *W* 1.2–1.4 m.
Status: fairly common in the boreal plain ecozone and northward from mid-April to mid-November; uncommon in the prairie ecozone from mid-April to late May and from early August to mid-November.
Habitat: large wetlands and lakes, often those with islands that provide undisturbed shorelines for nesting and with healthy populations of small fish.
Nesting: on a muskrat lodge, small island or peninsula; always near water; nest is built from aquatic vegetation; 2 olive brown eggs are

incubated for 29–30 days; pair shares all parental duties, including nest construction, egg incubation and the rearing of young.
Feeding: pursues small fish underwater; occasionally eats large, aquatic invertebrates and larval and adult amphibians.
Voice: alarm call is a quavering wail, often called "loon laughter"; contact call is a long but simple wailing note; intimate calls are soft, short hoots. *Male:* territorial call is an undulating, complex yodel.
Similar Species: *Yellow-billed Loon:* similar in all plumages; lighter, upturned bill. *Red-throated Loon:* smaller; slender, upturned bill; red throat in breeding plumage; extensive white on face in non-breeding plumage. *Pacific Loon:* smaller; slender bill; grey head and nape in breeding plumage; has dark necklace in non-breeding plumage.
Best Sites: *Breeding:* Besnard Lake; Candle Lake PP; Duck Mountain PP; Meadow Lake PP; Moose Mountain PP; Prince Albert NP. *In migration:* Blackstrap Reservoir; Regina Beach.

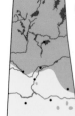

PIED-BILLED GREBE

Podilymbus podiceps

The Pied-billed Grebe is the smallest and least colourful of Saskatchewan's grebes. It is a shy and wary bird that prefers ponds and marshes offering extensive vegetative cover. Although it is not often seen, its loud *cow cow* calls reveal that it is common in most of the province. • The Pied-billed Grebe builds a floating nest in deep water. This strategy reduces the risk of flooding when water levels rise and allows parents easy escape from danger. When threatened, these grebes quickly cover their eggs and slide underwater—they can slowly submerge their bodies so that only their bills remain above water. Unattended, the nest looks like nothing more than a mat of debris. • Unlike other grebes in Saskatchewan, the Pied-billed has a thick, blunt bill and lacks white wing patches.

breeding

ID: *Breeding:* all-brown body; black ring on thick, blunt, light-coloured bill; black "chin"; short tail; white undertail coverts; pale belly; white ring around black eyes. *Non-breeding:* lacks black bill and "chin" markings. *Immature:* also lacks black markings; marbled brown-and-white head.

Size: *L* 30–38 cm.

Status: fairly common in the prairie ecozone and uncommon elsewhere from late April to late October.

Habitat: lakes, ponds, marshes and dugouts with thick emergent vegetation.

Nesting: a floating platform nest is anchored to, or placed among, emergent vegetation; pair incubates 4–5 bluish-white eggs for about 23 days and raises the striped young together.

Feeding: makes shallow dives and skims the surface for aquatic invertebrates, small fish, adult and larval amphibians and occasionally aquatic plants.

Voice: loud, whooping call that begins quickly, then slows down: *kuk-kuk-kuk cow cow cow cowp cowp.*

Similar Species: *Other Grebes:* thin bills. *American Coot* (p. 61): adults have all-black body and white of bill extends to forehead; young are more similar to Pied-billed Grebes, but their chicken-like bills are held at a downward tilt.

Best Sites: Chaplin Lake/Marsh; Buffalo Pound PP; Duck Mountain PP; Eastend; Greenwater Lake PP; Last Mountain Lake NWA; Luck Lake; Nicolle Flats; Pike Lake PP; Regina; Yorkton.

HORNED GREBE

Podiceps auritus

Cold, mucky wetlands seem very uninviting to most people, but nothing is more appealing to a Horned Grebe than a quiet, well-vegetated marsh. This grebe's propensity for this habitat starts early in life—even eggs often lie in a shallow pool of water at the bottom of the floating nest, the wet vegetation and tea-coloured water staining the eggs and improving their camouflage. After hatching, the striped chicks spend much of their time riding around on their parents' backs until, after several weeks, they are able to use their tiny wings to take short flights around their pond. • Grebes have the unique habit of swallowing their own feathers. The feathers often pack the digestive tract, and they may protect the stomach lining and intestines from sharp fish bones or parasites, or they may slow the passage of food, allowing more time for complete digestion. • Grebes appear to be relatively weak fliers, but they migrate long distances every year.

breeding

ID: *Breeding:* rufous neck and flanks; black cheek and forehead; golden "ear" tufts ("horns"); black back; white underparts; red eyes; flat crown. *Non-breeding:* black crown and nape; white cheek; pale grey neck; dark grey upperparts; white underparts. *In flight:* wings beat constantly; hunchbacked appearance; legs trail behind tail.
Size: *L* 30–38 cm.
Status: common in the prairie ecozone and uncommon and local elsewhere from late April to late October.
Habitat: *Breeding:* in thick vegetation along lake edges, ponds, marshes and reservoirs. *In migration:* also found on larger, more open waterbodies.
Nesting: floating mat of vegetation in shallow water; usually nest singly or in groups of 2–3 pairs; pair

incubates 4–7 bluish-white eggs for about 24 days and raises the young together.
Feeding: makes shallow dives or skims the surface for aquatic insects, crustaceans, mollusks, small fish and adult and larval amphibians.
Voice: loud series of croaks and shrieking notes and a sharp *keark keark* during courtship; usually quiet outside the breeding season.
Similar Species: *Eared Grebe:* black neck in breeding plumage; dark cheek in non-breeding plumage. *Pied-billed Grebe* (p. 21): stubbier bill; mostly brown body. *Red-necked Grebe* (p. 23): larger; more vocal; white cheek.
Best Sites: Buffalo Pound PP; Chaplin Lake/Marsh; Duck Mountain PP; Greenwater Lake PP; Last Mountain Lake NWA; Yorkton.

RED-NECKED GREBE

Podiceps grisegena

The whinnying of the Red-necked Grebe is commonly heard around lake-margin marshes in central Saskatchewan and the Cypress Hills. Although their laugh-like calls may not be as refined as the calls of loons, few loons can match the verbal vigour exhibited by a pair of Red-necks romancing the passions of spring. Typically, their wild laughter can be heard throughout the night in late May. • All grebes perform impressive courtship rituals, and Red-necked Grebes are no exception. Courting pairs present each other with bits of nesting material and simultaneously "dance" upright as they patter over the surface of the water. • Most of this bird's North American breeding range lies in western Canada. • The scientific name *grisegena* means "grey cheek"—a distinctive field mark of this bird.

breeding

ID: *Breeding:* reddish neck; whitish cheek; black crown; straight, heavy, yellow bill; black upperparts; light underparts; black eyes. *Non-breeding:* greyish-white throat and cheek.
Size: *L* 43–56 cm.
Status: fairly common in the aspen parkland ecoregion and northward from late April to late October; uncommon in the grasslands from late April to late May and from late August to late October.
Habitat: *Breeding:* the emergent vegetation zone of lakes and ponds. *In migration:* open, deep lakes.
Nesting: usually singly; occasionally in loosely scattered colonies; floating platform nest of aquatic vegetation is anchored to submerged plants; 4–6 eggs are incubated for 22–23 days; eggs are initially white but

often become stained by the wet vegetation.
Feeding: dives and skims the water surface for small fish, aquatic invertebrates and amphibians.
Voice: often-repeated, laugh-like *ah-ooo ah-ooo ah-ooo ah-ah-ah-ah-ah.*
Similar Species: *Horned Grebe* (p. 22): dark cheek. *Eared Grebe:* black neck. *Pied-billed Grebe* (p. 21): thicker bill; mostly brown body. *Western* and *Clark's grebes:* black upperparts; white underparts. *American Coot* (p. 61): all-black body; often seen on land.
Best Sites: Besnard Lake; Candle Lake PP; Cypress Hills PP; Duck Mountain PP; Greenwater Lake PP; Last Mountain Lake NWA; Meadow Lake PP; Moose Mountain PP; Pike Lake PP; Prince Albert NP.

AMERICAN WHITE PELICAN

Pelecanus erythrorhynchos

Most of us associate pelicans with saltwater habitats, but this pelican is a common visitor to inland lakes and rivers in all but the northern third of our province. Pelicans are often seen flying low over lakes and rivers, their bellies almost touching the water's surface, or circling high above woodlands or prairies. It is estimated that Saskatchewan hosts one-quarter of the world's American White Pelican population. • With wingspans of nearly 3 m, pelicans are massive waterbirds with large appetites for fish. These clever birds work co-operatively to herd fish into schools. Once the fish are concentrated in one place, each bird simply dips its bill into the water to scoop up its prize. In a single scoop, a pelican can hold up to 12 *l* of water and fish! Before consuming its meal, the pelican holds the fish in its large throat pouch and squeezes water out through the sides of its bill.

non-breeding

ID: very large, stocky white bird; long, orange bill and throat pouch; black primary and secondary wing feathers; short tail; naked, orange skin patch around eye. *Breeding:* small, keeled plate on upper mandible; pale yellow crest on back of head; yellow on upper chest. *Non-breeding* and *Immature:* white plumage is tinged with brown.
Size: *L* 1.4–1.8 m; *W* 2.8 m.
Status: fairly common from mid-April to late September.
Habitat: rivers and freshwater lakes.
Nesting: colonial; on bare, low-lying islands; nest scrape is lined with pebbles and debris or is completely unlined; 2 white eggs hatch

asynchronously after approximately 33 days; young are born naked and helpless.
Feeding: surface-dips for small fish and amphibians; small groups of pelicans often feed co-operatively by herding fish into large congregations.
Voice: generally quiet.
Similar Species: *Snow Goose* (p. 30): smaller; much smaller bill. *Tundra Swan* (p. 32) and *Trumpeter Swan:* white wing tips; longer, thinner neck.
Best Sites: *Breeding:* Last Mountain Lake NWA; Prince Albert NP; Quill Lakes; Redberry Lake. *Foraging:* Candle Lake PP; Chaplin Lake/Marsh; Duck Mountain PP; Greenwater Lake PP; Meadow Lake PP; Regina; Saskatoon.

DOUBLE-CRESTED CORMORANT

Phalacrocorax auritus

The Double-crested Cormorant's beauty can take longer to appreciate than the beauty of other birds. These slick-feathered birds often appear dishevelled, and extra-close encounters typically reveal the foul stench of fish oil. Their mastery of the aquatic environment, however, is virtually complete. The fact that their uropygial glands do not produce enough oil to fully waterproof their feathers works to their advantage during underwater dives by decreasing their buoyancy. After a bout of diving, however, they need to air-dry their wings and are often seen in a tree or on a pier with their wings partially extended. Their long, rudder-like tails, excellent underwater vision and sealed nostrils are other adaptations to an aquatic lifestyle. • Cormorants sit low in the water like loons. However, they are easily distinguished from other birds because they possess a strongly hooked bill that they tilt upward when swimming. • Double-crested Cormorants are a common sight around many lakes in Saskatchewan. Contrary to popular belief among fishermen, they feed mainly on suckers and other rough fish.

breeding

ID: all-black body; long, crooked neck; thin bill, hooked at tip; blue eyes. *Breeding:* throat pouch becomes intense orange-yellow; fine, black plumes trail from eyebrows. *Immature:* brown upperparts; buff throat and breast; yellowish throat patch. *In flight:* rapid wingbeats; kinked neck.
Size: *L* 66–81 cm; *W* 1.3 m.
Status: fairly common from mid-April to early October.
Habitat: rivers and freshwater lakes.
Nesting: colonial; on low-lying islands, often with pelicans, or precariously high in trees; nest is made of sticks, aquatic vegetation and bird droppings; 3–4 bluish-white eggs hatch after 25–33 days.

Feeding: long underwater dives to 9 m or more; pursues small schooling fish or, rarely, amphibians and invertebrates; feeds its young by regurgitation.
Voice: generally quiet; may issue grunts and groans, especially near nest colonies.
Similar Species: *Common Loon* (p. 20): shorter neck; black bill lacks hooked tip; spotted back in breeding plumage; white underparts in nonbreeding plumage. *Canada Goose* (p. 31): white cheek; brown overall.
Best Sites: *Breeding:* Last Mountain Lake NWA; Prince Albert NP; Quill Lakes; Redberry Lake. *Foraging:* Besnard Lake; Buffalo Pound PP; Candle Lake PP; Greenwater Lake PP; Meadow Lake PP; Prince Albert NP.

AMERICAN BITTERN

Botaurus lentiginosus

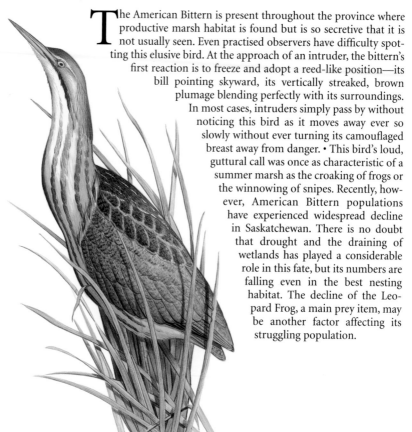

The American Bittern is present throughout the province where productive marsh habitat is found but is so secretive that it is not usually seen. Even practised observers have difficulty spotting this elusive bird. At the approach of an intruder, the bittern's first reaction is to freeze and adopt a reed-like position—its bill pointing skyward, its vertically streaked, brown plumage blending perfectly with its surroundings. In most cases, intruders simply pass by without noticing this bird as it moves away ever so slowly without ever turning its camouflaged breast away from danger. • This bird's loud, guttural call was once as characteristic of a summer marsh as the croaking of frogs or the winnowing of snipes. Recently, however, American Bittern populations have experienced widespread decline in Saskatchewan. There is no doubt that drought and the draining of wetlands has played a considerable role in this fate, but its numbers are falling even in the best nesting habitat. The decline of the Leopard Frog, a main prey item, may be another factor affecting its struggling population.

ID: brown upperparts; brown streaking from "chin" through to breast; straight, stout bill; yellow legs and feet; black flight feathers; adults have prominent, black neck streak.

Size: *L* 59–69 cm; *W* 1.1 m.

Status: uncommon from late April to early October.

Habitat: marshes, wetlands and lake edges with tall, dense grass, sedges, bulrushes and cattails.

Nesting: singly; above water in dense vegetation; nest platform is made of grass, sedges and dead reeds; nest often has separate entrance and exit paths; 3–5 pale brown eggs hatch after 24–28 days.

Feeding: patient, stand-and-wait predator; strikes at small fish, crayfish, amphibians, reptiles, mammals and insects.

Voice: deep, slow, resonant, repetitive *pomper-lunk* or *onk-a-BLONK*; most often heard in the evening or at night.

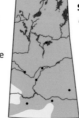

Similar Species: *Black-crowned Night-Heron* (p. 28), *Least Bittern* and *Green Heron:* immatures lack black neck streak; immature night-herons also have white flecking on upperparts.

Best Sites: Duck Mountain PP; Last Mountain Lake NWA; Quill Lakes; Nicolle Flats; Pike Lake PP; Prince Albert NP; Yorkton.

GREAT BLUE HERON

Ardea herodias

The Great Blue Heron is Saskatchewan's largest heron. Few of us can say we've never seen a Great Blue because its commanding stance and preference for open, shallow water and lake edges makes it a difficult bird to miss. It is a common visitor in summer south of the Precambrian Shield. • Great Blue Herons breed in colonies numbering from a few to hundreds of pairs. Their treetop colonies, known as heronries, are sensitive to human disturbance, so if you are fortunate enough to discover one, it is best to observe the birds from a distance. • In the wetlands, the Great Blue Heron is a patient sentry—it stands statuesquely, surveying shallow waters for its next meal. Most of its prey is grasped within its mandibles and swallowed whole, but larger items may be speared with a quick jab of its long, sharply pointed bill. • This heron is often mistaken for a crane, but cranes hold their necks outstretched in flight, whereas the Great Blue folds its neck back over its shoulders.

breeding

ID: large, grey-blue bird; long, curving neck; long, dark legs; blue-grey wing coverts and back; straight, long, yellow bill; chestnut thighs. *Breeding:* colours are more intense; plumes streak from crown to throat. *In flight:* neck folds back over shoulders; legs trail behind body; strongly bowed wings beat deeply and lazily.
Size: *L* 1.3–1.4 m; *W* 1.8 m.
Status: locally common from early April to early November.
Habitat: along the edges of rivers, lakes and marshes; also seen in fields and wet meadows.
Nesting: colonial; in a tree, often along a water course or on an island; flimsy to elaborate stick and twig platform nest is added onto, often over years, and can be up to 1.2 m in diameter; pair incubates 3–5 light bluish eggs for approximately 28 days.
Feeding: patient, stand-and-wait predator; strikes at small fish, amphibians, small mammals, aquatic invertebrates and reptiles; occasionally scavenges; occasionally feeds in fields.
Voice: usually quiet away from the nest; occasionally a deep, harsh *frahnk frahnk frahnk* (usually during takeoff).
Similar Species: *Black-crowned Night-Heron* (p. 28): much smaller; shorter legs. *Egrets:* all are predominantly white. *Sandhill Crane* (p. 62): red cap; flies with neck outstretched.
Best Sites: Buffalo Pound PP; Cypress Hills PP; Duck Mountain PP; Last Mountain Lake NWA; Leader; Nicolle Flats; Prince Albert NP; Quill Lakes.

BLACK-CROWNED NIGHT-HERON

Nycticorax nycticorax

When the setting sun has driven most wetland waders to their nightly roosts, Black-crowned Night-Herons scatter over the marshes, voicing their characteristic squawks. *Nycticorax,* meaning "night raven," refers to these distinctive nighttime calls. Black-crowned Night-Herons patrol shallow water in the dim light, searching for prey with their large, light-sensitive eyes. • A popular hunting strategy for day-active Black-crowned Night Herons is to sit motionless atop a few bent-over cattails, waiting for anything to pass below them—they will even prey on ducklings, small shorebirds or young muskrats. • Young night-herons are commonly seen around large cattail marshes in autumn. Because of their heavily streaked underparts, they can be easily confused with American Bitterns and other immature herons.

breeding

ID: black cap and back; white cheek and underparts; grey wings; dull yellow legs; stout, black bill; large, red eyes. *Breeding:* 2 white plumes trail down from crown. *Immature:* heavily streaked underparts; dull upperparts with light brown spots. **Size:** *L* 58–66 cm; *W* 1.1 m. **Status:** locally common from mid-April to early October. **Habitat:** shallow cattail and bulrush marshes, small lakes and slow rivers. **Nesting:** colonial; in willows and marshes; loose platform nest is made of twigs and sticks and lined with finer materials; male gathers the nest material; female constructs the nest; pair incubates 3–4 pale green eggs for 21–26 days. **Feeding:** often at dusk; stands motionlessly and waits for prey; stabs for small fish, amphibians, aquatic invertebrates, reptiles, young birds and small mammals.

Voice: deep, guttural *quark* or *wok,* often heard as the bird takes flight. **Similar Species:** *Great Blue Heron* (p. 27): much larger; longer legs; back is not black. **Best Sites:** Chaplin Lake/Marsh; Last Mountain Lake NWA; Nicolle Flats; Yorkton.

TURKEY VULTURE

Cathartes aura

At impressive heights, Turkey Vultures stay aloft for hours, using their long, broad wings to ride thermal updrafts as they scour the Saskatchewan landscape for carrion. Because soaring is a very efficient flight style, these birds have relatively underdeveloped flight muscles. They only need to adjust their wings slightly to account for major changes in air currents. • Turkey Vultures use their acute eyesight to locate dead animals, which they can spot from kilometres away. Because vultures depend heavily on carrion and rarely capture live prey, their bills and talons are not nearly as powerful as those of hawks or falcons. The Turkey Vulture's featherless head allows it to remain relatively clean while digging into messy carcasses. Although scavenging may seem like a repulsive lifestyle, vultures perform a valuable service to the environment by cleaning up the remains of dead animals. • Vultures are renowned for their ability to regurgitate meals, allowing parents to transfer food to their young or enabling startled birds to "lighten up" for a quick takeoff.

ID: all black; bare, red head. *Immature:* grey head. *In flight:* tilts side-to-side while soaring; silver-grey flight feathers; black wing linings; wings are held in a shallow "V"; head appears small.

Size: *L* 66–81 cm; *W* 1.7–1.8 m.

Status: fairly common and local from early April to early October.

Habitat: usually seen flying over open country, shorelines or roads, often seen at garbage dumps; rarely seen over densely forested areas.

Nesting: in a cave, brushpile or abandoned building; no nest material is used; female lays 2 dull white eggs on bare ground; pair incubates the eggs for up to 41 days.

Feeding: scavenges for carrion (mostly mammalian); young are fed by regurgitation; commonly seen at roadkills.

Voice: generally silent; occasionally produces a hiss or grunt if threatened.

Similar Species: *Bald Eagle* (p. 46) and *Golden Eagle:* wings are held flat in flight; often show white on underside of wings and tail; do not rock from side to side when soaring; head is larger and feathered.

Best Sites: Cypress Hills PP; Duck Mountain PP; eastern Qu'Appelle Valley; Moose Mountain PP.

SNOW GOOSE

Chen caerulescens

Each April and May, large, arctic-bound flocks of Snow Geese stop for days at various staging sites in our province to rest and refuel on new sprouts and waste grain. The birds arrive in the thousands, covering the brown fields and turning them white again. When a flock takes flight, the birds' black wing tips contrast with their white plumage, so that the entire flock can appear dark one moment and white the next. • The darker "blue" morph was once thought to be a different species. It is seen less commonly in Saskatchewan than the more familiar "white" morph, illustrated here. • Snow Geese migrating through Saskatchewan nest as far west as eastern Siberia and as far east as Baffin Island. Unlike Canada Geese, which fly in V-formations, migrating Snow Geese usually fly in oscillating, wavy lines. • These birds occasionally dig in the mud for rootstocks, and their heads may be stained a rusty colour as a result.

ID: white overall; black wing tips; dark pink feet and bill; dark "grinning patch" on bill; plumage is occasionally stained rusty by iron in the water. *"Blue Goose":* white head; blue-grey body. *Immature:* grey plumage; dark bill and feet.
Size: *L* 71–84 cm; *W* 1.4–1.5 m.
Status: common to abundant from late March to mid-May and from mid-September to mid-November.
Habitat: shallow wetlands, lakes and fields.
Nesting: does not nest in Saskatchewan.
Feeding: grazes on waste grain and new sprouts; also eats aquatic vegetation, grass and roots.
Voice: loud, nasal, constant *houk-houk* in flight.
Similar Species: *Ross's Goose:* smaller; shorter bill lacks black "grin." *Tundra Swan* (p. 32) and *Trumpeter Swan:* larger; white wing tips. *American White Pelican* (p. 24): much larger; larger bill; black in wings extends much farther towards body.
Best Sites: widespread; most abundant in the Kindersley area and at Last Mountain Lake NWA and Quill Lakes.

CANADA GOOSE

Branta canadensis

The Canada Goose is the most ubiquitous goose in Saskatchewan, and it can be encountered in a spring field, city park, golf course or wetland. Although the sight of these wetland giants can become commonplace by the end of summer, a flock breaking the horizon is still a breathtaking experience. • The first large flocks of geese arrive in early April, and the first downy goslings are normally encountered before mid-May. • The loyalty between pairs of Canada Geese is legendary, but if a bird's chosen mate passes away, it will usually find a new partner. • Two types of Canada Geese occur in Saskatchewan: a large form nests here, and a smaller, arctic-nesting form (which may soon be considered a separate species, the Tundra Goose), is only found here in migration.

ID: long, black neck; white "chin" strap; white undertail coverts; light brown underparts; dark brown upperparts; short, black tail.

Size: *L* 55–122 cm; *W* up to 1.8 m.

Status: common from late March to mid-November; locally common at Saskatoon, Regina and Estevan from late November to mid-March.

Habitat: lakeshores, riverbanks, ponds, farmlands and city parks.

Nesting: on islands and shorelines; usually on the ground; female builds a nest of plant material lined with down; female incubates 4–7 white eggs for 20–25 days while the male stands guard.

Feeding: grazes on new sprouts, aquatic vegetation, grass and roots; tips up for aquatic roots and tubers.

Voice: loud, familiar *ah-honk*.

Similar Species: *Greater White-fronted Goose:* neck is not black; lacks white "chin" strap; orange legs; adult has white around base of bill; dark speckling on belly.

Best Sites: *Breeding:* widespread around nearly every waterbody in the south. *Winter:* Estevan; Regina.

31

TUNDRA SWAN

Cygnus columbianus

In early April, before the winter snow melts away completely, Tundra Swans arrive in southern Saskatchewan to forage in flooded fields and pastures. They can be seen passing over rural areas and cities in spectacular numbers. The snow and ice that they encounter here will not be the last on their trip north—Tundra Swans usually reach their arctic breeding grounds well before the spring thaw. • Like the Trumpeter Swan, the Tundra Swan's windpipe loops through the bird's sternum, amplifying its call. The Tundra Swan is called the Whistling Swan in Europe. • Early in the 19th century, the Lewis and Clark exploration team first encountered this bird near the Columbia River, a fact that is reflected in its scientific name.

ID: white plumage; large, black bill; black feet; all-white wings; yellow "teardrop" usually in front of eye; neck is held straight up. *Immature:* grey-brown plumage; grey bill.
Size: *L* 1.2–1.5 m; *W* 2 m.
Status: common from late March to early May and from late September to mid-November.
Habitat: shallow areas of lakes and wetlands, agricultural fields and flooded pastures.
Nesting: does not nest in Saskatchewan except for one nesting record at Stoney Lake near Glaslyn from 1973 to 1980.
Feeding: tips up, dabbles and skims the water's surface for aquatic

vegetation and aquatic invertebrates; grazes for tubers, roots and waste grain.
Voice: high-pitched, quavering *oo-oo-whoo* is constantly repeated by migrating flocks.
Similar Species: *Trumpeter Swan:* larger; loud, bugle-like voice; lacks yellow lores, but upper bill has fleshy strip along gape; neck tends to be straighter and head tends to be more angular in profile; rare in Saskatchewan. *Snow Goose* (p. 30) and *Ross's Goose:* smaller; black wing tips.
Best Sites: Kindersley; Last Mountain Lake NWA; Luck Lake; Quill Lakes; Regina.

GADWALL

Anas strepera

M ale Gadwalls have a dignified appearance and subtle beauty, even though their plumage is not as striking as that of many other male ducks. Gadwalls are easily confused with female Mallards, but male Gadwalls have black hindquarters, and both sexes have a distinctive, white speculum. Once you learn their field marks, Gadwalls are easy to identify on land, on water or in the air. • Unlike many species of ducks, whose numbers have declined in southern Saskatchewan in recent years, the Gadwall has prospered. • This duck feeds almost entirely on vegetable matter. It prefers stems and leaves of pondweeds, which it usually acquires by dipping its head below the water's surface or dabbling its bill at the edges of ponds and sloughs. Ducks in the genus *Anas* (the dabbling ducks) share the habit of tipping up their hindquarters and submerging their heads to feed, but Gadwalls will also readily dive for food.

ID: black-and-white wing patches (often seen in resting birds); white belly. *Male:* mostly grey; black hindquarters; dark bill. *Female:* mottled brown; brown bill with orange sides.

Size: *L* 46–56 cm.

Status: common from mid-April to early November.

Habitat: shallow wetlands, lake borders and beaver ponds.

Nesting: in tall vegetation, sometimes far from water; nest is well concealed in a scraped hollow, often with grass arching overhead; nest is made of grass and other dry vegetation and lined with down; female incubates 8–11 white eggs for 24–27 days.

Feeding: dabbles and tips up for the leaves, stems, tubers and roots of water plants; grazes on grass and waste grain in migration; one of the few dabblers to routinely dive for food; also eats aquatic invertebrates, tadpoles and small fish.

Voice: *Male:* simple, singular *quack*; often whistles harshly. *Female:* high *kaak kaaak kak-kak-kak*, in series and oscillating in volume.

Similar Species: *American Wigeon* (p. 34): green speculum; male has white forehead and green eye swipe; female lacks black hindquarters. *Mallard* (p. 35), *Northern Pintail* (p. 38) and *other dabbling ducks:* females all generally lack black hindquarters and black-and-white wing patch.

Best Sites: widespread; especially common on shallow alkali ponds and lakes.

AMERICAN WIGEON

Anas americana

Although the American Wigeon frequently dabbles for food, nothing seems to please it more than the succulent stems and leaves of plants that dwell at the bottom of ponds. These plants grow far too deep to reach by dabbling, however, so wigeons often keep company with accomplished divers, such as American Coots (p. 61), Canvasbacks (p. 39), scaups and Redheads and pirate the food they bring to the surface. • American Wigeons are also commonly observed grazing on shore. They walk with relative ease, in contrast to other ducks. Lightly grazed fields and city parks with sources of water usually support at least a few American Wigeons. • Surveys have shown that American Wigeon numbers have declined in recent years, a common trend among southern Saskatchewan waterfowl.

ID: large, white wing patch; cinnamon breast and sides; white belly; black-tipped, grey-blue bill; green speculum. *Male:* white forehead; green swipe running back from each eye. *Female:* greyish head; brown underparts.
Size: *L* 46–58 cm.
Status: common from early April to early November.
Habitat: pothole, sloughs, marshes and lake edges.
Nesting: nest is well concealed in tall vegetation; it is built with grass and leaves and lined with down; female incubates 8–11 white eggs for 23–25 days.

Feeding: dabbles and tips up for aquatic leaves and the stems of pondweeds; also grazes and uproots young shoots in fields; may eat invertebrates.
Voice: *Male:* nasal, frequently repeated whistle: *whew WHEW wheew. Female:* soft, seldom heard *quack* reminiscent of a rubber bath duck.
Similar Species: *Gadwall* (p. 33): lacks large, white forewing patch; male has all-black hindquarters and lacks green eye swipe.
Best Sites: widespread; especially common on wetlands bordered by grassland.

MALLARD

Anas platyrhynchos

The male Mallard, with his iridescent, green head and chestnut breast, is undoubtedly the best-known duck in Saskatchewan. Mallards are widespread in our province and can quite literally be seen every day of the year, wherever open water is available. • Male Mallards are indiscriminate when it comes to mating, and they will approach almost any duck that catches their fancy. Wild Mallards will freely hybridize with domestic ducks (which were originally derived from Mallards in Europe), and the resulting offspring, often seen in city parks, are a confusing blend of both parents. • After breeding, males moult to look much like females. This "eclipse" plumage lasts briefly before they moult again into their distinctive breeding plumage, usually by early autumn. • The Mallard's familiar quacks are considered by many to be the classic duck call.

ID: dark blue speculum bordered by white; orange feet. *Male:* glossy, green head; yellow bill; chestnut breast; white "necklace." *Female:* mottled brown overall; orange bill splattered with black.

Size: *L* 50–70 cm; *W* 75–100 cm.

Status: common from late March to early November; uncommon and local where open water persists from mid-November to mid-March.

Habitat: widespread; in beaver ponds, lakes, rivers, city parks, agricultural areas and sewage lagoons.

Nesting: in tall vegetation or under a bush; usually near water; in an artificial structure or an abandoned stick nest in a tree; nest is made of grass and other material and is lined with down; female incubates 8–12 light green to white eggs for 26–30 days.

Feeding: tips up and dabbles in shallows for the seeds of sedges, willows and pondweeds; also eats aquatic invertebrates, larval amphibians and fish eggs.

Voice: *Female:* loud *quack*; very vocal. *Male:* deeper *quack*.

Similar Species: *Northern Shoveler* (p. 37): much larger bill; male has white breast and chestnut sides (reverse of male Mallard). *American Black Duck:* both sexes are darker than female Mallard; purple speculum lacks white borders; uncommon in Saskatchewan. *Common Merganser* (p. 43): male lacks chestnut breast; blood red bill.

Best Sites: *Breeding:* widespread around waterbodies. *Winter:* regular at Gardiner Dam; sporadic elsewhere.

BLUE-WINGED TEAL

Anas discors

Blue-winged Teals are quick, evasive fliers. Groups of teals can be identified in flight by their small size, colourful upperwing patches and the sharp twists and turns that they execute with great precision, often just above the water's surface. • The Blue-winged Teal is closely related to the Northern Shoveler and the Cinnamon Teal. All three of these species have broad, flat bills, pale blue forewing patches and green speculums. The female Cinnamon Teal and the female Blue-winged Teal are so similar in appearance that even expert birders have difficulty distinguishing the two species in the field. • Each autumn, Blue-winged Teals travel thousands of miles to their wintering grounds in Central and South America, making them champion migrants among waterfowl. • Like all ducks, Blue-winged Teals are flightless during their summer moult.

ID: *Male:* blue-grey head; white crescent on face; black-spotted breast and sides. *Female:* mottled brown overall. *In flight:* blue forewing patch; green speculum.
Size: *L* 35–40 cm; *W* 60–80 cm.
Status: common from mid-April to mid-October.
Habitat: wetland edges, shallow lakes, flooded fields and ditches.
Nesting: in grass along shorelines and in wet meadows; usually near water; nest is usually concealed by vegetation and is built of grass and considerable amounts of down; female incubates 9–12 white eggs (may be tinged with olive) for 23–24 days.

Feeding: skims the water's surface for sedge and grass seeds, pondweeds, duckweeds and aquatic invertebrates.
Voice: *Male:* soft *keck-keck-keck*. *Female:* soft *quack*.
Similar Species: *Cinnamon Teal* and *Green-winged Teal:* males lack white crescent on cheek; females are difficult to tell apart from female Blue-winged Teal. *Northern Shoveler* (p. 37): much larger bill; male has green head, lacks white crescent on face and spotting on body.
Best Sites: widespread; especially common on waterbodies in roadside ditches.

NORTHERN SHOVELER

Anas clypeata

An extra large, spoon-like bill equipped with specialized comb-like "teeth" allows this handsome duck to strain tiny invertebrates from the bottom of muddy ponds and sloughs. Shovelers eat more small, hard-bodied invertebrates than most other waterfowl do, and their intestines are elongated to prolong the digestion of these hard-to-digest items. • Like the Gadwall (p. 33), the Northern Shoveler is prefers warm, nutrient-rich waters. As a result, the number of breeding shovelers in Saskatchewan has increased significantly in recent years, making this bird a common breeder in southern parts of the province. • Shovelers usually build their nests on high ground, often far from water. • The scientific name *clypeata* is Latin for "furnished with a shield," most likely referring to the reddish patch on the male's belly and sides, vaguely resembling the shape of a shield when seen in flight from below. The Northern Shoveler's green head makes it easy to confuse with a Mallard, but a closer look quickly confirms its identity. Even when the bird is flying overhead, it is difficult not to notice its exceptionally large bill.

ID: large, spatulate bill; blue forewing patch; green speculum. *Male:* green head; white breast; chestnut sides. *Female:* mottled brown overall; orange-tinged bill.
Size: *L* 46–51 cm.
Status: common from early April to early November.
Habitat: temporary wetlands, temporary wetlands, sewage lagoons and shallow lakes with muddy bottoms and emergent vegetation.
Nesting: in a shallow hollow on dry ground, usually within 50 m of water; female builds the nest with dry grass and down and incubates 10–12 pale buff-olive eggs for 21–28 days.

Feeding: dabbles in shallows; strains out plant and animal matter, especially aquatic crustaceans, insect larvae and seeds; rarely tips up.
Voice: generally quiet. *Male:* has a distinctive *took took took* spring courtship call. *Female:* occasionally utters a raspy *chuckle* or *quack*.
Similar Species: *Mallard* (p. 35): blue speculum bordered by white; lacks pale blue forewing; male has chestnut breast and white flanks (the reverse of Northern Shoveler). *Other ducks:* females have smaller bills.
Best Sites: widespread; especially common on shallow waterbodies, including those in roadside ditches.

NORTHERN PINTAIL

Anas acuta

As elegant and graceful on the water as it is in the air, the male Northern Pintail has a beauty that is unsurpassed by most Saskatchewan birds. Its two long, upward slanting tail feathers, which are easily seen in flight and point skyward when the bird dabbles, are its trademark. • The Northern Pintail is the most widely distributed North American duck, and it is second in abundance only to the Mallard. Despite the pintail's impressive numbers in Saskatchewan, its population numbers are in decline in the southern portions of its range. • Northern Pintails usually travel in groups of 20 to 40 birds, but larger flocks are not uncommon. Open sloughs and flooded fields are particularly attractive to migrating pintails, and flocks containing thousands of birds have been known to alight in a single field.

ID: long, slender neck and pointed tail are distinctive; dark, glossy bill. *Male:* chocolate brown head; long, tapering tail feathers; white of breast extends up sides of neck; dusty grey body plumage; black-and-white hindquarters. *Female:* mottled light brown overall; shorter, pointed tail; grey bill. *In flight:* brownish speculum with white trailing edge.
Size: *Male: L* 64–76 cm. *Female: L* 51–56 cm.
Status: common from late March to early November.
Habitat: widespread; shallow wetlands, flooded fields and lake edges.
Nesting: in a small depression of vegetation; nest of grass, leaves and moss is lined with down; female incubates 6–12 greenish-buff eggs for 22–25 days.
Feeding: tips up and dabbles in shallows for the seeds of sedges, willows and pondweeds; also eats aquatic invertebrates and larval amphibians; eats waste grain in migration.
Voice: *Male:* soft, 2-toned whistle: *prrip prrip. Female:* rough *qua-ack.*
Similar Species: *Mallard* (p. 35) and *Gadwall* (p. 33): females are chunkier and lack tapering tail and long, slender neck. *Blue-winged Teal* (p. 36): female is smaller; green speculum; blue forewing patch.
Best Sites: widespread; especially common on shallow wetlands bordered by grassland.

CANVASBACK

Aythya valisineria

Canvasbacks are members of a sizable genus of ducks that are typically found in deepwater marshes and larger freshwater bodies. The various *Aythya* ducks are deep divers that seldom stray into the shallow areas of wetlands and typically tend to be "dark at both ends and pale in the middle." They are clumsy on land, owing to their rearward-set legs, which aid them in diving, and they require a brief running start in order to become airborne. • The Canvasback's unique, sloping bill is an unmistakable field mark, allowing birds of either sex to be easily identified: the long bill meets the forecrown with no apparent break in angle. • From a distance, males can be distinguished from similar Redheads by their white bodies (those of male Redheads are mostly grey).

ID: long, sloping forehead and bill; dark grey bill. *Male:* canvas white back; dark red head and eyes; black breast and hindquarters. *Female:* dull brownish grey overall; brown eyes.
Size: *L* 48–60 cm; *W* 70–90 cm.
Status: fairly common from mid-April to early November.
Habitat: open marshes and wetlands bordered by emergent vegetation.
Nesting: suspended above shallow water in dense stands of aquatic plants; may also nest on a muskrat house or on dry ground; basket nest is built of reeds and vegetation and is lined with down; female incubates

7–12 olive green eggs for up to 29 days.
Feeding: dives for roots, tubers and the basal stems of plants; occasionally eats aquatic nvertebrates, seeds and clams.
Voice: *Male:* occasional coos and "growls" during courtship. *Female:* low, soft, purring *quack* or *kuck*; also "growls."
Similar Species: *Redhead:* rounded forehead; black-tipped, blue bill; male has greyer back; female is browner overall and has light patch near base of bill.
Best Sites: Buffalo Pound PP; Chaplin Lake/Marsh; Last Mountain Lake NWA; Luck Lake; Nicolle Flats; Quill Lakes; Yorkton.

LESSER SCAUP

Aythya affinis

The Lesser Scaup and its similar-looking relative, the Greater Scaup, are easy to spot—the "dark at both ends and whitish in the middle" pattern of diving ducks is particularly obvious on the plumage of the males of these species. The Lesser Scaup nests throughout most of Saskatchewan and is the more familiar of the two species. The Ring-necked Duck is another similar-looking relative; it can be distinguished by the white ring around its otherwise dark bill. • Lesser Scaups nest along island shorelines in lakes, on floating mats of vegetation in marshes and on deep-water lakes where the aquatic vegetation grows to within a foot of the water's surface. These diving ducks avoid the shallow prairie wetlands that are home to Mallards (p. 35), wigeons, teals and other dabbling ducks.

ID: yellow eyes. *Male:* dark, iridescent, purplish head; black breast and hindquarters; dirty white sides; greyish back; bluish-grey, black-tipped bill. *Female:* dark brown overall; white patch encircles base of bill.

Size: *L* 38–46 cm.

Status: common (increasingly scarce in the boreal plain ecozone and northward) from early April to early November.

Habitat: *Breeding:* woodland and tundra ponds, wetlands and lake edges with grassy margins. *In migration:* deep lakes, marshes and rivers.

Nesting: on the ground near water or over water on floating mats; a shallow scrape in concealing vegetation is lined with dry grass and down; female incubates 8–14 olive-buff eggs for 21–27 days; nests with more than 14 eggs generally include eggs from more than one female.

Feeding: dives underwater for aquatic vegetation and invertebrates, including mollusks, amphipods and insect larvae.

Voice: alarm call is a deep *scaup. Male:* soft, whistled *whee-oooh* in courtship. *Female:* purring *kwah.*

Similar Species: *Greater Scaup:* rounded head; slightly larger bill; longer, white wing edge; male has iridescent, green head. *Ring-necked Duck:* male has white shoulder slash, black back and white ring around bill; female has dark eyes, slight eye ring and ring on bill. *Redhead:* female has dark eyes and less white at base of bill.

Best Sites: Buffalo Pound PP; Candle Lake PP; Chaplin Lake/Marsh; Duck Mountain PP; Last Mountain Lake NWA; Luck Lake; Nicolle Flats; Quill Lakes; Yorkton.

BUFFLEHEAD

Bucephala albeola

The Bufflehead is closely related to Common and Barrow's goldeneyes, as similarities in its profile, behaviour and scientific name will attest. Like the goldeneyes, the Bufflehead chooses to breed in tree cavities or nest boxes—a fact that surprises most novice birdwatchers. • Buffleheads are common summer residents of woodland lakes in the boreal forest. • This bird's large head and sloped forehead are reminiscent in shape to those of a buffalo. This characteristic is reflected in both its common and scientific names—*Bucephala* means "ox-headed" in Greek. • Buffleheads are the smallest diving ducks in North America. Unlike other diving ducks, they can take off straight from the water, without the need for a running start.

ID: small, rounded duck; short, grey bill; puffy head; short neck. *Male:* large bonnet-like white wedge on dark, iridescent, green or purple head (often looks black); dark back; white neck, flanks and underparts. *Female* and *Immature:* dark brown head; white, oval "ear" patch; light brownish-grey to greyish-white underparts; small, white wing patch. *In flight:* large, white wing patch; rapid wingbeats.
Size: *L* 33–40 cm; *W* 50–60 cm.
Status: common in the boreal plain ecozone and northward from mid-April to early November; uncommon in the prairie ecozone from early April to early May and from late September to mid-November.
Habitat: woodlands near ponds and wetlands.

Nesting: in a natural tree cavity or artificial nest box, usually near water; nest cavity is lined with down; female incubates 6–12 ivory-coloured eggs for 28–33 days.
Feeding: dives for aquatic invertebrates; also eats invertebrate larvae, seeds and small fish.
Voice: *Male:* hoarse, growling call. *Female:* harsh *quack*.
Similar Species: *Hooded Merganser:* male has long, spike-like bill; dark sides; white head crest is outlined in black. *Common Goldeneye* (p. 42): males are larger and have white patch between eye and bill.
Best Sites: *Breeding:* Besnard Lake; Candle Lake PP; Duck Mountain PP; Moose Mountain PP; Pike Lake PP; Prince Albert NP. *In migration:* Blackstrap Reservoir; Regina Beach.

COMMON GOLDENEYE

Bucephala clangula

The courtship display of the male Common Goldeneye looks much like an avian slapstick routine, although to the bird itself it is probably a serious matter. In a spectacular display, the male circles the female, then arches his head backward almost to the tail while producing a strange *peent* and kicking up water. • Common Goldeneyes are abundant in Saskatchewan in summer. They search scrupulously for cavities in trees or elevated stumps near lakes and rivers, and they will even explore chimneys. When suitable sites are scarce, females may lay their eggs in other goldeneye nests (referred to as "nest parasitism"), sometimes resulting in clutches of over 30 eggs. • Goldeneyes are frequently called "whistlers," because of the musical whistle produced by their wings as they fly. • During winter, Common Goldeneyes are our most wide-spread duck—they may be found as far north as Cold Lake, La Ronge and Squaw Rapids. They provide life and colour in an otherwise frosty landscape but run the risk of being frozen to the ice or being taken by a Bald Eagle (p. 46).

ID: short neck; peaked, "puffy" head; steep forehead; black wings with large, white patches; golden eyes. *Male:* dark, iridescent, green head; round, white facial spot; dark bill and back; white sides and belly. *Female:* chocolate brown head; brownish-grey over-all with lighter breast and belly; dark bill, tipped with yellow in spring and summer; white collar not always visible. *Immature:* similar to female, but lacks white collar.
Size: *L* 41–51 cm.

Status: common in the boreal plain ecozone and northward from mid-April to early November; uncommon in the prairie ecozone from late March to early May and from late September to late November; uncommon and local where open water persists from early December to late March.
Habitat: *Breeding:* woodland marshes, ponds, lakes and rivers. *Non-breeding:* open water of lakes and rivers.

Nesting: in a tree cavity or nest box, usually close to water; nest cavity is lined with wood chips and down; female incubates 6–15 greyish-green eggs for 28–32 days.
Feeding: dives underwater for crustaceans, mollusks and aquatic insect larvae; may also eat tubers, leeches, frogs and small fish.
Voice: wings whistle in flight. *Male:* courtship calls are a nasal *peent* and a hoarse *kraaagh. Female:* harsh *croak*.
Similar Species: *Barrow's Goldeneye:* male has large, white, crescent-shaped cheek patch and smaller, white marks on wings; rare in Saskatchewan. *Bufflehead* (p. 41): smaller; male has white head crest; female has white, oval "ear" patch.
Best Sites: *Breeding:* Besnard Lake; Candle Lake PP; Duck Mountain PP; Meadow Lake PP; Pike Lake PP; Prince Albert NP. *In migration:* Blackstrap Reservoir; Regina Beach. *Winter:* Gardiner Dam; Saskatoon; Tobin Lake.

COMMON MERGANSER

Mergus merganser

Straining like a jumbo jet during takeoff, the Common Merganser runs a considerable distance along the surface of the water, beating its wings until it gains sufficient speed to become airborne. Once up and away, this great duck flies arrow-straight, low over the water, and makes broad sweeping turns to follow the meanderings of rivers and lake shorelines. • During the breeding season, the Common Merganser is most common on the fish-rich lakes and rivers of northern Saskatchewan. • All mergansers have thin bills equipped with tooth-like serrations to help them keep a firm grasp on slippery prey, which they usually swallow whole. A single, successful dive by one merganser may cause pandemonium, as nearby birds attempt to steal the catch before it is swallowed headfirst by its owner. • Common Mergansers are the most widespread and abundant mergansers in North America. These highly social birds often gather in large groups in migration. While most mergansers retreat from the province for the winter, a few overwinter below dams or rapids.

ID: large, elongated body. *Male:* long, whitish body; black back; glossy, greenish-black, uncrested head; blood red bill and feet; dark eyes. *Female:* grey body; rusty neck and crested head; sharply defined white throat and breast; reddish bill and feet; orangish eyes. *In flight:* shallow wingbeats; arrow-like flight.
Size: L 56–69 cm.
Status: common in the boreal plain ecozone and northward from mid-April to early November; uncommon in the prairie ecozone from early April to early May and from late October to mid-November; regular at E.B. Campbell and Gardiner dams from mid-November to late March.
Habitat: large, forest-lined rivers and deep lakes.
Nesting: in a tree cavity 4.5–6 m high; occasionally on the ground under a bush or log, on a cliff ledge or in a large nest box; usually near water; female incubates 8–11 pale buff eggs for 30–35 days.
Feeding: dives underwater to 9 m for fish, usually whitefish, trout, suckers, perch or minnows; may eat amphibians and aquatic invertebrates.
Voice: *Male:* harsh *uig-a*, like a guitar twang. *Female:* harsh *karr karr*.
Similar Species: *Red-breasted Merganser:* male has shaggy, green head crest and spotted, red breast; female has poorly defined, white throat and foreneck. *Hooded Merganser:* male has black-and-white head and dark sides; female has bushy crest and brownish head. *Common Loon* (p. 20): white spotting on back; dark bill; red eyes.
Best Sites: *Breeding:* Besnard Lake; Candle Lake PP; Eastend; Greenwater Lake PP; Meadow Lake PP; Prince Albert NP. *In migration:* Blackstrap Reservoir; Regina Beach. *Winter:* E.B. Campbell and Gardiner dams.

RUDDY DUCK

Oxyura jamaicensis

Ruddy Ducks display energetically on their breeding ponds. In an attempt to attract a female, the male cocks his tail, puffs out his chest and vigorously pumps his bright blue bill up and down. During the breeding season, he is intolerant of competing males, but later in the summer he seeks their company, leaving the female with the full responsibility of nesting and rearing young. • Although the Ruddy is one of our smallest ducks, the female lays enormous eggs—her eggs are bigger than those of a Mallard (p. 35), even though a Mallard is twice the size of a Ruddy Duck! • Like most diving ducks, Ruddies must patter along the water's surface for quite a distance before they become airborne. • The Ruddy Duck is essentially a western duck, breeding primarily in the Prairie Provinces and on the Great Plains. It is the only member of the stiff-tailed duck group found in Saskatchewan.

breeding

ID: small, chubby duck; large bill and head; short neck; long tail (often cocked upward); greyish-white underparts. *Breeding male:* white cheeks; rusty red body; bright blue bill; black tail and crown. *Female:* brownish-grey overall; white cheek with dark stripe; darker crown and back; greyish bill. *Non-breeding male:* like female, but with unmarked white cheek.
Size: *L* 38–41 cm.
Status: common in the prairie ecozone and uncommon elsewhere from mid-April to early October.
Habitat: shallow marshes with dense emergent vegetation and muddy bottoms.
Nesting: in emergent vegetation; may use an abandoned duck or coot nest, a muskrat lodge or an exposed log; platform nest of reeds is built over water and is lined with fine materials; female incubates 5–10 rough, whitish eggs for about 26 days; may parasitize other waterbird nests.
Feeding: dives to wetland bottoms for insect larvae, invertebrates, seeds and the leafy parts of aquatic plants.
Voice: *Male:* courtship call is a sputtering *Chick-ik-ik-ik-k-k-kurrrrr*; "buzzy" in flight.
Similar Species: *Other diving ducks:* males lack bright blue bill and rusty red plumage; females lack long, stiff tail and dark facial stripe.
Best Sites: Buffalo Pound PP; Chaplin Lake/Marsh; Last Mountain Lake NWA; Nicolle Flats; Pike Lake PP; Quill Lakes; Yorkton.

OSPREY

Pandion haliaetus

Ospreys eat fish almost exclusively, so they are usually found near water. Their primarily white underparts help them blend in with the sky as they soar on broad wings high above lakes in search of prey. Spotting a flash of silver or a slowly moving shadow near the surface of the water, the Osprey locks itself in a perilous headfirst dive towards its target, and thrusts its talons forward an instant before striking the water. Sometimes it will make a tremendous splash, and it may even disappear beneath the water's surface. As it rises into the air and shakes its soggy feathers, the Osprey re-positions the catch, if necessary, to face forward for optimum aerodynamics. An Osprey's talons are specialized to prevent fish from making a squirmy escape: two toes face forward, two face backward, and the soles are covered with sharp spines.

ID: large raptor; dark upperparts; white underparts; head is mostly white with dark eye line; yellow eyes. *Male:* all-white throat. *Female:* fine, dark "necklace." *In flight:* long wings are held in a shallow "M" (held slightly bent at both joints instead of fully extended); dark "wrist" patches.
Size: *L* 53–63 cm; *W* 1.4–1.8 m.
Status: uncommon in the boreal plain ecozone and northward from mid-April to early October; uncommon in the prairie ecozone from mid-April to late May and from late August to mid-October.
Habitat: lakes and slow-moving rivers and streams.
Nesting: on treetops, usually near water; also on artificial platforms, utility poles or towers up to 27 m

high; massive stick nest is reused over many years; mostly the female incubates 2–4 white to pinkish eggs for 32–33 days.
Feeding: fish make up almost all of the diet; may take some rodents, birds and other small vertebrates.
Voice: series of melodious ascending whistles: *chewk-chewk-chewk*; also an often-heard *kip-kip-kip*.
Similar Species: *Bald Eagle* (p. 46): larger; holds its wings flat when soaring; adult has completely white head and tail on an otherwise dark body; immatures lack white underparts and dark "wrist" patches.
Best Sites: *Breeding:* Besnard Lake; Candle Lake PP. *In migration:* Last Mountain Lake NWA; Saskatoon.

BALD EAGLE

Haliaeetus leucocephalus

Because fish is their main food source, Bald Eagles are usually found near water. Although they are capable of killing their own prey, these eagles rely heavily on fish carrion and on prey stolen from Ospreys. In autumn and winter, they will also scavenge on moose and deer carcasses. • Today, Bald Eagles are common wilderness icons, but their mystical quality has always impressed people. They are frequently represented in the stories, rituals and clothing of native people. • Each summer, our province plays host to a large number of breeding Bald Eagles. In 1974, a survey revealed that northern Saskatchewan was blessed with one of the largest inland breeding concentrations of Bald Eagles in the world: an estimated 2500 pairs. • Bald Eagles mate for life, and a pair will renew its bonds each year by adding new sticks and branches to its massive nest. After years and years of additions, the nest becomes enormous. In fact, Bald Eagles build the largest nests of all North American birds.

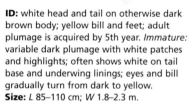

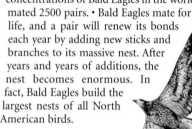

immature

ID: white head and tail on otherwise dark brown body; yellow bill and feet; adult plumage is acquired by 5th year. *Immature:* variable dark plumage with white patches and highlights; often shows white on tail base and underwing linings; eyes and bill gradually turn from dark to yellow.
Size: *L* 85–110 cm; *W* 1.8–2.3 m.
Status: fairly common in the boreal plain ecozone and northward from late March to late November; fairly common in the prairie ecozone from mid-March to late April and from mid-September to late November; uncommon and local around Cold and Tobin lakes and in the southern prairie from early December to mid-March.
Habitat: *Breeding:* large northern lakes and rivers. *In migration:* widespread but especially common along major river valleys. *In winter:* open-water areas and plains.

Nesting: in shoreline trees; occasionally on cliffs; sometimes far from water; huge stick nest (up to 2 m across) is reused for many years; pair incubates 1–3 white eggs for about 35 days.
Feeding: waterbirds, small mammals and fish captured at the water's surface; frequently feeds on carrion; pirates fish from Ospreys.
Voice: thin, weak squeal or gull-like cackle: *kleek-kik-kik-kik* or *kah-kah-kah.*
Similar Species: Adult is distinctive. *Golden Eagle:* adult is dark overall with golden nape, smaller bill and shorter neck; immature Golden has prominent white patch on primary flight feathers and base of tail. *Osprey* (p. 45): M-shaped wings in flight; dark "wrist" patches; dark bill.
Best Sites: *Breeding:* Besnard Lake; Prince Albert NP. *Winter:* Gardiner Dam; Tobin Lake.

NORTHERN HARRIER

Circus cyaneus

The Northern Harrier may be the easiest raptor to identify on the wing, because no other hawk routinely flies so close to the ground. When hunting, it cruises low over fields, meadows and marshes, grazing the tops of long grass and cattails and relying on surprise attacks to capture its prey. Although the harrier has excellent vision, its owl-like, parabolic facial discs allow it to hunt easily by sound as well. • The Northern Harrier's courtship flight is an impressive spring event. Males perform huge looping dives to secure the attentions of onlooking females. • Nesting populations of Northern Harriers, like those of the Short-eared Owl (p. 86), have declined as roadsides and field margins have become increasingly cultivated and as pastures have become more heavily grazed. Nonetheless, it remains a common summer resident throughout the agricultural portion of our province. In more northern regions, it is also present in recent burns, dry bogs and open areas.

ID: distinctive, white rump patch; long wings; long, narrow tail. *Male:* blue-grey to silvery grey upperparts; white underparts; tail bands indistinct except for dark subterminal band. *Female:* dark brown upperparts; streaky, brown-and-buff underparts. *Immature:* rich reddish-brown underparts; dark tail bands; streaked breast, sides and flanks. *In flight:* wings held in a "V."
Size: *L* 43–58 cm; *W* 97–122 cm.
Status: common in the prairie ecozone and uncommon elsewhere from late March to early November; occasional in the prairie ecozone from mid-November to mid-March.
Habitat: open country, including scrubby areas, hayfields, wet meadows, marshes and bogs.
Nesting: on the ground, usually in long grass, cattails or dense scrub; nest is lined with weeds, sticks and cattails; female incubates 4–7 bluish-white eggs for 30–32 days.

Feeding: hunts in low flights, often skimming just above ground vegetation; eats small mammals, birds, amphibians, reptiles and large insects.
Voice: generally quiet; high-pitched *ke-ke-ke-ke-ke-ke* near its nest.
Similar Species: *Swainson's Hawk* (p. 50): dark bib; dark flight feathers contrast with pale underbody and underwing linings. *Rough-legged Hawk:* broader wings; dark "wrist" patches; fan-like tail with white base and broad, dark subterminal band; dark belly band. *Red-tailed Hawk* (p. 51): lacks white rump and long, narrow tail.
Best Sites: widespread wherever grasslands or marshes remain.

SHARP-SHINNED HAWK

Accipiter striatus

Like all accipiters, or woodland hawks, "Sharpies" have short, rounded wings and long, rudder-like, banded tails that give them the manoeuverability they need to weave their way through forest foliage. They hunt silently, using stealth and speed to ambush wary prey and catching the quarry in mid-air with their long legs and sharp talons. After a successful hunt, Sharpies usually perch on a "plucking post" to feast. • Of the three *Accipiter* species in Saskatchewan, the Sharp-shinned is the smallest and by far the most widespread, and it nests in a variety of forest types throughout the province. When not chasing down songbirds, it will flap and glide through mixed forests, either scouting over treetops or crossing small forest openings. • The male Sharp-shinned Hawk is cautious around his mate when delivering food to his nestlings—she is typically one-third larger him and frequently bad tempered. There is such a difference in the sizes of the two sexes, in fact, that they prey on differently sized animals.

ID: small hawk; short, rounded wings; long, straight, heavily barred tail is squared at tip; dark barring on pale undertail and underwings. *Adult:* blue-grey back; red horizontal bars on underparts; red eyes. *Immature:* brown upperparts; yellowish eyes; brown, vertical streaking on breast and belly. *In flight:* flap-and-glide flier.

Size: *Male:* L 25–30 cm; W 51–61 cm. *Female:* L 30–36 cm; W 61–71 cm.

Status: fairly common in the aspen parkland ecoregion and northward from early April to early October; fairly common in the rest of the prairie ecozone from early April to late May and from late August to early October.

Habitat: *Breeding:* dense to semi-open forests and large woodlots; favours dense, deciduous or mixed

forests and bogs. *In migration:* wooded rivers and valleys, farmsteads and urban woodlots, especially near birdfeeders.

Nesting: in trees along woodland edges and clearings; usually builds a new stick nest each year; sometimes remodels an abandoned crow, squirrel or magpie nest; nest is lined with bark strips and vegetation; female incubates 4–5 whitish eggs for up to 35 days.

Feeding: small birds, such as chickadees, finches and sparrows; rarely takes small mammals, amphibians and insects.

Voice: generally silent; intense, shrill *kik-kik-kik-kik* is occasionally issued.

Similar Species: *Cooper's Hawk:* usually larger; tail has broader terminal band and tip is more rounded. *American Kestrel* (p. 53): pointed wings; 2 dark facial stripes. *Merlin* (p. 54): dark eyes; 1 dark facial stripe; brown streaking on buff underparts; pointed wings; rapid wingbeats.

Best Sites: *Breeding:* widespread but secretive during nesting; especially common in Cypress Hills PP, Duck Mountain PP, and Meadow Lake PP. *In migration:* Last Mountain Lake NWA.

NORTHERN GOSHAWK

Accipiter gentilis

A hungry goshawk may be the boldest, most aggressive bird in Saskatchewan. Northern Goshawks will prey on any animal they can overtake, and once a capture has been made, they stab repeatedly at their victim's internal organs with their long, sharp talons. These raptors have even been known to chase their quarry on foot when elusive prey disappear under the cover of dense thickets.
• Goshawks are devoted parents and are equally fierce when defending their nest sites as they are when capturing prey; unfortunate souls who wander too close to a goshawk nest are assaulted by an almost deafening, squawking dive-bomb attack. • In the air, accipiters can be distinguished from buteos and falcons by their flap-and-glide flight style. • The clearing of forests for agricultural and residential development has caused goshawk populations to decline significantly throughout their range in northern Europe, Asia and parts of North America. These birds require extensive forested territories for hunting and raising their families.

ID: large hawk; rounded wings; long, banded tail with 1 white, terminal band; white eyebrow stripe. *Adult:* red eyes; dark crown; blue-grey back; fine, grey, vertical streaking on pale breast and belly; grey barring on pale undertail and underwings. *Immature:* yellow eyes; brown overall; brown streaking on whitish breast and belly; irregular brown barring on pale undertail and underwings; pale eyebrow stripe.
Size: *Male:* L 53–58 cm; W 1–1.1 m. *Female:* L 58–64 cm; W 1.1–1.2 m.
Status: uncommon in the boreal plain ecozone and northward year-round; uncommon and erratic in the prairie ecozone from mid-September to early April.
Habitat: *Breeding:* prefers mature mixed woodlands; also found in extensive deciduous forests. *Non-breeding:* forest edges, semi-open parklands and farmlands.

Nesting: in a deciduous tree in deep woods; large, bulky stick platform nest is often reused for several years; female incubates 2–5 bluish-white eggs for 35–36 days.
Feeding: eats grouse, rabbits, ground and tree squirrels; may take pigeons in winter.
Voice: generally silent; adults utter a loud and fast *kak-kak-kak-kak* or *kuk-kuk-kuk-kuk* (deeper than the call of the Cooper's Hawk or the Sharp-shinned Hawk) during the nesting season.
Similar Species: *Cooper's Hawk* and *Sharp-shinned Hawk* (p. 48): smaller; adults have reddish breast bars and no white eyebrow stripe. *Buteo hawks:* shorter tails; broader wings. *Gyrfalcon:* wings are more pointed; dark eyes have "tearstreak."
Best Sites: Besnard Lake; Candle Lake PP; Duck Mountain PP; Hudson Bay; Meadow Lake PP; Prince Albert NP.

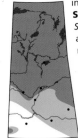

49

SWAINSON'S HAWK

Buteo swainsoni

The Swainson's Hawk is the common buteo of the prairies, and in Saskatchewan its distribution and abundance are strongly correlated with those of its main prey item, the Richardson's ground squirrel. A nesting pair of Swainson's Hawks may catch up to 300 ground squirrels in a single summer. • Swainson's Hawks are social birds, gathering into large flocks in migration and feeding in groups on their wintering grounds. These hawks winter mainly in the Pampas of southern South America, thus undertaking the longest migration of any Saskatchewan raptor. Many of our hawks are killed on their wintering grounds by the incautious use of pesticides, reminding us that the conservation of migratory species requires international cooperation. • Buteos are relatively large hawks with long, broad wings and wide, fanned tails when flying. They hunt principally in open country, watching for prey from a prominent perch or while soaring in wide circles high above the ground.

light morph

dark morph

ID: long, narrow wings; fan-shaped tail. *Light morph:* dark bib; white wing linings contrast with dark flight feathers; white belly; finely barred tail; white uppertail coverts. *Dark morph:* brown overall; dark wing linings blend with brown flight feathers. *In flight:* wings are held in a shallow "V."
Size: *L* 48–51 cm; *W* 1.3 m (female is slightly larger).
Status: common from mid-April to late September.
Habitat: open fields and grasslands with scattered trees or large shrubs for nesting.
Nesting: in a tree or shrub adjacent to open habitat; nest is made of sticks, twigs and forbs (Russian

thistle in particular) and is lined with bark and fresh leaves; pair incubates 2–4 brown-spotted, whitish eggs for 28–35 days.
Feeding: dives to the ground for voles, mice and ground squirrels; also eats large numbers of grasshoppers and other insects; eats some snakes, small birds and rabbits.
Voice: typical call, *keeeeeeer,* is higher-pitched than the Red-tailed Hawk's call.
Similar Species: *Red-tailed Hawk* (p. 51): wings are held flat in flight; more rounded wing tips; dark leading edge on underwing; dark belly band. *Other buteos:* flight feathers are lighter than wing linings; all lack dark bib.
Best Sites: *Breeding:* Eastend; Grasslands NP; Kindersley area; Maple Creek.

RED-TAILED HAWK

Buteo jamaicensis

Red-tails are one of the most commonly seen hawks in Saskatchewan, especially in the aspen parkland ecoregion. A drive through the country will likely reveal numerous Red-tails perching on exposed tree limbs, fenceposts or utility poles overlooking open fields and road-sides. From their perches, these birds scan the terrain, looking for unsuspecting prey to pounce on. Like other soaring hawks, they use their acute vision to spot prey from great distances. • The Red-tail's diet consists primarily of small mammals, and in settled areas this bird helps to control rodent populations. • In spring courtship, male and female Red-tailed Hawks will dive at each other, sometimes locking talons and tumbling through the air together before swooping down to land in a tree. • The Red-tailed Hawk's unforgettable piercing call is more impressive than the weak call of an eagle. For this reason, movie producers often pair the visual image of an eagle with the Red-tail's impressive call for a more powerful effect.

ID: *Typical adult:* streaky, dark brown abdominal "belt"; dark brown head. *Harlan's:* dark, mottled tail can have traces of red. *Krider's:* light, almost white tail with reddish wash. *Immature:* extremely variable; greyish tail is generally barred. *In flight:* fan-shaped tail; dark leading edge on underside of wings is distinctive when present.
Size: *Male: L* 48–58 cm; *W* 1.2–1.5 m. *Female: L* 51–65 cm; *W* 1.2–1.5 m.
Status: common, except uncommon and local in the grasslands, from late March to mid-October.
Habitat: semi-open country with some trees to forested terrain with openings, including roadsides and fields near woodlots, hedgerows and open mixed forests.
Nesting: usually high in a deciduous tree adjacent to open areas; rarely in conifers; pair incubates 2–4 brown-spotted, whitish eggs; female raises the young.

Feeding: scans for food while perched or soaring; takes primarily rodents; also takes some insects, birds, amphibians, reptiles and small rabbits.
Voice: powerful, descending scream: *keener.*
Similar Species: *Rough-legged Hawk:* white tail base; dark underwing "wrist" patches; broad, dark terminal tail band; belly patch is larger and lower on belly than that of Red-tail. *Ferruginous Hawk* (p. 52): adult's dark legs contrast with light underparts. *Broad-winged Hawk:* broad, banded tail; broader wings with pointed tips; lacks dark "belt." *Swainson's Hawk* (p. 50): dark bib; dark flight feathers and pale underwing linings; holds its wings in a shallow "V"; more pointed wing tips.
Best Sites: widespread; especially common in the aspen parkland ecoregion.

FERRUGINOUS HAWK

Buteo regalis

Although greatly reduced in numbers, the Ferruginous Hawk still holds dominion over the grasslands of Saskatchewan. It is a common summer resident in the south, where it can be found cruising low over the bald prairie or circling high in the sky in search of prey. Its combination of huge size, rich colour and limited distribution makes this the favourite buteo of many birders in the province. • The Ferruginous Hawk prefers to nest in a tree where available, but it will also settle on a cliff, in a low bush or on the ground. In the prairies, this might mean that each and every cottonwood grove has a nesting pair of Swainson's or Ferruginous hawks. Some of this species' more unusual nest sites have included old buildings, gravel piles, windmills, farm machinery and gravel stock piles. In true hawk-like fashion, the female spends most of her time tending to the young while the male brings food to the nest.

light morph

dark morph

ID: *Light morph:* rusty red shoulders and back; light windows (base of upper flight feathers), light underparts; dark legs; light tail is tipped with rufous. *Dark morph:* dark underparts; white tail; dark wing linings; light flight feathers. *Immature:* very light; light-coloured legs.

Size: *L* 56–69 cm; *W* 1.4 m.

Status: fairly common and local in the grasslands from late March to late September.

Habitat: open grasslands and croplands.

Nesting: usually in a solitary tree, grove or abandoned farmstead, less commonly on a cliff or on the ground; large, compact nest is made of sticks, weeds and cow dung and lined with finer materials; female

incubates 2–4 eggs for 32–33 days; male provides the food.

Feeding: dives from high, soaring flights; feeds primarily on Richardson's ground squirrels in Saskatchewan; also takes rabbits, hares, snakes and small birds.

Voice: *kureha*, dropping at the end, is much softer than the calls of other species.

Similar Species: *Red-tailed Hawk* (p.51): underparts generally have streaks across belly; dark leading edge on underwing near body; usually has red tail. *Swainson's Hawk* (p.50): dark flight feathers; light wing linings. *Rough-legged Hawk:* dark "elbow" and belly patches.

Best Sites: Chaplin Lake/Marsh; Estevan; Grasslands NP; Kindersley; Maple Creek.

AMERICAN KESTREL

Falco sparverius

The American Kestrel is widespread in our province, making appearances from the grasslands north to the southern fringes of the taiga shield ecozone. It is the smallest of our falcons, but it is not merely a miniature version of its relatives. Kestrels are more buoyant in flight, and they are less inclined towards the all-out aerial attacks that have made other falcons such revered predators. • Kestrels often hover while hunting for ground-dwelling prey, stopping in mid-air with rapidly beating wings and a fanned tail before dropping onto the grass below. Studies have shown that the Eurasian Kestrel can detect ultraviolet reflections from rodent urine on the ground, but it is not known if the American Kestrel has the same ability. • Like all falcons, kestrels fly with a combination of rapid wingbeats and short glides. • The American Kestrel was formerly called the Sparrow Hawk, a misleading name since the kestrel is not a hawk and rarely hunts small birds. • American Kestrels commonly nest in tree cavities but will also use nest boxes.

ID: small, colourful falcon; 2 distinctive, dark facial stripes. *Male:* rusty back; blue-grey wings; blue-grey crown with rusty cap; lightly spotted underparts. *Female:* rusty back, wings and breast streaking. *In flight:* frequently hovers; long, rusty tail.
Size: *L* 23–30 cm; *W* 50–62 cm.
Status: common in the boreal plain ecozone and northward and uncommon and local elsewhere from late March to mid-October.
Habitat: open or partly open habitats with scattered trees; hunts along roadside ditches, grasslands and croplands; in the north, favours burns or logged areas.
Nesting: in a cavity or nest box; rarely on a building or cliff; little nest material is added; pair incubates 4–7 white or pinkish eggs blotched with reddish-brown for about 30 days.

Feeding: swoops from a perch or from a hovering position; mainly eats insects and small rodents; may take some small birds, reptiles and amphibians.
Voice: high-pitched, rapid *killy-killy-killy* or *klee-klee-klee*; female's voice is lower pitched.
Similar Species: *Merlin* (p. 54): less colourful; lacks double facial stripes; has proportionately shorter tail; does not hover; flight is more direct. *Sharp-shinned Hawk* (p. 48): short, rounded wings; red barring on underparts; lacks facial stripes; flap-and-glide flight style.
Best Sites: *Breeding:* Besnard Lake; Candle Lake PP; Duck Mountain PP; Maple Creek; Prince Albert NP. *In migration:* commonly seen perched on power lines in April.

MERLIN

Falco columbarius

Like all its falcon relatives, this small raptor's main weapons are speed, surprise and sharp talons. The Merlin's sleek body, long, narrow tail and pointed wings increase its aerodynamic efficiency during high-speed pursuits. It often snatches birds in mid-air, and it is frequently seen flying low and fast over trees and urban neighbourhoods, hoping to surprise unwary songbirds. • Most Merlins migrate as far as Central and South America each autumn, but many remain in our province over winter. They are enticed to stay here by mild urban climates and an abundance of overwintering songbirds, which in turn are attracted by numerous fruitbearing trees and backyard feeders. • The Merlin was formerly known as the Pigeon Hawk, and the scientific name *columbarius* comes from the Latin for "pigeon," which it only remotely resembles in flight. • In Saskatchewan, the Merlin is represented by two races: the pale "Richardson's Merlin" is a fairly common summer resident over most of the agricultural zone; the darker "Taiga Merlin" breeds uncommonly through northern parts of the province. The former is the race most commonly found in winter.

"Taiga Merlin"

ID: heavily banded tail; heavily streaked underparts; indistinct facial stripe; long, narrow wings and tail. *Male:* blue-grey back and crown. *Female* and *Immature:* brown back and crown. *In flight:* very rapid, shallow wingbeats.
Size: *L* 25–35 cm; *W* 60–68 cm.
Status: fairly common from late March to early November; uncommon in the prairie ecozone (mainly in cities) from late November to mid-March.
Habitat: *Breeding:* Taiga Merlins nest in mixed and coniferous forests adjacent to open hunting grounds; Richardson's Merlins use native groves, abandoned farmsteads and cemeteries in rural areas, while in urban areas they nest in conifers and feed miles away in open country. *In migration:* frequents open fields and lakeshores.

Nesting: in a conifer where available; uses abandoned crow or magpie nests or more rarely jay, raptor, or squirrel nests; pair incubates 4–7 white eggs, with reddish-brown markings, for 28–31 days.
Feeding: hunts smaller birds in flight; also eats some rodents and large insects; rarely takes birds as large as a Rock Dove (p. 80).
Voice: loud, noisy, cackling cry: *kek-kek-kek-kek-kek* or *ki-ki-ki-ki*; calls in flight or while perched, often around the nest.
Similar Species: *American Kestrel* (p. 53): prominent facial stripes; longer tail more colourful; often hovers. *Peregrine Falcon* (p. 55): larger; prominent, dark helmet; black flecking on pale undersides. *Sharp-shinned Hawk* (p. 48) and *Cooper's Hawk:* short, rounded wings; reddish barring on breast and belly. *Rock Dove* (p. 80): broader wings in flight; shorter tail; often glides with its wings held in a "V."
Best Sites: *Breeding:* most large prairie towns have a pair. *Winter:* Regina; Saskatoon.

PEREGRINE FALCON

Falco peregrinus

In a perilous headfirst dive, a hunting Peregrine Falcon targets an unsuspecting group of shorebirds. As it reaches its top speed, which in a dive is up to 360 km/h, the Peregrine clenches its talons and then strikes its prey with an irreparable blow. Peregrines eat birds almost exclusively and typically capture them in mid-air. • The Peregrine's awesome speed and hunting skills could not defend it against the pesticide DDT, which caused contaminated birds to lay eggs with thin shells that crushed under the weight of incubating birds or failed to hatch. DDT was banned in North America in 1972, but it still persists in the food chain and is still used in parts of Latin America. Despite its recovery, the subspecies of Peregrine Falcon found in Saskatchewan is still considered a threatened species. • The Peregrine Falcon can be seen almost anywhere and at any time in our province. It is most frequently observed in spring and autumn when northern breeding birds are fairly common, often chasing waterfowl or shorebirds along lakeshores.

immature

ID: blue-grey back; broad "moustache"; dark hood; light underparts with dark spots. *Immature:* similar patterning but brown where adult is blue-grey; heavier breast streaks; grey (rather than yellow) feet and base of bill. *In flight:* pointed wings; long, narrow, dark-banded tail.
Size: *Male: L* 38–43 cm; *W* 94–109 cm. *Female: L* 43–48 cm; *W* 1.1–1.2 m.
Status: fairly common from late April to late May and from mid-August to mid-October; rare in the settled south from mid-November to mid-April and from early June to early August.
Habitat: *Breeding:* lakeshores, river valleys, urban areas, alpine meadows, river mouths and open fields.
In migration: open areas, especially areas where shorebirds and waterfowl concentrate.
Nesting: usually on rocky cliffs or cutbanks; no material is added, but

the nest is littered with prey remains, leaves and grass; nest sites are traditionally reused; female (mainly) incubates 3–4 eggs for 32–34 days.
Feeding: high-speed, diving swoops; strikes birds in mid-air and guides them to a perch for consumption; pigeons, waterfowl, grebes, shorebirds, jays, flickers, swallows and larger songbirds are the primary prey.
Voice: loud, harsh, continuous *cack-cack-cack-cack-cack* near the nest site.
Similar Species: *Prairie Falcon:* dark "wing pits"; lacks dark hood. *Gyrfalcon:* lacks dark hood; typically seen only in winter in Saskatchewan. *Merlin* (p. 54): smaller; lacks broad "moustache" stripe.
Best Sites: widespread; most regularly seen in areas where waterbirds congregate, such as Chaplin Lake/Marsh, Last Mountain Lake NWA and Quill Lakes.

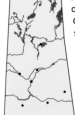

GRAY PARTRIDGE

Perdix perdix

Throughout much of the year, Gray Partridges are probably best seen "gravelling up" along quiet country roads. Like other seed-eating birds, this bird regularly swallows bits of gravel that remain in its gizzard, a muscular grinding pouch of its stomach, and help to crush the hard seeds it feeds on. • During cold weather, Gray Partridges huddle together in a circle with each bird facing outward, ready to burst into flight at the first sign of danger. Although they are relatively hardy birds, many perish in harsh weather, and some birds become trapped under layers of hardened snow when taking refuge from the cold. • Unlike the Ring-necked Pheasant, the Gray Partridge was not introduced directly into our province. It was released near Calgary, Alberta in 1908 and reached Saskatchewan in 1921. Today, it is a common, permanent resident found throughout agricultural portions of the province.

ID: small, rounded, greyish bird; short tail; chestnut outer tail feathers; chestnut barring on flanks; orange-brown face and throat; grey breast; mottled brown back; bare, yellowish legs. *Male:* dark, chestnut brown patch on white belly. *Female:* lacks dark belly patch; has paler face and throat.
Size: *L* 28–36 cm.
Status: fairly common year-round.
Habitat: grassy ditches, weedy fields and agricultural croplands, often near hedgerows, farmsteads or other cover.
Nesting: on the ground; in hayfields, pastures and overgrown fencelines and field margins; a scratched-out depression is lined with grass;

female incubates 15–20 olive-coloured eggs for about 24 days.
Feeding: probes fields for waste grain and seeds; may eat leaves, buds and large insects; feeds among livestock manure piles in winter; forages at dawn and dusk in summer.
Voice: at dawn and dusk; sounds like a rusty gate hinge: *kee-uck* or *scirl;* call is *kuta-kut-kut-kut* when excited; also utters a loud *kar-wit kar-wit.*
Similar Species: *Ruffed Grouse* (p. 57): lacks rusty face and outer tail feathers.
Best Sites: widespread; especially common in areas with numerous hedgerows, such as north of Gardiner Dam.

RUFFED GROUSE

Bonasa umbellus

The mating display of the male Ruffed Grouse is more often heard than seen. He announces his presence by beating the air with accelerating wing strokes that end suddenly, while strutting on a fallen log with his tail fanned and his neck ruffed. Drumming is mostly heard during the spring courtship season, but Ruffed Grouse also drum for a few weeks in autumn. Males are promiscuous, often mating with several females in a breeding season. • Ruffed Grouse are well adapted to their northern habitat. In autumn and early winter, scales on the toes of these grouse grow out along the sides, providing them with temporary snowshoes. • The Ruffed Grouse is named for the black "ruffs" on the sides of its neck. Males erect these black patches when displaying to females. • Both a rufous-tailed morph and a grey-tailed morph are found in the forests of Saskatchewan. It is believed that the rufous-tailed morph is more prevalent in deciduous woodlands, the grey-tailed in mixedwoods.

grey morph

♂

ID: small head crest; mottled grey-brown overall; black feathers on sides of lower neck (visible when fluffed out in courtship); fan-shaped, barred tail with distinctive, dark subterminal band and white tip. *Female:* incomplete, subterminal tail band.
Size: *L* 38–48 cm; *W* 56–64 cm.
Status: fluctuates; generally common in the boreal plain ecozone and northward, the Cypress upland ecoregion and larger forest patches within the aspen parkland ecoregion year-round.
Habitat: deciduous and mixed forests and woodlands with a dense, brushy understorey; favours young second-growth stands with birch and poplar.
Nesting: in a shallow scrape among leaf litter; often beside a boulder, shrub, fallen log or tree; nest is lined with feathers; female incubates 9–15 buff-coloured eggs for about 24 days.

Feeding: omnivorous diet includes seeds, buds, flowers, berries, catkins, leaves, insects, spiders and snails.
Voice: *Male:* deep "drumming" courtship call suggests an accelerating motor: *bup...bup...bup...bup, bup, up, r-rrrrrr.* *Female:* clucks and hisses around her chicks.
Similar Species: *Spruce Grouse* (p. 58): lacks head crest; lacks white tip and barring on tail; male has red eye combs. *Sharp-tailed Grouse* (p. 59): lacks fan-shaped tail and black feathers on lower neck.
Best Sites: Besnard Lake; Buffalo Pound PP; Candle Lake PP; Cypress Hills PP; Duck Mountain PP; Greenwater Lake PP; Hudson Bay; Meadow Lake PP; Moose Mountain PP; Pike Lake PP; Prince Albert NP.

SPRUCE GROUSE

Falcipennis canadensis

Spruce Grouse trust their camouflaged plumage even in open areas, which is one of the reasons they are often called "fool hens." They are tame and easily approached, but we probably overlook more of them than we realize. Setting out to find a Spruce Grouse is nowhere near as easy as bumping into one by accident. • Spruce Grouse are most conspicuous in late April and early May, when females issue their vehement calls and strutting males magically appear in open areas along walking trails, roads and campgrounds. Their deep call is nearly undetectable to the human ear, but a displaying male attracts attention as he transforms from his usual dull camouflage to a red-eyebrowed, puff-necked, fan-tailed splendour. • Because of this bird's trusting nature, which makes it easy prey for hunters, and its requirement for extensive tracts of undisturbed forest, it has not adjusted well to civilization.

♀ *grey morph*

♂

ID: black, unbarred tail with chestnut tip; mottled grey, brown and black overall; feathered legs. *Male:* red comb over eye; black throat, neck and breast; dark back; white-tipped undertail, lower neck and belly feathers. *Female:* brownish overall; mottled and barred underparts.
Size: *L* 38–44 cm.
Status: fairly common year-round.
Habitat: moist, conifer-dominated forest, usually with a dense understorey; sometimes disperses into deciduous forests.
Nesting: on the forest floor; in a well-hidden, shallow scrape lined with grass and conifer needles; female incubates

7–12 buff-coloured eggs for about 24 days.
Feeding: live buds and needles of spruce, pine and fir trees; also eats berries, seeds and a few insects in summer.
Voice: very low, guttural *krrrk krrrk krrrk.*
Similar Species: *Ruffed Grouse* (p. 57): head is crested; white-tipped tail has broad, dark subterminal band; lacks black throat and breast. *Sharp-tailed Grouse* (p. 59): has thinner, sharper tail; white throat; yellow eye combs.
Best Sites: Besnard Lake; Candle Lake PP; Hudson Bay; Meadow Lake PP; Prince Albert NP; Tobin Lake.

SHARP-TAILED GROUSE

Tympanuchus phasianellus

The courtship display of the male Sharp-tailed Grouse has been emulated in the traditional dance of many native cultures on the prairies. In spring, male Sharp-tails gather at traditional dancing grounds (leks) to perform their mating rituals. With wings drooping at their sides, tails pointing skyward and purple air sacs inflated, males furiously pummel the ground with their feet, vigorously cooing and cackling for a crowd of prospective mates. Each male has a small stage within the circular lek that he defends against rival males with kicks and warning calls. • The Sharp-tailed Grouse is Saskatchewan's bird emblem. It is a common, permanent resident in the settled south, where it is most abundant in lightly grazed to ungrazed pastures with patches of snowberry and rose bushes. The few records that exist in the north suggest that it is a widespread but uncommon bird of recent burns and dry bogs. • As with other grouse, Sharp-tail numbers rise and fall dramatically over time. In years of high abundance, large numbers of Sharp-tails move great distances, often colonizing new areas of suitable habitat.

ID: mottled brown-and-black neck, breast and upperparts; dark crescents on white belly; white undertail coverts and outer tail feathers; long, central tail feathers; yellow eye combs; white throat; feathered legs. *Male:* purple-pink air sacs on neck are inflated during courtship displays.
Size: *L* 40–48 cm; *W* 56–64 cm.
Status: common and local in the prairie ecozone and uncommon and local elsewhere year-round.
Habitat: grasslands and lightly grazed pastures with patches of snowberry and wild rose, open bogs, fens and forest clearings.
Nesting: on the ground; usually under cover near the lek; in a depression lined with grass and feathers;

female incubates 10–13 light brown eggs dotted with reddish-brown for about 24 days.
Feeding: eats buds, seeds, flowers, green shoots and berries; also eats insects.
Voice: male gives a mournful *coo-oo* call and a cackling *cac-cac-cac-cac* during courtship.
Similar Species: *Ruffed Grouse* (p. 57): slight head crest; broad, fan-shaped tail with broad, dark subterminal band; black patches on neck. *Ring-necked Pheasant:* unfeathered legs; paler markings on underparts; female has longer tail. *Spruce Grouse* (p. 58): black, fan-shaped tail; black or mottled throat; male has red eye combs.
Best Sites: Besnard Lake; Buffalo Pound PP; Last Mountain Lake NWA; Meadow Lake PP; Pike Lake PP.

SORA

Porzana carolina

Two ascending whistles followed by a strange, descending whinny abruptly announce the presence of the often undetectable Sora. Although it is the most common and widespread rail in North America, the Sora is seldom seen by birders. Its skulking habits and preference for dense marshlands force most would-be observers to settle for a quick look at this small bird. • When disturbed, rails will almost always attempt to scurry away through dense, concealing vegetation, instead of risking exposure in a getaway flight. When they do fly, it is only for a moment before they plunge into the reeds again. • Soras have remarkably narrow bodies, making it easy for them to squeeze through the narrow confines of their marshy homes. When they reach deep water, they climb about on reeds with their long legs and large feet. • Soras swim quite well over short distances, even though their feet are not webbed or lobed.

ID: short, yellow bill; black patch on throat and front of face; grey neck and breast; short, cocked tail; long, greenish legs. *Immature:* brown overall; no black patch.
Size: *L* 20–25 cm; *W* 30–36 cm.
Status: common in the prairie ecozone and uncommon elsewhere from late April to late September.
Habitat: marshes and sloughs with abundant emergent vegetation.
Nesting: usually over water under concealing vegetation, but occasionally in a moist meadow; basket nest is made of reeds and aquatic vegetation; pair incubates 8–12 buffy-brown eggs for up to 20 days.
Feeding: seeds, plants, aquatic insects and mollusks.

Voice: alarm call is a sharp *keek*; courtship song is a plaintive *ker-wee*, often followed by a descending whinny.
Similar Species: *Virginia Rail:* long, down-curved, reddish bill; chestnut wing patch; rusty breast; call is a telegraph-like *kik, kik, ki-dik, ki-dik, ki-dik, ki-dik. Yellow Rail:* smaller; upperparts are streaked with black and tan; white throat; white trailing edges of the wings are seen in flight; call is like two stones being clicked together: *tik, tik, tik-tik-tik;* uncommon in Saskatchewan.
Best Sites: Besnard Lake; Buffalo Pound PP; Candle Lake PP; Eastend; Last Mountain Lake NWA; Luck Lake; Moose Mountain PP; Nicolle Flats; Pike Lake PP; Prince Albert NP; Yorkton.

AMERICAN COOT

Fulica americana

The coot is truly an all-terrain bird: in its quest for food it dives and dabbles like a duck, grazes confidently on land and swims around skillfully with its lobed feet. • American Coots are noisy birds. They are constantly grunting and cackling, and they commonly squabble with one another. These odd birds can often be seen scooting across the water's surface, charging rivals with flailing, splashing wings in an attempt to intimidate them. Outside the breeding season, coots gather in large groups. In spring and autumn, thousands of these birds congregate at a few select staging sites. • When swimming, a coot is often mistaken for a duck, but the coot's bobbing head and short bill are distinctly rail-like. • On occasion, a few coots will overwinter on open water in Saskatchewan.

ID: grey-black overall; white bill extends onto forehead; red forehead spot; long, green-yellow legs; lobed toes; white patches under tail; red eyes. *Immature:* lighter overall; darker bill and legs; less prominent forehead shield.

Size: *L* 33–40 cm; *W* 58–70 cm.

Status: common to abundant in the prairie ecozone, uncommon in the boreal plain ecozone and rare and local in the boreal shield ecozone from mid-April to early November.

Habitat: shallow marshes, ponds and semi-permanent wetlands with open water and emergent vegetation; also sewage lagoons.

Nesting: in emergent vegetation usually over water; floating or anchored nest is made of reeds and aquatic

vegetation; pair incubates 8–12 brown-spotted, pinkish-buff eggs for about 24 days.

Feeding: eats insects, snails, worms, tadpoles and fish; also eats aquatic and terrestrial vegetation.

Voice: calls frequently in summer: *kuk-kuk-kuk-kuk-kuk*; also *kakakakaka* and a variety of croaks, cackles and grunts.

Similar Species: *Ducks:* all lack the coot's extended white bill and uniform, blackish body colour. *Grebes:* lack white forehead shield and all-dark plumage; swim without pumping their heads back and forth.

Best Sites: *Breeding:* all permanent waterbodies. *In migration:* widespread; especially noticeable at Last Mountain Lake NWA in autumn.

SANDHILL CRANE

Grus canadensis

Deep, resonant, rattling calls announce the approach of a flock of migrating Sandhill Cranes long before they pass overhead. Cranes can sail effortlessly for hours using thermal updrafts, and they sometimes circle and glide at such heights that they can scarcely be seen. • Cranes mate for life and reinforce their pair bond each spring with an elaborate courtship dance. Their courtship rituals involve calling, bobbing, bowing, tossing grass, running with their wings extended and making spectacular leaps into the air with partially raised wings. Immature birds may also get caught up in the excitement and join in on the dance. • During their travels through Saskatchewan, arctic-nesting Sandhill Cranes merge with Saskatchewan-nesting birds, making this bird a common transient throughout the province. Spectacular autumn concentrations of thousands of birds occur in the Kindersley, Outlook, Last Mountain and Quill Lakes areas.

ID: very large, grey bird; plumage is often stained rusty red; long legs and neck; naked, red crown; long, straight bill; "bustle" of shaggy feathers hangs over rump of standing bird. *Immature:* lacks red crown; reddish-brown plumage may appear patchy. *In flight:* fully extended neck and legs; glides, soars and circles in flocks.
Size: *L* 85–120 cm; *W* 1.8–2.1 m.
Status: fairly common in the boreal plain ecozone and northward and uncommon and local elsewhere from mid-April to early October; common and locally abundant from early April to early May and from late August to early November.
Habitat: *Breeding:* isolated, open marshes, fens and bogs lined with trees or shrubs and coastal tundra. *In migration:* agricultural fields and shorelines.

Nesting: in water or along undisturbed shorelines; nest is a large mound of sticks, reeds and aquatic vegetation; pair incubates 2 large, buff-olive eggs for 29–32 days.
Feeding: opportunistic; takes insects, soft-bodied invertebrates, waste grain, shoots, tubers and even small mammals and eggs.
Voice: loud, resonant, rattling *gu-rrroo gu-rrroo gurrroo*.

Similar Species: *Great Blue Heron* (p. 27): crooked neck in flight; lacks tufted tail and red forehead patch. *Whooping Crane* (p. 63): all-white plumage with black flight feathers.
Best Sites: *Breeding:* Besnard Lake; Candle Lake PP; Duck Mountain PP; Hudson Bay; Nisbet PF; Prince Albert NP. *In migration:* widespread; most abundant in Kindersley area, north of Gardiner Dam and around Last Mountain and Quill Lakes.

WHOOPING CRANE

Grus americana

In the 1940s, the Whooping Crane was on the verge of extinction, its wild population numbering only 15 birds. Habitat destruction and losses from hunting had compounded with a naturally low population growth rate to take a toll on the species. Since then, one of the most intensive conservation and public education programs in history has managed to increase that number to just over 200. • At over 1 m in height, the Whooping Crane is the tallest Canadian breeding bird. Although the young aquire their adult plumage in their second year, they do not breed until they are four to six years of age (they can live up to 24 years). • Aside from its wintering grounds in Texas at the Aransas National Wildlife Refuge, the Whooping Crane is most readily seen in Saskatchewan. A population of around 135 birds makes it a rare but regular transient here. Try looking for this bird in open fields near large shallow lakes northwest and southeast of Saskatoon.

breeding

ID: tall, very large bird; mostly white; black primary feathers; bare, red skin on forehead and "chin"; long, pointed bill; black legs. *Immature:* orange-red head and neck. *In flight:* neck and legs are extended.
Size: *L* 1.3–1.5 m; *W* 2–2.3 m.
Status: uncommon from mid-April to early May and from mid-September to early November.
Habitat: wetlands, croplands and fields.
Nesting: does not nest in Saskatchewan now, but formerly nested here in large marshes.
Feeding: picks food from the water or the ground; eats amphibians, small mammals and plant material on breeding grounds; eats waste grain and some animal material in migration.
Voice: gravelly rattle: *ker-loo ker-lee-loo*; similar to Sandhill Crane.
Similar Species: *Sandhill Crane* (p. 62): grey, not white and black. *American White Pelican* (p. 24): much shorter legs; secondary feathers are also black. *Snow Goose* (p. 30): much shorter legs and bill; much smaller overall. *Swans:* all-white wings.
Best Sites: Buffer Lake; Last Mountain Lake NWA; Radisson Lake.

BLACK-BELLIED PLOVER

Pluvialis squatarola

In spring migration, the Black-bellied Plover's black-and-white plumage stands out against the still-bleak Saskatchewan soil. For a brief period, small groups of these arctic breeders pass through Saskatchewan and, fortunately for birders, congregate in open areas where they are easily identifiable. Flocks of Black-bellied Plovers often include rarer shorebirds such as Red Knots, Ruddy Turnstones and Buff-breasted Sandpipers. • The autumn passage of Black-bellied Plovers begins at the end of July with adults in worn-out breeding plumage. It is often not until late October that the last of the plain grey immatures have moved through our province. • This bird's habit of travelling in comparatively small flocks may have saved it from the fate of its close relative the American Golden-Plover, whose population suffered because of market hunters in the 19th century and has never returned to its former numbers. • Unlike other plovers, which have three toes, the Black-belly has a fourth toe high on its ankle, similar to sandpipers.

breeding

ID: short, black bill; long, black legs. *Breeding:* black face, breast and belly; grey-spotted back; white crown, collar and undertail coverts. *Non-breeding:* grey-brown upperparts; light underparts. *In flight:* black "wing pits"; white rump and wing stripe.
Size: L 27–34 cm.
Status: fairly common from mid-May to early June and from mid-July to early November.
Habitat: ploughed fields, meadows, mudflats and lakeshores.

Nesting: does not nest in Saskatchewan.
Feeding: run-and-stop foraging technique; eats insects, mollusks and crustaceans.
Voice: rich, plaintive whistle: *pee-oo-ee.*
Similar Species: *American Golden-Plover:* upperparts are golden rather than grey; black undertail coverts in breeding plumage; lacks black "wing pits."
Best Sites: Buffer Lake; Luck Lake; Last Mountain Lake NWA; Regina.

PIPING PLOVER

Charadrius melodus

The Piping Plover is hardly noticeable when it settles on shorelines. Its plumage blends in perfectly with a sandy beach, and the dark bands across its forehead and neckline resemble the shadows cast by scattered pebbles or strips of washed-up vegetation. • Within about 24 hours of hatching, young Piping Plovers are able to walk, although they rarely venture far for the first month. These young puffballs match their surroundings perfectly and are even tougher to spot than their parents. • The Piping Plover is considered endangered in Canada. Recent surveys have shown that the numbers of Piping Plovers in our province have remained stable. This fact is impressive considering the increasing disturbance of their habitat by cattle and people and the perennial flooding of nest sites at a major breeding area on Lake Diefenbaker. These same surveys have shown that Saskatchewan hosts about 20 percent of the world's population of Piping Plovers—the most by far of any jurisdiction.

♂

breeding

ID: pale sandy upperparts; white underparts; orange legs. *Breeding:* black-tipped, orange bill; black forehead band; black "necklace" (sometimes incomplete, especially on female). *Non-breeding:* no breast or forehead band; all-black bill.
Size: L 18–19 cm.
Status: uncommon and local from early May to early September.
Habitat: sandy beaches on freshwater lakes and open shorelines on saline lakes.
Nesting: on bare ground on an open shoreline; the shallow scrape is sometimes lined with pebbles; pair incubates 4 eggs for up to 28 days.

Feeding: run-and-stop feeding; eats worms and insects; almost all of its food is taken from land.
Voice: clear, whistled melody: *peep peep peep-lo.*
Similar Species: *Semipalmated Plover:* much darker upperparts, dark patch through eye. *Killdeer* (p. 66): larger; 2 breast bands; much darker upperparts.
Best Sites: Chaplin Lake/Marsh; Douglas PP; Gardiner Dam; Quill Lakes; Redberry Lake.

KILLDEER

Charadrius vociferus

The ubiquitous Killdeer is often the first shorebird a beginning birder will learn to identify. It is one of our most familiar birds, occurring in all but the extreme northeastern part of the province. It has adapted well to urbanization, and it finds open fields, golf courses and abandoned industrial areas as much to its liking as shorelines. • If you happen to wander too close to a Killdeer nest, the parents will try to lure you away, issuing loud alarm calls and feigning a broken wing. Similar distraction displays are widespread phenomena in the bird world, but in Saskatchewan, the Killdeer's broken wing act is by far the best known. These birds nest on open ground, usually in a slight depression lined with pebbles and grass. Their eggs are cryptically patterned, making them difficult for predators to see. • Killdeers are usually seen singly or in small groups. • The scientific name *vociferus* aptly describes this vocal bird. When disturbed or while in flight the Killdeer continuously calls its own name, *kill-dee, kill-deer, kill-deer!*

ID: long, dark yellow legs; white breast with 2 black bands; brown upperparts; white collar and underparts; white eyebrow; tail projects beyond wing tips; black forehead band; rusty rump. *Immature:* downy; only 1 breast band.
Size: *L* 22–28 cm; *W* 48–53 cm.
Status: common from late March to mid-October.
Habitat: various open areas including gravel parking lots and roadsides, lakeshores, sandy beaches, mudflats, streambeds, wet meadows and grasslands.
Nesting: on open ground; in a shallow, usually unlined depression;

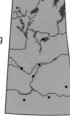

pair incubates 4 speckled, buff eggs for 28 days; occasionally has 2 broods per year.
Feeding: run-and-stop feeder; mainly eats insects; also takes spiders, snails and earthworms.
Voice: loud and distinctive *kill-dee killdeer kill-deer* and variations; also a plaintive, rising *dee-dee-dee-dee* and trill.
Similar Species: *Semipalmated Plover:* smaller; only 1 breast band. *Piping Plover* (p. 65): smaller; much lighter upperparts; 1 breast band.
Best Sites: widespread in disturbed areas; local in the north along roads and in and around settlements and airports.

AMERICAN AVOCET

Recurvirostra americana

Saline lakes and flooded cultivated fields, commonly found in the southern parts of our province, are the favourite breeding haunts of the handsome American Avocet. An American Avocet in breeding plumage is truly an elegant bird, and for many birders in Saskatchewan, seeing an avocet for the first time is an exciting event. • An avocet's upturned bill is just the right shape for skimming food off the surface of the water. This bird typically forages in shallow water and probes in shoreline mud, but it may also wade into deep water, where it dips its head beneath the water's surface or "tips-up" like a surface-feeding duck. • During courtship, the female avocet extends her bill forward and lowers her "chin" until it just clears the water's surface. The male struts around her patiently, waiting for the best moment to approach her. After mating, the pair cross their slender bills and then walk away in unison. • Before autumn migration, American Avocets stage in large flocks on our large, shallow lakes. By this time their peachy hoods have been replaced by subtler winter greys.

breeding

ID: long, upturned, black bill; long, pale blue legs; black wings with wide, white patches; white underparts; female's bill is slightly shorter and more upturned than the male's. *Breeding:* peachy tan head, neck and breast; white eye ring. *Non-breeding:* pale grey head, neck and breast. *In flight:* long legs and neck; boldly striped black-and-white wings.
Size: *L* 42–48 cm; *W* 68–96 cm.
Status: common from late April to late September.
Habitat: exposed, sparsely vegetated shorelines, saline sloughs and mud-flats.
Nesting: often colonial; on sparsely vegetated islands, mudflats or culti-vated fields, always near water; in a

shallow depression or on a raised mound; sparsely lined with vegetation; pair incubates 4 brown-spotted, olive-buff eggs for up to 29 days.
Feeding: sweeps its bill along or beneath the water's surface for crustaceans, aquatic insects and larvae; eats some aquatic vegetation and seeds.
Voice: harsh, shrill *wheek* or *kleet* is excitedly repeated near the nest.
Similar Species: *Willet* (p. 69): greyish overall, including back; straight bill. *Marbled Godwit* (p. 72): brownish overall; thicker, long, bicoloured, slightly upturned bill.
Best Sites: Buffer Lake; Chaplin Lake/Marsh; Luck Lake; Quill Lakes; Radisson Lake; Regina.

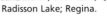

LESSER YELLOWLEGS

Tringa flavipes

Lesser Yellowlegs are among the first shorebirds to arrive in spring and often the last to leave in autumn. They arrive on their breeding grounds in the northern part of the province in April and stay until October. • When disturbed from their forested nesting areas, Lesser Yellowlegs retreat to the tops of spruce trees to scan the surroundings. A treetop perch may seem an odd place for a shorebird, but the yellowlegs and its relatives seem right at home there. • Lesser Yellowlegs and Greater Yellowlegs look very similar, and many birders find it a challenge to distinguish between them in the field. With practice, you will come to recognize the slightly upturned, somewhat heavier bill of the Greater, and the Lesser's finer, straighter, slightly shorter bill. If you still find the bird's identity puzzling, it is perfectly acceptable to simply write "yellowlegs" in your field notes.

ID: bright yellow legs; all-dark bill is shorter than head length; brown-black back and wing coverts; fine, dense, dark streaking on head, neck and breast; subtle, dark eye line; light lores.

Size: *L* 25–28 cm.

Status: common in the boreal plain ecozone and northward from early April to early October; common in the prairie ecozone from early April to early June and from mid-July to early October.

Habitat: *Breeding:* muskegs, grassy ponds in open forest. *In migration:* shorelines of lakes, rivers and ponds.

Nesting: usually in open muskegs or natural openings in forests; in a depression on a dry mound; nest is

sparsely lined with leaves and grass; pair incubates 4 blotched eggs for 22–23 days.

Feeding: snatches prey from the water's surface; frequently wades in shallow water; eats mostly aquatic invertebrates, but will also take small fish and tadpoles.

Voice: high-pitched *tew-tew*, typically a pair of notes.

Similar Species: *Greater Yellowlegs:* larger; slightly longer, upturned bill; call is typically 3–5 notes. *Solitary Sandpiper:* white eye ring; heavily barred tail; greenish legs.

Best Sites: *Breeding:* Candle Lake PP; Duck Mountain PP; Hudson Bay; Meadow Lake PP; Nisbet PF; Prince Albert NP. *In migration:* may be found on almost any waterbody.

WILLET

Catoptrophorus semipalmatus

On the ground, the Willet cuts a rather dull figure. The moment it takes flight, however, its black-and-white wings flash in harmony while it calls out a loud, rolling *will-will willet, will-will willet!* It is thought that the bright, bold flashes of the Willet's wings may serve as danger warnings to other Willets or may intimidate predators during the bird's dive-bombing defence of its young. Willets are perhaps the most intimidating of the dive bombers in a typical prairie marsh. Their large size, heavy bill, scolding calls and arm's-length approaches effectively scare off most invaders. • Willets are summer residents of wet meadows, sloughs and grassy lakeshores, and they rarely wander far from water the way some other shorebirds, such as the Long-billed Curlew (p. 71), will often do. Willets move around in small groups until their nesting territories are established and then gather together again in autumn on larger saline lakes. Birds that nest in Saskatchewan winter along the rocky shores of the West Coast.

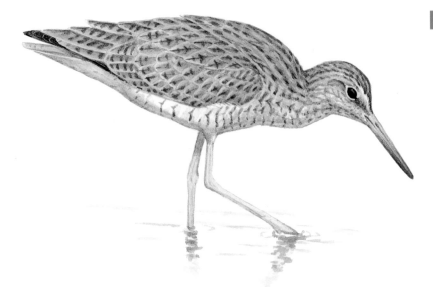

ID: plump; heavy, straight, black bill; lightly mottled, grey-brown plumage; light throat and belly. *In flight:* black-and-white wing pattern.

Size: *L* 26–41 cm.

Status: common from late April to late September.

Habitat: shores of marshes, wet fields and lakes; they do not require much water and may inhabit drier areas than some other shorebirds.

Nesting: in open, dry areas and sandy flats, only occasionally far from water; in a shallow depression lined with grass and other vegetation; occasionally builds a cup nest; pair incubates 4 olive-buff eggs blotched with brown for 22–29 days.

Feeding: feeds by probing muddy areas; also skims the ground for insects; occasionally eats shoots and seeds.

Voice: loud, rolling *will-will willet, will-willet* on breeding grounds.

Similar Species: *Marbled Godwit* (p. 72): much longer, slightly upturned bill; browner overall. *Greater Yellowlegs:* long, yellow legs; lacks bold wing pattern.

Best Sites: Buffer Lake; Chaplin Lake/Marsh; Eastend; Last Mountain Lake NWA; Luck Lake; Radisson Lake; Regina; Yorkton.

SPOTTED SANDPIPER

Actitis macularia

It wasn't until 1972 that the unexpected truths about the Spotted Sandpiper's breeding activities were realized. The female defends a territory and mates with several males in a single breeding season, and the male incubates the eggs and raises the young. This unusual behaviour, known as "polyandry," is found in only 1 percent of all bird species. • The Spotted Sandpiper's breast spots aren't noticeable from a distance, but its flight pattern is easily recognized. It flies with stiff, downcurved wings and has a tendency to burst from shore when closely approached. On land, these birds teeter constantly, bobbing their tails up and down. • Spotted Sandpipers are rarely found in flocks. They are solitary birds, preferring to feed singly or in pairs along rocky or sandy shores of rivers and freshwater lakes.

breeding

ID: teeters almost continuously. *Breeding:* white underparts with heavy, dark spotting; yellow-orange legs; yellowish, black-tipped bill; white eyebrow stripe. *Non-breeding* and *Immature:* pure white breast, foreneck and throat; brown bill; dull yellow legs. *In flight:* flies close to the water's surface with very rapid, shallow, stiff wingbeats; white upperwing stripe.
Size: *L* 18–20 cm.
Status: uncommon and local in dry grasslands and common elsewhere from early May to mid-September.
Habitat: shorelines of ponds, marshes, rivers, streams and sewage lagoons.
Nesting: usually near water; often under overhanging vegetation among logs or pebbles; in a shallow depression lined with grass and

moss; male incubates 4 eggs for 20–22 days and raises the young.
Feeding: probes along shorelines for terrestrial and aquatic invertebrates; also snatches flying insects from the air.
Voice: sharp, crisp *eat-wheat, eat-wheat*, or a rapidly repeated *wheat-wheat-wheat-wheat*.
Similar Species: *Solitary Sandpiper:* complete eye ring; greenish legs; lacks breast spotting. *Other sandpipers:* all lack breast spotting; most have black bills and legs, none fly with shallow, stiff wingbeats.
Best Sites: Candle Lake PP; Chaplin Lake/Marsh; Duck Mountain PP; Eastend; Greenwater Lake PP; Last Mountain Lake NWA; Meadow Lake PP; Regina.

LONG-BILLED CURLEW

Numenius americanus

On the prairies, Long-billed Curlews are fun to watch during the breeding season. Male curlews put on spectacular displays over their nesting territories, issuing loud ringing calls as they flutter higher and higher, and then glide down again in an undulating flight. • The Long-billed Curlew occasionally visits shorelines, but it is more commonly seen in pastures and stubble fields. Its long, downcurved bill is a wonderfully dexterous tool for picking up grasshoppers while it keeps a watchful eye above the prairie grass. • Habitat loss has led to the decline of the Long-billed Curlew in Canada. Its future concerns conservationists, who point out that our current abundance of rangeland habitats should not be taken for granted.

ID: very long, downcurved bill (female's bill is distinctly longer); buff-brown underparts; brown upperparts; mottled back; unstriped head; long legs.
Size: *L* 51–66 cm.
Status: fairly common and local in the prairie ecozone from early April to early August.
Habitat: short-grass prairie and tame pastures; less commonly grainfields, fallow or stubble; often near water in migration.
Nesting: usually on dry prairie; in a slight depression sparsely lined with grass and debris; pair incubates 4 eggs for 27–30 days.

Feeding: *Breeding:* picks grasshoppers and other invertebrates from grass and sloughs; also known to feed on the nestlings of grassland songbirds. *In migration:* probes shorelines and mudflats for soft-bodied invertebrates.
Voice: most common call in summer is a loud whistle: *cur-lee cur-lee cur-lee;* also a melodious, rolling *cuurrleeeuuu.*
Similar Species: *Whimbrel:* striped head; shorter bill. *Marbled Godwit* (p. 72): slightly upturned, bicoloured bill.
Best Sites: Douglas PP; Grasslands NP; Leader; Maple Creek; Pike Lake PP.

MARBLED GODWIT

Limosa fedoa

The Marbled Godwit forages in grasslands and wet meadows, but it also feeds on muddy shorelines, sometimes wandering into deep water and dipping its head beneath the water's surface, where it uses its long bill to probe deep into soil and mud. Its bill is sensitive to underground movements, so it is adept at locating and extracting worms and mollusks. • Marbled Godwits are found primarily in southern parts of our province. They draw attention to themselves with their loud, incessant calls, so they are often easy birds to find. In autumn, godwits stage on large prairie lakes, where they may be seen in flocks of up to 1000 birds, often in the company of Hudsonian Godwits.

• Godwits are large members of the sandpiper family, and three species—the Bar-tailed, Marbled and Hudsonian—nest in North America. Next to the Long-billed Curlew (p. 71), the godwit is the largest shorebird in Saskatchewan.

breeding

ID: long, slightly upturned bill is dark and has orange base; long neck; mottled buff-brown plumage is darkest on upperparts; long, black-blue legs. *In flight:* cinnamon wing linings.
Size: *L* 40–50 cm; *W* 80 cm.
Status: common from late April to late September.
Habitat: *Breeding:* marshes and saline lakes, with a preference for at least some prairie upland. *In migration:* flooded fields, wet meadows, marshes and mudflats and lakeshores.
Nesting: often in loose colonies; on dry ground in short grass, usually near water; in a slight depression lined with dry grass; may have a canopy; pair incubates 4 brown-spotted, olive-brown eggs for 21–23 days.

Feeding: probes deeply in soft substrates for worms, insect larvae, crustaceans and mollusks; picks insects from grass.
Voice: loud squawks: *co-rect co-rect* or *god-wit god-wit*; also *raddica-raddica-raddica*.
Similar Species: *Hudsonian Godwit:* smaller; in spring, chestnut red neck and underparts; in autumn, much greyer; white rump and wing stripe; black "wing pits" and wing linings in all plumages. *Greater Yellowlegs:* shorter, all-dark bill; long, bright yellow legs. *Dowitchers:* smaller; straight, all-dark bill; white rump wedge; yellow-green legs. *Long-billed Curlew* (p. 71): long, downcurved bill.
Best Sites: Buffer Lake; Chaplin Lake/Marsh; Eastend; Last Mountain Lake NWA; Luck Lake; Quill Lakes; Radisson Lake; Regina; Yorkton.

SEMIPALMATED SANDPIPER

Calidris pusilla

In spring and autumn migrations, the Semipalmated Sandpiper is probably the most abundant shorebird in Saskatchewan. It occurs in small numbers on almost any waterbody with an open shoreline, but its highest concentrations are recorded along the barren shorelines of the large, saline lakes of southern Saskatchewan. Flocks of several thousand are not unusual in such areas. • The Semipalmated Sandpiper is one of the "peep" sandpipers (small sandpipers in the genus *Calidris*). Members of this group are notoriously difficult to identify in the field. In Saskatchewan, the commonly occurring peeps include the Least, White-rumped and Baird's sandpipers. • The term "semiplamated" refers to the partial webbing between this bird's front toes, an unusual feature in sandpipers.

breeding

ID: dark, short, straight bill; dark legs. *Breeding:* mottled upperparts; rufous "ear" patch; faint streaks on upper breast and flanks. *Non-breeding:* grey-brown upperparts; white underparts; faint, white eyebrow. *In flight:* narrow, white wing stripe; white rump is split by 1 black line.
Size: *L* 14–18 cm.
Status: common to abundant from early May to early June and from mid-July to early September.
Habitat: mudflats and the shores of ponds and lakes.
Nesting: does not nest in Saskatchewan.
Feeding: probes soft substrates for aquatic insects and crustaceans.

Voice: flight call is a harsh *cherk*.
Similar Species: *Least Sandpiper:* yellowish legs; darker upperparts. *Western Sandpiper:* longer, slightly downcurved bill; in breeding plumage, has bright rufous wash on crown and "ear" patch. *Sanderling:* paler grey upperparts in non-breeding plumage; much rustier upperparts in breeding plumage; more prominent wing stripe in flight. *White-rumped Sandpiper:* larger; white rump; folded wings extend beyond tail. *Baird's Sandpiper:* larger; longer bill; folded wings extend beyond tail.
Best Sites: Besnard Lake; Buffer Lake; Luck Lake; Meadow Lake PP; Moose Mountain PP; Yorkton.

73

COMMON SNIPE

Gallinago gallinago

Visit a wetland at dusk in spring or early summer and there is a good chance that you will hear the "winnowing" of courting Common Snipes. Snipes perform these territorial flights over their breeding grounds, swooping and diving at great heights with their tails spread. Their outer tail feathers vibrate as they catch air to make a loud winnowing sound much like the whistling of a duck's wings. Between flights, male snipes are commonly seen scanning their territory from atop a fencepost. • Outside the courtship season, this well-camouflaged bird is shy and secretive. Only when an intruder approaches too closely will a snipe flush from cover, performing a series of zig-zag manoeuvers and uttering a grating *skawp* call. • The snipe's long bill is extremely flexible, and it is sensitive enough to detect the movements of earthworms and larval insects buried deep within the mud. Its long, spiked tongue moves food to the back of the mouth so that it can be swallowed.

ID: extremely long, straight bill; short legs; heavily striped head and back; dark barring on sides and flanks; unmarked, white belly. *In flight:* zig-zag flight pattern; short, orange tail.

Size: *L* 26–29 cm; *W* 44–50 cm.

Status: uncommon and local in dry grassland areas and fairly common elsewhere from mid-April to early October.

Habitat: marshes, sedge meadows, grassy margins of creeks and sloughs, poorly drained floodplains, bogs and fens.

Nesting: in dry grass, usually under vegetation; often on a raised hummock in marshes and fens; nest is made of grass, moss and leaves; female incubates 4 darkly spotted olive-buff eggs for about 20 days.

Feeding: probes soft substrates for larvae, earthworms and other soft-bodied invertebrates; also eats mollusks, crustaceans, spiders, small amphibians and some seeds.

Voice: accelerating aerial courtship display sound is a winnowing *woo-woo-woo-woo-woo-woo*; often sings *wheat wheat wheat* or *chip-a, chip-a, chip-a; scaip* alarm call.

Similar Species: *Dowitchers:* lack heavy striping on head, back, neck and breast; longer legs; white wedge up back; reddish underparts in spring; usually travel in flocks. *Marbled Godwit* (p. 72): much larger; slightly upturned bill; much longer legs.

Best Sites: Chaplin Lake/Marsh; Duck Mountain PP; Hudson Bay; Meadow Lake PP; Nicolle Flats; Regina; Yorkton.

WILSON'S PHALAROPE

Phalaropus tricolor

In addition to its bright colours, which are unusual for a shorebird, the Wilson's Phalarope is known for its peculiar mating strategy. Phalaropes practise polyandry, a mating system in which a female mates with several males. After laying a clutch of eggs, the female usually abandons her partner, leaving him to incubate the eggs and tend the young. She may either continue to "play the field" or may act as a lookout for one of her males. This reversal of traditional gender roles also includes a reversal of plumage characteristics—females are more brightly coloured than their male counterparts, whose pale plumage allows them to remain inconspicuous while sitting on their nests.
• Phalaropes are small, colourful, sandpiper-like birds with lobed feet. They are equally at home on water and on land, and unlike other shorebirds, they obtain most of their food while swimming. When foraging, phalaropes can be singled out among other shorebirds because they spin and whirl around in tight circles, using their feet to stir up tiny crustaceans, mollusks and other aquatic invertebrates.

breeding

ID: dark, needle-like bill; white eyebrow; light underparts; black legs. *Breeding female:* very defined colours; grey cap; chestnut throat; black eye line extends down side of neck; white line down back of neck. *Breeding male:* duller overall; dark cap. *Non-breeding birds:* very plain.
Size: *L* 21–24 cm; *W* 36–40 cm.
Status: common in the prairie eco-zone and uncommon elsewhere from late April to early September.
Habitat: *Breeding:* marshes, wet meadows and margins of sewage lagoons. *In migration:* lakeshores, marshes and sewage lagoons.
Nesting: on the ground, often near water; in a depression lined with grass and other vegetation; nest is often well concealed; male incubates 4 brown-spotted, buff eggs for

about 20 days; male takes care of the young.
Feeding: whirls in tight circles in water to stir up prey, then picks out aquatic insects, worms and small crustaceans; on land, makes short jabs to pick up insects, crustaceans and some seeds.
Voice: deep, grunting *work work* or *wu wu wu*, issued on the nesting grounds.

Similar Species: *Red-necked Phalarope:* in breeding plumage, dark nape with red stripe down side of neck; in winter plumage, black "ear" and crown patches; wing stripes are obvious in flight in all plumages. *Lesser Yellowlegs* (p. 68): larger; yellow legs; streaked neck; mottled upperparts.
Best Sites: Buffer Lake; Chaplin Lake/Marsh; Eastend; Luck Lake; Radisson Lake; Regina; Yorkton.

FRANKLIN'S GULL

Larus pipixcan

Although we refer to the Franklin's Gull as a "sea gull," this bird spends much of its life away from salt water. It is a common prairie gull—often called the "Prairie Dove" because it has a dove-like profile—that nests on inland lakes and only in winter is it found along coastlines. The Franklin's Gull often follows tractors across agricultural fields, snatching up insects from the tractor's path in much the same way its cousins follow fishing boats. On warm summer evenings, you will often see huge flocks of Franklin's Gulls circling gracefully overhead. Large emergences of midges and flying ants are usually the source of this excitement. Watch one bird, and you will see it flutter up to catch a flying insect and continue circling. These gulls will also scavenge at dumps but not to the same extent as some other gulls will.

breeding

ID: grey mantle; white underparts; full or partial hood with broken, white eye ring. *Breeding:* black head; orange-red bill and legs; breast may have pinkish tinge. *Non-breeding:* white head; dark patch on back of head. *In flight:* black crescent through white wing tips.
Size: *L* 33–38 cm; *W* 90 cm.
Status: common from mid-April to early October.
Habitat: agricultural fields, marshy lakes, landfills and large river and lake shorelines.
Nesting: colonial; on a floating platform of reeds; nest is made of coarse marsh vegetation and lined with fine grass and plant down; pair incubates 2–4 greenish-buff eggs for 24 days.

Feeding: opportunistic; probes fields for grasshoppers and other insects; often catches insects in mid-air; also eats small fish and some crustaceans.
Voice: mewing, shrill *weeeh-ah weeeh-ah* while feeding and in migration; also a shrill *kuk-kuk-kuk*.
Similar Species: *Bonaparte's Gull:* black bill; conspicuous, white wedge on forewing; breeding adult has black hood and narrow, white eye ring; non-breeding and immature birds have small black spot behind ear. *Sabine's Gull:* large black, white and grey triangles on upper-wings; dark bill with yellow tip; rare in Saskatchewan.
Best Sites: *Breeding:* Chaplin Lake/Marsh; Luck Lake. *Foraging:* widespread and often abundant; follows machinery at spring seeding.

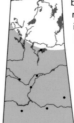

RING-BILLED GULL

Larus delawarensis

Few of us can claim that we've never seen a Ring-billed Gull in Saskatchewan. Ring-bills are the most frequently encountered "white-headed gull" in our province, appearing everywhere except in the extreme north. From the shores of lakes and rivers, where they roost, Ring-bills fly to dumps and city parks to scavenge for food scraps. Some people feel that they have become pests, but few species have fared as well as the Ring-billed Gull in the face of human development, which, in itself, is something to appreciate. • Autumn migration is a prolonged affair, typically with the last of the Ring-bills waiting for the first bitter cold snap to chase them from the province, usually sometime in November. • Ring-billed Gulls do not attain their adult plumage or reproduce until they are at least three years old.

breeding

ID: medium-sized gull; white head; yellow bill and legs; black ring around bill tip; pale grey mantle; yellow eyes; white underparts. *Immature:* variable amounts of grey and/or brown on back and wings; brown flecking on head, neck, breast, sides and flanks. *First-year:* small size and black-tipped, whitish tail are distinctive.
Size: *L* 45–50 cm; *W* 1.2 m (male is slightly larger).
Status: common from late March to early November.
Habitat: *Breeding:* on small, barren islands. *In migration:* lakes, rivers, landfills, parks, parking lots and cultivated fields.
Nesting: colonial; on the ground in a shallow scrape lined with reeds, debris, grass and sticks; pair incubates 2–4 buff-white eggs for 26–27 days.

Feeding: probes the ground for garbage, spiders, insects, rodents, earthworms, grubs and some waste grain; scavenges for carrion; surface-tips for aquatic invertebrates and fish while swimming; will take mice, eggs and young birds.
Voice: high-pitched *kakakaka-akakaka*; also a low, laughing *yook-yook-yook*.
Similar Species: *California Gull:* larger; no bill ring; black-and-red spot near tip of lower mandible; dark eyes. *Herring Gull* and *Glaucous Gull:* much larger; adults have pinkish legs, red spot near tip of lower mandible and lack bill ring. *Mew Gull:* dark eyes; darker mantle; lacks bill ring; adults have less black on wing tips; rare except in northern Saskatchewan.
Best Sites: widespread; especially common along lakeshores and in landfills and parks.

COMMON TERN

Sterna hirundo

Unlike gulls, terns arrive on their breeding grounds after the spring break-up and depart well before the autumn freeze-up. Perhaps they must wait until temperatures are warm enough for the fish upon which they feed to move to the water's surface. When hunting, this tern hovers briefly over its intended target and then plunges into the water. Its dive may take it underwater momentarily, but then it pops to the surface carrying a minnow or other small fish in its bill. Terns eat fish almost exclusively, but they will occasionally take crustaceans and insects. • Recently, a Common Tern banded in Great Britain was recovered in Australia—a record travelling distance for any bird. Terns are effortless fliers, and they are some of the greatest migrants. • Common Terns nest on barren shorelines in colonies or, less commonly, in single pairs. Should an intruder approach a tern nest, the parent will dive repeatedly, often defecating on the offender. Needless to say, it is best to keep a respectful distance from nesting terns, and from all nesting birds, for that matter.

breeding

ID: *Breeding:* black cap; white underparts; pearl grey mantle; red, black-tipped bill; red legs; white rump; white tail with grey outer edges. *Non-breeding:* black nape; lacks black cap. *In flight:* shallowly forked tail; long, pointed wings; darker wedge near upper-wing tips.
Size: *L* 33–41 cm; *W* 76 cm.
Status: locally common from early May to early September.
Habitat: *Breeding:* barren islands in larger lakes. *In migration:* large lakes, open wetlands and slow-moving rivers.
Nesting: colonial, often nesting with other colonial birds; in open areas without vegetation; nest scrape is lined with pebbles, vegetation, debris or shells; pair incubates 1–3 variably marked brown eggs for 21–30 days.

Feeding: hovers over the water and plunges headfirst after small fish; also takes insects and aquatic invertebrates.
Voice: drawn-out *keee-arrrr* with a downward inflection; also *kik-kik-kik* and *kirri-kirri*.
Similar Species: *Forster's Tern:* grey tail with white outer edges; upper primaries have silvery look. *Arctic Tern:* all-red bill; deeply forked tail; upper primaries lack dark grey wedge; greyer underparts, rare except in far northern Saskatchewan. *Caspian Tern:* much larger overall; much heavier red-orange bill.
Best Sites: Besnard Lake; Candle Lake PP; Duck Mountain PP; Meadow Lake PP; Radisson Lake; Prince Albert NP; Yorkton.

BLACK TERN

Chlidonias niger

The dizzying, buoyant flight of the Black Tern is a classic sight above cattail marshes and adjacent fields and meadows. It dips, dives and swoops, picking insects neatly off the water's surface or catching them in mid-air. Even on stormy days, the Black Tern slices through the air with grace. • Black Terns are finicky nesters and do not return to areas that show slight changes in water level or density of emergent vegetation. Foraging flocks of Black Terns occasionally number in the hundreds, but their population numbers have declined in recent years. A commitment to restoring and protecting wetland habitat will help this bird maintain its prominent place in our province. • In order to spell this bird's genus name correctly, one must misspell *chelidonias*, the Greek word for "swallow."

breeding

ID: *Breeding:* black head and underparts; grey back, tail and wings; white undertail coverts; black bill; reddish-black legs. *Non-breeding:* white forehead and underparts; moulting autumn birds may be mottled with brown. *In flight:* long, pointed wings; shallowly forked tail.
Size: *L* 23–25 cm; *W* 61 cm.
Status: rare in the boreal shield ecozone and common and local elsewhere from mid-May to early September.
Habitat: shallow, marshes, wet meadows, lake edges and sewage ponds with emergent vegetation.
Nesting: in loose colonies; in emergent vegetation, usually over water;

nest of dead plant material is built on floating vegetation, a muddy mound or a muskrat lodge; pair incubates 2–4 blotched dark olive-buff eggs for about 22 days.
Feeding: snatches insects from the air, from tall grass or from the water's surface; also takes small fish.
Voice: shrill, metallic *kik-kik-kik-kik-kik;* typical alarm call is *kreea.*
Similar Species: *Other terns:* all are light in colour, not dark.
Best Sites: Buffalo Pound PP; Candle Lake PP; Duck Mountain PP; Meadow Lake PP; Moose Mountain PP; Nicolle Flats; Pike Lake PP; Prince Albert NP; Yorkton.

ROCK DOVE

Columba livia

The Rock Dove was introduced to North America in the 17th century, and it has since settled wherever cities, towns, farms and grain elevators are found. Most Rock Doves seem content to nest on buildings or farmhouses, but "wilder" members of this species can occasionally be seen nesting on cliffs, usually along lakeshores. • Rock Doves are believed to have been domesticated from Eurasian birds in about 4500 BC as a source of meat. Since then, they have been used as message couriers—both Caesar and Napoleon used them—as scientific subjects and even as pets. Much of our understanding of bird migration, endocrinology (the study of hormones) and sensory perception derives from experiments involving Rock Doves. • No other "wild bird" varies as much in coloration, a result of semi-domestication and extensive inbreeding in recent times.

ID: all have red feet; typical birds are blue-grey with white rump, 2 black wing bars, and dark-tipped tail; atypical birds may be dark grey, "checkered" or mottled with reddish-brown. *In flight*: claps wings on takeoff; holds wings in a deep "V" while gliding.
Size: *L* 33–36 cm (male is usually larger).
Status: common and local year-round.
Habitat: urban areas, railway yards, farmyards and grain elevators; high cliffs are used by some.
Nesting: on the ledges of barns, bridges, buildings and towers; rarely on cliffs; flimsy nest is made of sticks, grass and assorted vegetation; pair incubates 1–2 white unmarked eggs for about 18 days.
Feeding: probes the ground for waste grain, seeds and fruits; occasionally eats insects.
Voice: soft, gurgling *coorrr-coorrr-coorrr*.
Similar Species: *Merlin* (p. 54): not as heavy-bodied; longer tail; does not hold its wings in a "V"; wings do not clap on takeoff.
Best Sites: widespread at occupied farmsteads with livestock, around grain terminals and in cities.

MOURNING DOVE

Zenaida macroura

With increasing human settlement, Mourning Doves have dramatically expanded their range in Saskatchewan. Today, their soft, cooing calls are common sounds heard filtering through woodlands, farmlands and suburban parks and gardens in the southern and central parts of our province. In the south, the spread of aspen groves and the establishment of shelterbelts have helped increase their numbers, and land clearing for agriculture and forestry have allowed them to extend the northern part of their range. In both areas, humans have assisted them by creating the semi-open landscapes they prefer. • Despite its fragile appearance, the Mourning Dove is a swift, direct flier whose wings whistle as it cuts through the air at high speed. • All members of the pigeon family (including doves) feed "milk" to their young. It isn't true milk, but a nutritious liquid produced by glands in the bird's crop. The chicks insert their bills down the adult's throat to eat the thick liquid.

ID: buffy grey-brown plumage; small head; long, white-edged, pointed tail; sleek body; dark, shiny patch below ear; dull red legs; dark bill; pale rosy underparts; nods its head while walking.

Size: *L* 28–33 cm; *W* 43–48 cm.

Status: common in the prairie ecozone and uncommon and local in the boreal plain ecozone from mid-April to early October; occasional in the prairie ecozone from November to March.

Habitat: open woodlands, forest edges, hedgerows, farmyards, suburban areas and open parks.

Nesting: in the fork of a tree or shrub; rarely on the ground; fragile, shallow platform nest is made of

twigs, weeds and grass; pair incubates 2 white eggs for 14 days.

Feeding: probes the ground and vegetation for seeds, waste grain, berries or insects; occasionally seen in winter at feeders or feedlots.

Voice: mournful, soft *co-ooooooh coo-coo-coo*.

Similar Species: *Rock Dove* (p. 80): stockier; more colourful; white rump; shorter, fan-shaped tail. *Black-billed Cuckoo* (p. 82): curved bill; larger head; red eyes; long tail with broad, rounded tip; brown upperparts, white underparts.

Best Sites: widespread in all wooded areas, especially in shelterbelts and farmsteads.

BLACK-BILLED CUCKOO

Coccyzus erythropthalmus

The Black-billed Cuckoo does not sound anything like its famous European relative, nor does it sound quite like any other bird in Saskatchewan. Cuckoos vocalize in loud bursts from shrubby thickets, repeating deep *ca*, *coo* and *cow* notes in tangled melodies. In some parts of their range they are called "Rain Crows" because their calls are thought to predict rain. • This infrequently seen bird nests in shrubby areas, where it forages mostly on insects and berries. It is one of the few birds that eats tent caterpillars, and its numbers vary markedly with population fluctuations of this prey item. • Cuckoos are essentially southern birds, and of the five species found in North America, only two regularly occur in Canada.

ID: brown upperparts; white underparts; long, white-spotted undertail; downcurved, dark bill; reddish eye ring.

Size: *L* 30 cm.

Status: fairly common in the aspen parkland ecoregion but uncommon and local elsewhere from late May to early September.

Habitat: densely vegetated woodlands, shrubs and thickets; often in riparian areas.

Nesting: in a shrub or small tree; nest of twigs is lined with grass and other vegetation; occasionally lays eggs in other birds' nests; pair incubates 2–3 eggs for up to 13 days.

Feeding: probes hairy caterpillars from leaves, branches and trunks; also eats other insects and berries.

Voice: fast *cu-cu-cu* or *cu-cu-cu-cu-cu*; also a series of *ca*, *cow* and *coo* notes.

Similar Species: *Mourning Dove* (p. 81): slender neck; peach-coloured underparts. *Yellow-billed Cuckoo:* yellow bill; prominent, white spots on undertail; lacks red eye ring; rare in Saskatchewan.

Best Sites: eastern Qu'Appelle Valley; Estevan; Regina; most common in the southeast especially during tent caterpillar outbreaks.

GREAT HORNED OWL

Bubo virginianus

The familiar *hoo-hoo-hoooo hoo-hoo* that resounds through campgrounds, suburban parks and farmyards is the call of the adaptable and superbly camouflaged Great Horned Owl. This formidable, primarily nocturnal, hunter uses its acute hearing and powerful vision to hunt a wide variety of prey, including grouse, ducks, snakes, hares, mice and even fish. Its poorly developed sense of smell may explain why it is the only consistent predator of skunks. • Great Horned Owls often begin courtship as early as January, when their hooting calls make them quite conspicuous. By February and March, they are already incubating their eggs, and by the time the last migratory birds have arrived in Saskatchewan, Great Horned owlets have already fledged. • Although Great Horned Owl population numbers vary considerably, this bird has the distinction of being the only permanent resident that can be found in any part of the province.

ID: large owl; prominent "ear" tufts set wide apart on head; yellow eyes; fine, horizontal barring on breast; facial disc outlined in black; white "chin"; overall colour varies from light grey to dark brown.
Size: *L* 46–64 cm; *W* 90–150 cm.
Status: uncommon to fairly common year-round.
Habitat: deciduous or coniferous forests, scattered trees in agricultural areas, riparian woodlands and suburban parks; widespread among fragmented or open woodlands; absent from large areas of continuous forest.
Nesting: in the abandoned stick nest of a crow, raven or hawk; rarely in abandoned buildings; little material is added to the nest; mostly the female incubates 2–6 dull, whitish eggs for about 33 days; nests as early as February.
Feeding: nocturnal; may also hunt at dusk and dawn or by day in winter; usually swoops from a perch; eats small mammals, birds, snakes and amphibians.

Voice: 4–6 deep, resonant hoots: *huu-hu-hu hooo-hooo* or *eat-my-food, I'll-eat you*; female's hoots are faster and higher-pitched.
Similar Species: *Long-eared Owl:* much smaller; tall, thin body and head; vertical breast streaks; "ear" tufts are close-set. *Eastern Screech-Owl:* much smaller; vertical breast streaks. *Other large owls:* lack prominent "ear" tufts.
Best Sites: widespread; most common in the aspen parkland ecoregion and in years when snowshoe hare populations are high.

83

SNOWY OWL

Nyctea scandiaca

W hen the mercury drops and the landscape hardens with winter's icy grip, ghostly white Snowy Owls appear on fenceposts, utility poles, fields and lakeshores. Motorists and landowners with an eye for these diurnal birds often spot them, even though they blend almost perfectly with nearly any flat, open, snow-covered landscape. In most winters, this arctic-breeding owl is a common resident in settled areas of our province. • Feathered to the toes, a Snowy Owl can remain active at cold temperatures and wind chill levels that send other owls to the woods for shelter. • As Snowy Owls age, their plumage becomes lighter in colour; old males are the most characteristic in their nearly all-white plumage.

ID: mostly white with varying amounts of dark flecking; white face and throat; yellow eyes; black bill and talons; rounded head with no "ear" tufts. *Male:* very little dark barring. *Female:* prominent dark barring on breast and upperparts. *Immature:* heavier barring than adult female.
Size: *L* 50–70 cm; *W* 1.4–1.7 m (female is noticeably larger).
Status: uncommon to fairly common, except in extensive forest, from late October to late April.
Habitat: in open country, including large forest clearings and fields.

Nesting: does not nest in Saskatchewan.
Feeding: usually hunts during daylight hours; eats mice, voles, grouse, partridges, hares and weasels in winter.
Voice: quiet in winter; barking *krow-ow* or repeated *rick* call on nesting grounds.
Similar Species: *Great Gray Owl:* grey plumage. *Great Horned Owl* (p. 83): prominent "ear" tufts; usually brown-grey overall; lacks white face. *Short-eared Owl* (p. 86): brownish breast streaking and upperparts; black eye sockets; dark "wrist" crescents.
Best Sites: widespread; especially common in open farmland with high Gray Partridge populations.

BURROWING OWL

Athene cunicularia

The Burrowing Owl is a loyal inhabitant of the prairies. Its favourite haunts are heavily grazed pastures in intensively cultivated regions and disturbed areas in extensive grasslands. Burrowing Owls nest underground in abandoned burrows, and during the day they are often seen atop fenceposts or on the dirt mound beside their lair. • The Burrowing Owl is considered an endangered species in Canada. Its range and population numbers have decreased drastically in recent years. Collisions with vehicles, the diminishing number of ground squirrels, the effect of agricultural chemicals and the conversion of native grasslands to cropland are thought to be some of the challenges facing this bird. Today the species' strongholds are the Regina Plains, the Cabri and Weyburn areas and Grasslands National Park.

ID: long legs; short tail; rounded head; no "ear" tufts; white around eyes; yellow bill; bold, white "chin" stripe; horizontal barring on underparts; brown upperparts are flecked with white. *Immature:* brownish band across breast; pale, unbarred underparts.

Size: *L* 23–28 cm; *W* 50–60 cm.

Status: uncommon and local from early April to late September.

Habitat: open, short-grass haylands, pastures and prairies; occasionally on lawns and golf courses.

Nesting: singly or in loose colonies; in an abandoned natural or artificial burrow; nest is lined with bits of dry manure, food debris, feathers and fine grass; female incubates 5–11 white eggs.

Feeding: eats mostly ground insects, such as grasshoppers, beetles and crickets; also eats small rodents, some birds, amphibians and reptiles.

Voice: call is a harsh *chuk*; chattering *quick-quick-quick*; rattlesnake-like warning call when inside its burrow. *Male: coo-hooo* courtship call is higher than, but similar to, the *coo* of the Mourning Dove (p. 81).

Similar Species: *Short-eared Owl* (p. 86): heavy, vertical streaks on underparts; small "ear" tufts; long wings with dark "wrist" marks; black eye sockets; doesn't nest in burrows. *Northern Saw-whet Owl:* bold, vertical, reddish streaks on underparts; short legs.

Best Sites: increasingly difficult to find but most readily seen in Grasslands NP and south of Regina.

85

SHORT-EARED OWL

Asio flammeus

The Short-eared Owl is a recent casualty of intensive agriculture in southern Saskatchewan. Although it has always been erratic in its numbers and distribution, it was once at least an uncommon summer resident. Except in a few areas, this owl has now declined to the point of rarity in our province. • Like the Snowy Owl (p. 84), the Short-eared Owl lacks conspicuous "ear" tufts and fills a niche that has been left unoccupied by forest-dwelling owls. This bird of open country occupies such habitats as wet meadows, marshes, fields, bogs and tundra, and it can be surprisingly difficult to locate, especially during the summer breeding season when females sit tightly on their ground nests. • In spring, Short-eared Owls perform visually dramatic courtship displays. Courting pairs fly together, and the male claps his wings on each downstroke as he performs short, periodic dives. Short-ears do not "hoot" like forest-dwelling owls because visual displays provide a more effective means of communicating in open environments.

ID: yellow eyes set in black sockets; heavy, dark vertical streaking on pale buff belly; straw-coloured upperparts; short "ear" tufts are often hidden. *In flight:* dark "wrist" crescents; buff upperwing patches; irregular, "flopping" flight pattern; deep wingbeats; long wings.

Size: *L* 33–43 cm; *W* 1–1.2 m (female is slightly larger).

Status: uncommon, local and erratic year-round.

Habitat: open areas, including grasslands, wet meadows, marshes, airports, muskegs and tundra.

Nesting: on the ground; in a slight depression sparsely lined with grass; female incubates 4–12 white eggs for up to 37 days.

Feeding: usually hunts at dawn and dusk; eats mainly voles and other small rodents; some insects, small birds and amphibians are taken.

Voice: generally quiet; produces a soft *toot-toot-toot* during nesting; also sneezy "barks" like a dog: *kee-yow, wow* or *waow.*

Similar Species: *Burrowing Owl* (p. 85): smaller; much longer legs; shorter wings and tail; brown, horizontal barring on white underparts; bold, white "chin" stripe; white-spotted upperparts. *Great Horned Owl* (p. 83) and *Long-eared Owl:* long "ear" tufts; rarely hunts during daylight hours.

Best Sites: widespread but usually erratic and local; Last Mountain Lake NWA.

COMMON NIGHTHAWK

Chordeiles minor

Each June and July, male nighthawks fly high above towns and cities, forest clearings, fields and lakeshores snatching up insects and gaining elevation in preparation for the climax of their noisy aerial display. High above, males dive swiftly and then thrust their wings forward in a braking action to pull out of the steep dive. This quick thrust of the wings produces a deep, hollow *vroom* that attracts female nighthawks. • Nighthawks are generally less nocturnal than other nightjars, but they still spend most of the day resting on a tree limb or on the ground. These birds have very short legs and small feet, and they sit along the length of tree branches, rather than across the branch as most perched birds do. • Like other members of the nightjar family, the Common Nighthawk is adapted for catching insects in midair: its gaping mouth is surrounded by feather shafts that help to funnel insects into its mouth.

ID: cryptic, mottled light and dark plumage; barred underparts. *Male:* white throat and undertail stripe. *Female:* buff throat. *In flight:* bold, white patches on long, pointed wings; shallowly forked, barred tail; erratic flight pattern.
Size: *L* 22–25 cm.
Status: fairly common, except in heavily cultivated areas, from late May to early September.
Habitat: open and semi-open habitats, such as forest openings, meadows, badlands, lakeshores, gravel pits and rooftops.
Nesting: on bare ground; on sand or gravel or on a rooftop; may use a stump or an abandoned robin's nest; pair incubates 2 olive white eggs for about 19 days.

Feeding: feeds primarily at dawn and dusk, but will also feed during the day and night; catches insects in flight; eats mosquitoes, moths and other flying insects.
Voice: frequently repeated, nasal *peent peent*; also makes a deep, booming *vroom* with its wings during courtship flights.
Similar Species: *Whip-poor-will* and *Common Poor-will:* lack white wing patches; shorter wings; rounded tail and wing tips; each species calls its own name; Whip-poor-will is uncommon in east-central Saskatchewan, Common Poorwill in southwestern Saskatchewan.
Best Sites: Besnard Lake; Candle Lake PP; Duck Mountain PP; Eastend; Meadow Lake PP; Moose Mountain PP; Prince Albert NP; Saskatchewan Landing PP; Saskatoon.

RUBY-THROATED HUMMINGBIRD

Archilochus colubris

The Ruby-throated Hummingbird spans the ecological gap between birds and bees—it feeds on the sweet, energy-rich nectar that flowers provide in exchange for pollination. While hovering, the Ruby-throat probes its long, thin bill deep into the heart of the flower, its extendible tongue lapping up the nectar. Many avid gardeners and birders have long understood the nature of this co-dependence and have planted nectar-producing plants in their yards in hopes of attracting these delightful birds. • Almost everything about hummingbirds is unique. Weighing about as much as a quarter, these birds are capable of speeds of up to 100 km/h for brief periods; in direct flight, they beat their wings up to 1200 times per minute. They are among the few birds that are able to fly vertically and in reverse and many have migration routes that take them hundreds of miles from their breeding grounds. • There are over 300 species of hummingbird in the world, all of which are restricted to the Western Hemisphere.

ID: size of a large moth or butterfly; long bill; iridescent, green back; light underparts; dark tail. *Male:* iridescent, ruby red throat (appears black in poor light); forked tail. *Female* and *Immature:* fine, dark throat streaking; rounded tail has white spots.
Size: *L* 7.5–9.5 cm.
Status: fairly common in the boreal plain ecozone, the aspen parkland ecoregion, and the Cypress upland ecoregion from late May to early September; uncommon and local in the grasslands from late May to early June and from late July to early September.
Habitat: open deciduous or mixed woodlands, orchards, parks and flower gardens.
Nesting: on a horizontal tree limb; bottlecap-sized cup nest of lichen,

moss and plant fibres is bound with spider silk; female incubates 2 white, pea-sized eggs for 13–16 days; often has 2–3 broods per year.
Feeding: drinks nectar from blooming flowers and sugar-sweetened water from special feeders; also eats small insects and spiders and feeds at sapsucker wells.
Voice: soft buzzing of the wings in flight; loud *chick* and other high squeaks when in courtship or territorial battles.
Similar Species: *Rufous Hummingbird:* male has rufous-coloured back and flanks; female has rufous patches on tail; uncommon in Saskatchewan.
Best Sites: *Breeding:* Candle Lake PP; Duck Mountain PP; Meadow Lake PP; Moose Mountain PP; Pike Lake PP; Prince Albert NP. *In migration:* Regina; Saskatoon.

BELTED KINGFISHER

Ceryle alcyon

Many of Saskatchewan's lakes, rivers, marshes and beaver ponds are monitored closely by the boisterous Belted Kingfisher. Never far from water, this bird is often found uttering its distinctive, rattling call while strategically perched on a bare branch that extends over a productive pool of water. The kingfisher dives head-first from its perch or hovers briefly before diving in. When it finally takes the plunge, it may disappear momentarily under the water's surface before quickly resurfacing with a fish in its bill. • A pair of kingfishers will typically take turns excavating their nest burrow. They use their bills to chip away at an exposed sandbank and then kick loose material out of the tunnel with their feet. Females have the traditional female reproductive role for birds, but, like phalaropes, are more colourful than their mates. • Kingfishers are found around the world, but the Belted Kingfisher is the only species found in Canada.

ID: long, dagger-like bill; large, blue head with shaggy crest; white collar; greyish-blue upperparts; blue breast band; white underparts. *Female:* has additional rust-coloured "belt" (may be incomplete), sides and flanks. *Male:* lacks rust-coloured belt, sides and flanks.

Size: *L* 27–36 cm.

Status: fairly common, except rare and local in the grasslands, from mid-April to mid-October.

Habitat: rivers, large streams, lakes and marshes, especially near exposed soil banks.

Nesting: along riverbanks and dirt cliffs; in a cavity at the end of an earth burrow, up to 4 m deep, dug by the pair with their bills and claws; nest cavity is lined with grass and leaves; pair incubates 6–8 white eggs.

Feeding: eats mostly small fish, frogs and tadpoles; may eat aquatic invertebrates, small rodents and birds; young are fed by regurgitation.

Voice: fast, repetitive, cackling rattle, a little like a teacup shaking on a saucer.

Similar Species: *Blue Jay* (p. 102): brighter blue overall; much smaller bill; neatly crested head; behaves in a completely different fashion.

Best Sites: Besnard Lake; Candle Lake PP; Duck Mountain PP; Yorkton; Estevan;Meadow Lake PP; Prince Albert NP.

YELLOW-BELLIED SAPSUCKER

Sphyrapicus varius

Yellow-bellied Sapsuckers arrive in our province in late April and early May, proclaiming their territories by drumming on tree trunks. Their irregular, Morse-code-like drumming is easily distinguished from the drumming of other woodpeckers. • Lines of parallel "wells" drilled in tree bark are a sure sign that a sapsucker is nearby. When the wells fill with sticky sap, they attract insects, and the sapsuckers make their rounds, eating both the trapped bugs and the pooled sap. Sapsuckers don't actually suck sap; they lap it up with a fringed tongue that resembles a paintbrush. Within their forest territory, a pair of sapsuckers often drill wells at a number of sites. This variation of the typical woodpecker foraging strategy has proven to be quite successful for the sapsucker.

ID: broad, black bib; red forecrown; black-and-white facial stripes; black overall with white barring on back, wings and tail; large, white shoulder patch; yellow wash on lower breast and belly. *Male:* red "chin" and throat. *Female:* white "chin" and throat. *Immature:* brownish overall; distinctive, white shoulder patch.
Size: *L* 20–23 cm; *W* 35–40 cm.
Status: fairly common in the boreal plain ecozone and northward and uncommon in the aspen parkland ecoregion and the Cypress upland ecoregion from late April to late September; uncommon in the grasslands from late April to early May and from mid-September to early October.
Habitat: deciduous and mixed forests, especially second-growth woodlands.
Nesting: in a cavity; usually in a live poplar or birch with heart-rot; lines the cavity with wood chips; pair

incubates 4–7 white eggs; nest trees are often reused.
Feeding: hammers trees for insects; drills "wells" in live trees where it collects sap and trapped insects; also eats wild fruit and flycatches for insects.
Voice: a cat-like *meow* or a nasal squeal; territorial/courtship hammering has a Morse-code-like quality and rhythm; hammering is rapid then slows near the end.
Similar Species: *Red-naped Sapsucker:* the Cypress Hills; nape red, female has white "chin," red throat. *Downy Woodpecker* (p. 91) and *Hairy Woodpecker:* lack large, white wing patch and red forecrown; red nape; white back patch. *Black-backed Woodpecker* and *Three-toed Woodpecker* (p. 92): lack white wing patch; yellow forecrown.
Best Sites: Besnard Lake; Candle Lake PP; Duck Mountain PP; Hudson Bay; Meadow Lake; Moose Mountain PP; Nisbet PF; Pike Lake PP; Prince Albert NP.

DOWNY WOODPECKER

Picoides pubescens

The Downy Woodpecker is the most common woodpecker in most regions of Saskatchewan. It is the most likely species to be attracted to backyard feeding stations during the colder months and is generally approachable and tolerant of human activities. Once you become familiar with its dainty appearance, you will also come to associate it with the soft taps and staccato calls that filter through your neighbourhood. Encounters are not confusion-free, however, because the Downy looks remarkably similar to its larger relative, the Hairy Woodpecker.
• The Downy's chisel-like bill is amazingly effective at poking into tiny crevices and exposing dormant invertebrates and wood-boring grubs. Like many woodpeckers, it has feathered nostrils to filter out the sawdust it produces by hammering. Woodpeckers also have to cushion their heads from the shock of all that hammering; they have evolved large bill, neck and skull muscles, a reinforced, flexible skull and a brain that is tightly packed in its cranium.

ID: clean, white belly and back; black wings are faintly barred with white; black eye line, "chin" stripe and crown; short, stubby bill; black tail; white outer tail feathers are spotted with black. *Male:* small, red nape patch. *Female:* no red nape patch.
Size: *L* 15–18 cm.
Status: common, except rare or absent in the grasslands, year-round.
Habitat: open deciduous or mixed forests, parks, orchards and riparian woodlots; avoids extensive forest.
Nesting: pair excavates a cavity in a dying or decaying trunk or limb; entrance hole is approximately 2.5 cm in diameter; cavity is lined with wood chips; pair incubates 3–6 white eggs.
Feeding: chips away at bark and probes trees for insect eggs, cocoons, larvae and adults; also eats nuts and seeds; attracted to sunflowers and suet feeders in winter.
Voice: a long trill or whinny that descends in pitch; calls are a sharp *pik*, *ki-ki-ki* or whiny *queek queek*.

Similar Species: *Hairy Woodpecker:* larger overall; bill is as long as head is wide; no spots on white outer tail feathers; harsher *peek* call. *Red-naped Sapsucker* and *Yellow-bellied Sapsucker* (p. 90): large, white shoulder patch; red forecrown; lacks red nape and clean, white back. *Black-backed Woodpecker* and *Three-toed Woodpecker* (p. 92): yellow forecrown; black barring on flanks.
Best Sites: widespread wherever there are woodlands; may move into smaller treed areas, such as farmsteads and cities, in winter.

THREE-TOED WOODPECKER

Picoides tridactylus

Evidence of the Three-toed Woodpecker's foraging activities is seen more commonly than the bird itself. In its search for insect eggs and invertebrates, it flakes off bits of bark from diseased, dead or dying conifers. After years of serving as forage sites, trees may be skirted with bark chips and take on a reddish look because of their exposed trunks. • While foraging, Three-toed Woodpeckers often listen for grubs under the bark and in the wood. These woodpeckers help to control infestations of the spruce bark beetle, a major forest pest. They may also feed on sap from wells dug by sapsuckers. • Both the Three-toed Woodpecker and the Black-backed Woodpecker have three toes instead of four, which is the usual number for woodpeckers. In Saskatchewan, the Three-toed Woodpecker outnumbers the Black-backed Woodpecker by a margin of about two to one.

ID: black-and-white barring down centre of back; white underparts; black barring on sides; predominantly black head with 2 white stripes; black tail with white outer tail feathers. *Male:* yellow crown. *Female:* black crown with occasional white spotting.
Size: *L* 21–24 cm.
Status: fairly common in the boreal plain ecozone and northward year-round; rare in aspen parkland ecoregion from early November to late February.
Habitat: mature spruce and fir forests, especially around concentrations of fire-killed or diseased trees.

Nesting: excavates a cavity in a dead or dying conifer trunk; excavation can take up to 12 days; pair incubates 4 eggs for up to 2 weeks.
Feeding: searches under bark flakes for larval and adult wood-boring insects; occasionally eats berries.
Voice: call is a low *pik*; drums in a prolonged series of steady bursts.
Species: *Black-backed Woodpecker:* solid black back. *Hairy Woodpecker:* clean white back; lacks barring on sides.
Best Sites: Besnard Lake; Candle Lake PP; Duck Mountain PP; Hudson Bay area; Nisbet PF; Prince Albert NP; Tobin Lake.

NORTHERN FLICKER

Colaptes auratus

Although woodpeckers are typically found in trees, the Northern Flicker is more apt to spend its time on the ground. It appears almost robin-like as it hops about on grassy meadows, fields and forest clearings searching for ants and other insects. On the wing, however, the flicker's powerful, undulating flight easily distinguishes it as a woodpecker. • Flickers are often seen bathing in dusty depressions. The dust particles absorb oils and bacteria that are harmful to the birds' feathers. To clean themselves more thoroughly, flickers will squish captured ants and then preen themselves with the remains (ants produce formic acid, which can kill small parasites on the flicker's skin and feathers). • All woodpeckers, including the Northern Flicker, can cling to vertical surfaces. Most have zygodactyl feet (two toes pointing forward and two toes pointing backward), hooked claws and a stiff tail to prop themselves upright. • There are two forms of Northern Flicker in Saskatchewan: the "Yellow-shafted Flicker" is more common and nests throughout much of the province; the "Red-shafted Flicker" is prevalent only in the extreme southwestern part of the province.

"Red-shafted Flicker"

"Yellow-shafted Flicker"

ID: barred, brown back and wings; black spots on buff underparts; black bib; white rump; long bill. *Yellow-shafted:* brownish to buff face; grey crown; red nape crescent; yellow underwings and undertail; male has black "moustache." *Red-shafted:* grey face; brownish crown; red underwings and undertail; male has red "moustache."
In flight: white rump is obvious.
Size: *L* 30–36 cm; *W* 47–53 cm.
Status: common from early April to mid-October; uncommon and local in the prairie ecozone (mainly in cities) from late October to late March.
Habitat: open deciduous, mixed and coniferous woodlands, forest edges, city parks and riparian woods.
Nesting: excavates a cavity in a dead or dying deciduous tree; may use a utility pole, nest box or may take over a nest tunnel in a dirt bank; nest is sometimes reused; lines the cavity with wood chips; pair incubates 5–12 white eggs for 11–16 days.
Feeding: searches the ground and bark on trees for ants; also eats worms, berries, nuts, beetles and other insects; may also flycatch; young are fed by regurgitation.
Voice: loud, laughing, rapid *kick-kick-kick-kick-kick-kick*; rapidly repeated *woika* or *flicker* call issued during courtship; also drums soft, muffled volleys.
Similar Species: none.
Best Sites: *Breeding:* widespread in most areas with at least some tree cover. *Winter:* larger cities.

PILEATED WOODPECKER

Dryocopus pileatus

With its flaming red crest, undulating flight and strident call, the Pileated Woodpecker can stop hikers in their tracks. This large, crow-sized woodpecker is uncommon, even in its preferred habitat, and because it maintains a large territory, it is not frequently encountered. If you do encounter a Pileated Woodpecker, however, it will be difficult to miss because it is often vocal and spends much of its time drumming on tree trunks and drilling for carpenter ants. A fist-sized cavity at the base of a large tree is also a telltale sign that a Pileated is nearby. • In March and April, pairs work in shifts to excavate a nesting cavity, which may take up to a month to complete. If you come across wood chips at the base of a large, mature poplar, shift your gaze upward and you may find an active Pileated Woodpecker nest. When the young fledge, they look like miniature versions of their parents. • As a primary cavity nester, the Pileated Woodpecker plays an important role in forest ecosystems. Other birds and even mammals depend on the activities of this woodpecker—ducks, owls, kestrels and flying squirrels are frequent nesters in Pileated cavities.

ID: black overall; flaming red crest; black-and-white striped head and neck; stout, dark bill. *Male:* red "moustache"; red crest extends from bill. *Female:* duller; black "moustache"; red crest starts on crown. *In flight:* white wing linings.
Size: *L* 40–50 cm; *W* 68–76 cm.
Status: fairly common in the boreal plain ecozone, uncommon in the boreal shield ecozone and the aspen parkland ecoregion and rare in the grasslands (Leader area) year-round.
Habitat: extensive tracts of mature, deciduous forest or dense, mature, deciduous stands; may also use extensive, heavily wooded river corridors in agricultural areas.

Nesting: excavates a cavity in a dead or dying tree; cavity is lined with wood chips; pair incubates 3–5 white eggs.
Feeding: often hammers at the base of rotting trees; creates fist-sized or larger, oblong (or rectangular) holes; eats ants, wood-boring beetles, larvae, berries and nuts.
Voice: much louder flicker-like call; irregular *kik-kik-kikkik-kik-kik*; fast, rolling *woika-woika-woika-woika*; long series of *kuk* notes; loud resonant drumming.
Similar Species: *Other woodpeckers:* much smaller; lack crest. *American Crow* (p. 104) and *Common Raven* (p. 105): lack white underwings and flaming red crest.
Best Sites: Besnard Lake; Candle Lake PP; Duck Mountain PP; Hudson Bay; Nisbet PF; Meadow Lake PP; Prince Albert NP; Tobin Lake.

LEAST FLYCATCHER

Empidonax minimus

This bird might not look like a bully, but the Least Flycatcher is one of the boldest and most pugnacious songbirds in Saskatchewan. During the nesting season, it is noisy and conspicuous, forcefully repeating its two-part call throughout much of the day and chasing any small bird that enters its territory. Intense song battles usually eliminate the need for physical aggression, but feather-flying fights are occasionally required to settle disputes. • Throughout most of Saskatchewan, the Least Flycatcher is the most abundant *Empidonax* flycatcher. It is less specific in its choice of habitat than most other flycatchers are, so it is more widely distributed and thus more likely to be seen. • There are two families of flycatchers: tyrant flycatchers and Old World flycatchers. Only tyrant flycatchers are found in Canada and they are an extremely successful family of birds, with 374 species found throughout the Western Hemisphere.

ID: olive grey upperparts; 2 white wing bars; bold, white eye ring; fairly long, narrow tail; dark upper mandible; yellow-orange lower mandible; white throat; whitish-grey breast; mostly white belly and undertail coverts; flicks its tail and wings. *Immature:* buff wing bars.
Size: *L* 13–15 cm.
Status: common, except uncommon and local in the grasslands, from mid-May to mid-September.
Nesting: on a horizontal limb or in the fork of a tree; small cup nest of grass, plant fibres and shredded bark is lined with fine grass, plant down and feathers; female incubates 3–6 creamy white eggs for about 15 days.
Feeding: flycatches, hovers and probes for ants, caterpillars and other insects; may eat some fruits and seeds.

Voice: constantly repeated, *che-bec che-bec* or *Quebec Quebec;* call note is a dry *whit.*
Similar Species: *Western Wood-Pewee:* stouter head; lacks distinct eye ring and conspicuous wing bars. *Alder Flycatcher:* faint eye ring; song is *free-beer;* mostly found near water. *Willow Flycatcher:* lacks distinct eye ring; greener upperparts; yellower underparts; song is *fwitch-be-hear;* less common in Saskatchewan. *Yellow-bellied Flycatcher:* yellowish eye ring; greener upperparts; yellower underparts; song is *je-bunk* or *per-wee.* *Ruby-crowned Kinglet* (p. 116): bold, broken eye ring; much daintier bill; shorter tail, more horizontal posture.
Best Sites: widespread in all but the smallest wooded areas (native or planted).

EASTERN PHOEBE

Sayornis phoebe

Eastern Phoebes once nested on cliffs and fallen trees, but their mud nests are now found primarily on buildings and under bridges. This species and the closely related Say's Phoebe are the earliest flycatchers to return to our province in spring, and their nest-building activities are normally well underway by the time many other songbirds make their first appearances here. With such an early start, phoebe pairs regularly raise two broods during the nesting season, often reusing the same nest. • Other birds pump their tails while perched, but few species can match the zest and frequency of the Eastern Phoebe's tail pumping and fanning. This habit is a valuable identification point, since the Eastern Phoebe is a drab, greyish bird with few conspicuous field marks. • The Say's Phoebe is also found in Saskatchewan, but it is less common and occurs mainly in the southwestern part of the province in drier, more open habitat.

ID: grey-brown upperparts; all-black bill; white underparts with grey wash on breast and sides; no eye ring or conspicuous wing bars; dark legs; frequently pumps and spreads its tail. *Immature:* browner upperparts; yellowish underparts; faint, buff wing bars.
Size: *L* 16–19 cm.
Status: common and local in the boreal plain ecozone and northward from late April to early October; uncommon migrant (and local nester) in the prairie ecozone from late April to early May and from early August to early October.
Habitat: open deciduous woodlands, riparian woods and forest edges; usually near a source of water and often near bridges or buildings.
Nesting: under the ledge of a building, culvert, bridge or cliff; often in an abandoned Barn Swallow (p. 110) nest; bulky nest of moss, grass,

rootlets, fur and feathers is often attached with mud to a ledge; female incubates 4–8 white eggs for 16 days; has 2 broods per year.
Feeding: flycatches flying beetles, flies, wasps, grasshoppers, mayflies and other insects; may eat some frogs and tiny fish.
Voice: hearty, snappy *phoe-be* or *fee-bee* (2nd note alternates from higher to lower than the first); call is a sharp *chip*.

Similar Species: *Western Wood-Pewee:* pale wing bars; bicoloured bill; does not wag its tail. *Olive-sided Flycatcher:* dark sides form an open "vest"; 2 white, fluffy rump patches. *Empidonax flycatchers:* most have eye ring and conspicuous wing bars. *Say's Phoebe:* larger; apricot belly.
Best Sites: Candle Lake PP; Duck Mountain PP; Meadow Lake PP; Nicolle Flats; Prince Albert NP; Yorkton.

WESTERN KINGBIRD

Tyrannus verticalis

The Western Kingbird's bickering call and aggressive nature make it a difficult bird to miss. This kingbird will attack large birds, such as crows and hawks that fly through its territory, and in some instances, it will even dive-bomb house cats that approach too closely to its nest. Witnesses to these brave attacks will find it easy to understand why this brawler was awarded the name "kingbird." • Western Kingbirds are adept at catching insects in mid-air, and they are commonly seen perched on fenceposts, powerlines and utility poles. • The tumbling aerial courtship display of the Western Kingbird often indicates that this bird is nesting nearby. Twisting and turning, the male rises up into the sky, stalls and then plummets back to earth. • Western Kingbirds were once confined to the wooded valleys of the Cypress Hills, but with human settlement they have spread to become common summer residents in farm shelterbelts, towns and cities of southern Saskatchewan.

ID: grey head and breast; dark grey eye line; thin, orange-red crown (rarely seen); white "chin"; black bill; yellow belly and undertail coverts; ash grey upperparts; darker wings and tail; white outer tail feathers.

Size: *L* 20–23 cm.

Status: common in the grasslands and uncommon elsewhere from mid-May to early September.

Habitat: riparian woodlands, towns, farm shelterbelts and open scrubland areas with scattered patches of brush or hedgerows.

Nesting: in a deciduous tree; sometimes on a utility post; bulky cup nest of grass, weeds, wool and twigs is lined with fur, plant down and feathers; female incubates 3–7 whitish, heavily blotched eggs for 14 days.

Feeding: flycatches for aerial insects, including bees, wasps, butterflies, moths, grasshoppers and flies; occasionally eats berries.

Voice: chatty, bickering calls: *whit-ker-whit*, a short *kit* or extended *kit-kit-keetle-dot*.

Similar Species: *Eastern Kingbird* (p. 98): black upperparts; white underparts; white-tipped tail. *Great Crested Flycatcher:* bushy crest on head; rufous tail and wings; faint wing bars; lacks white outer tail feathers.

Best Sites: Eastend; Grasslands NP; Kindersley; Last Mountain Lake NWA; Leader; Luck Lake; Maple Creek.

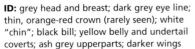

97

EASTERN KINGBIRD

Tyrannus tyrannus

The Eastern Kingbird could be referred to as a "Jekyll and Hyde bird" because it is a gregarious fruit-eater while wintering in South America and an antisocial, aggressive insect-eater while nesting in Canada. • This bird's tyrannical nature is reflected in its scientific name, *Tyrannus tyrannus*. Like the Western Kingbird, it will fearlessly attack crows, hawks and even humans that pass through its nesting territory, often vigorously pursuing intruders. It is not uncommon to see an Eastern Kingbird chase a soaring hawk and pull feathers from its head. • The kingbird's fluttery courtship flight, which is characterized by short, quivering wingbeats, belies the bird's aggressive nature. • In courtship displays, males tumble and hover, often revealing their red crown patch and white tail band.

ID: dark grey to blackish upperparts; white underparts; white-tipped tail; black bill; adults have thin, orange-red crown (rarely seen); no eye ring; black legs; quivering flight style.
Size: *L* 20–23 cm.
Status: common in the prairie ecozone and uncommon elsewhere from mid-May to early September.
Habitat: fields with scattered shrubs, trees or hedgerows, forest fringes, clearings, shrubby roadsides, towns and farmyards.
Nesting: on a horizontal limb of an isolated tree or shrub; rarely in cavities, on stumps, in artificial structures or fenceposts; cup nest composed of weeds, twigs, string, wool and grass is lined with soft materials; female incubates 3–5 darkly blotched, white to pinkish-white eggs for up to 14 days.

Feeding: flycatches aerial insects; infrequently eats berries.
Voice: call is a quick, loud, chattering *kit-kit-kitter-kitter;* also a buzzy *dzee-dzee-dzee;* also a nasal *dzeep.*
Similar Species: *Western Kingbird* (p. 97): yellow upperparts; grey underparts; white-edged tail. *Tree Swallow* (p. 108): iridescent, dark blue or green back; lacks white-tipped tail; smaller and more stream-lined; smaller bill. *Olive-sided Flycatcher:* lacks white-tipped tail; dark sides form an open "vest"; 2 white rump tufts. *Western Wood-Pewee:* smaller; bicoloured bill; lacks white-tipped tail; underparts are not uniformly white.
Best Sites: widespread in any brushy area in the south; restricted to shrubby riparian areas and muskegs in the north.

LOGGERHEAD SHRIKE

Lanius ludovicianus

Shrikes are predatory songbirds that will kill and eat small birds and rodents, as well as large insects. When they strike, these birds rely on their sharp, hooked bills to dispatch their quarry, although they may use their feet to help as well. A male Loggerhead Shrike will sing to establish a territory and attract a mate like most other songbirds, but he will also impale his prey on thorns and barbed wire around his territory. This habit might be a means of storing excess food items or of demonstrating his hunting competence to female shrikes. • Although a drive through southern Saskatchewan can produce a dozen Loggerhead Shrike sightings, conservationists are concerned about this species' future, and it is considered threatened in Canada. In recent years, its populations have declined in both range and number throughout North America. • The Northern Shrike, a close relative, is also found in Saskatchewan. It replaces the summer-resident Loggerhead Shrike in winter, making the task of distinguishing between the two species less onerous for the average birder.

ID: black tail and wings; grey crown and back; white underparts; barred flanks; black mask extends above hooked bill. *Immature:* brownish-grey, barred upperparts. *In flight:* white wing patches; white-edged tail.
Size: *L* 23 cm.
Status: fairly common in the grasslands and uncommon elsewhere from late April to early September.
Habitat: open areas with shrublands and grasslands.
Nesting: in a low crotch in a shrub or small tree; on rare occasions, nests have been found in piles of tumbleweeds and rolls of fencing wire; bulky cup nest is made with twigs and grass and lined with fine materials; female incubates 5–6 eggs for 15–17 days.

Feeding: swoops down on prey from a perch or attacks prey in pursuit; regularly eats small birds, rodents and shrews; will commonly take insects if they are available; also eats carrion.

Voice: *Male:* bouncy *hiccup, hugh-ee hugh-ee*, during summer; infrequently a harsh *shack-shack*.
Similar Species: *Northern Shrike:* winter resident; larger; finely barred underparts; immature has a faint mask and brown-grey, unbarred upperparts. *Northern Mockingbird:* lacks black mask; generally more sleek and slim; rare in Saskatchewan.
Best Sites: Last Mountain Lake NWA; Maple Creek.

RED-EYED VIREO

Vireo olivaceus

The Red-eyed Vireo is Saskatchewan's undisputed champion when it comes to vocal endurance. In spring and well into summer, males will sing continuously through the day until long after most songbirds have curtailed their courtship melodies. One particularly vigorous Red-eyed Vireo, although not from Saskatchewan, holds the current world record for the most songs delivered by an individual bird in a single day: 22,197! • Red-eyed Vireos sound a lot like American Robins (p. 119), and you might be surprised to discover this vireo hiding behind a "familiar" song right in front of your eyes. When learning these birds' calls, keep in mind that Red-eyed Vireos are not commonly heard in our province until mid-May (robins arrive here as early as mid-March). • Red-eyed Vireos are common throughout much of our province, but finding one may require a bit of effort. They are difficult to spot because, like most vireos, they blend in well with their leafy background and move slowly and deliberately among the upper forest canopy.

ID: dark eye line; white eyebrow; black-bordered, blue-grey crown; olive green back and wings; pale grey cheeks; white to pale grey underparts; may have a yellow wash on sides, flanks and undertail coverts, especially in autumn; no wing bars; adults have red eyes.
Size: *L* 14–16 cm.
Status: common, except uncommon and local in the grasslands, from mid-May to mid-September.
Habitat: pure or mixed deciduous groves and forests, especially those of aspen poplar; well-treed yards and towns; prefers a semi-open canopy and shrubby understorey.
Nesting: in the fork of a tree or shrub; nest is a hanging, basket-like cup of grass, rootlets, shredded bark, spider silk and lichen; female incubates 3–5 dark-spotted, white eggs for 11–14 days.

Feeding: skims foliage for insects, especially caterpillars; also hovers; rarely eats snails and berries.
Voice: song is a continuous, robin-like run of phrases, with pauses in-between: *Look-up way-up tree-top see-me here-I-am*; call note is a nasal, whining *chway*.
Similar Species: *Philadelphia Vireo:* yellow breast; lacks black border to blue-grey cap; song is very similar, slightly higher pitched. *Warbling Vireo:* incomplete, faint eye line; lacks contrast between cap and back. *Blue-headed* and *Yellow-throated vireos:* white spectacles and wing bars. *Tennessee Warbler* (p. 125): blue-grey cap and nape; white eyebrow; olive green back; slimmer bill; dark eyes.
Best Sites: *Breeding:* widespread in larger wooded tracts. *In migration:* any wooded area.

GRAY JAY

Perisoreus canadensis

Few birds exceed mischievous Gray Jays in curiosity and boldness. Attracted by any foreign sound or potential feeding opportunity, small family groups glide gently and unexpectedly out of spruce stands to introduce themselves to any passers-by. Gray Jays are well known to anyone who camps or picnics in the boreal forest, because these "camp robbers" will make themselves at home at your campsite; they will not hesitate to steal scraps of food off an unattended plate. While they might be bothersome at times, Gray Jays are likeable birds and are probably the most mild-mannered of the jays. • Gray Jays lay their eggs and begin incubation as early as late February. Their nests are well insulated to conserve heat, and nesting early allows young jays the time to learn how to forage efficiently and store food before the next cold season approaches. • The Gray Jay has some interesting nicknames: "Whiskey Jack," "Camp Robber" and "Canada Jay."

ID: fluffy, pale grey underparts; dark grey upperparts; white crown, forehead, cheek, throat and undertail coverts; dark grey nape; fairly long tail; dark bill. *Immature:* dark sooty grey overall; white whisker line is distinctive. *In flight:* flap-and-glide flier.
Size: *L* 25–33 cm.
Status: common in the boreal plain ecozone and northward year-round; uncommon in the aspen parkland ecoregion and rare in the grasslands from late November to early February.
Habitat: coniferous and mixed forests, bogs, picnic sites and campgrounds.
Nesting: usually in a coniferous tree; bulky, well-woven nest made of plant fibres, roots, moss and twigs is lined with feathers, hair and fur; female incubates 3–5 pale green,

brown-spotted eggs for about 17 days.
Feeding: diet includes insects, fruit, seeds, fungi, eggs, nestlings and carrion; stores food at scattered cache sites.
Voice: complex vocal repertoire includes a soft, whistled *quee-oo*, a chuckled *cla-cla-cla* and a *churr*; also imitates other birds.
Similar Species: *Loggerhead Shrike* (p. 99) and *Northern Shrike:* black mask; black-and-white wings and tail; hooked bill; Northern Shrike is rare in summer in northern Saskatchewan. *Northern Mockingbird:* white wing patch and outer tail feathers; longer, slimmer bill; rare in Saskatchewan.
Best Sites: Besnard Lake; Candle Lake PP; Duck Mountain PP; Hudson Bay; Meadow Lake PP; Prince Albert NP; Tobin Lake.

BLUE JAY

Cyanocitta cristata

The Blue Jay embodies all the admirable traits and aggressive qualities of the corvid family, which includes the magpie, crow, raven and other jays. Although it is beautiful and resourceful, the Blue Jay can at times prove to be one of the most annoying birds around. Whether on its own or gathered in a mob, a Blue Jay will rarely hesitate to drive away smaller birds, squirrels or even cats. It seems that no predator, not even the Great Horned Owl (p. 83), is too formidable for this bird to cajole or harass. Fortunately, this jay's intriguing character and enchanting boldness usually outweigh its rebellious behaviour. • For a short time during the breeding season, Blue Jays are quiet and unsociable as they tend to the duties of raising young. By late summer, however, they are back to their usual selves, frequenting gardens and backyards to satisfy their ravenous appetites and harass other birds. Blue Jays are most evident in winter, when they appear at feeders generously stocked with sunflower seeds and peanuts.

ID: blue crest; black "necklace"; blue upperparts; white underparts; white bar and flecking on wings; dark bars and white corners on blue tail; black bill.
Size: *L* 28–31 cm.
Status: fairly common in the boreal plain ecozone and aspen parkland ecoregion year-round; uncommon and local in the grasslands from mid-September to late March.
Habitat: mixed or deciduous forests and townsites.
Nesting: in the crotch of a tree or tall shrub; pair builds a bulky stick nest and

incubates 4–5 greenish, buff or pale blue eggs, spotted with grey and brown, for 16–18 days.
Feeding: forages on the ground and among vegetation for nuts, berries, eggs and nestlings; also eats insects and carrion; visits birdfeeders.
Voice: noisy, screaming *jay-jay-jay*; nasal *queedle, queedle-queedle* sounds a little like a muted trumpet; often imitates various sounds.
Similar Species: none.
Best Sites: widespread; inconspicuous in summer; conspicuous at feeders in winter.

BLACK-BILLED MAGPIE

Pica hudsonia

The saying "familiarity breeds contempt" is well illustrated by the Black-billed Magpie in Saskatchewan and across the prairies. Truly one of North America's most beautiful birds, magpies are too often maligned because of their raucous demeanor. Many of us are jaded by the omnipresence of the magpie, but this bird plays a valuable role in our environment by consuming large numbers of grasshoppers, grubs and other harmful insects. • Magpies became rare in the province after the great bison herds were slaughtered, but they soon returned to recolonize the southern half of our province, cleverly adapting to life in both rural and urban areas. • An exceptional architect, the Black-billed Magpie builds an elaborate domed nest that can be found in a spruce or deciduous tree or, on occasion, on an iron bridge. Constructed from sticks and held together with mud, the domed compartment conceals and protects eggs and young from predators and harsh weather. The nests are so well constructed that they may remain in trees for years, and non-building birds, such as Merlins (p. 54) and owls, often use them as nest sites.

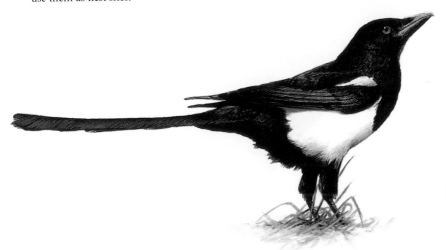

ID: colourful, iridescent wings and very long tail may appear black; black head, breast, back and undertail coverts; white belly; large, black bill. *In flight:* rounded, black-and-white wings.

Size: L 46–56 cm.

Status: common in the prairie ecozone and uncommon and local elsewhere year-round; spreads north in the winter.

Habitat: farmyards, hedgerows and open tree and shrub groves, often near human habitations.

Nesting: often colonial; in a tree or tall shrub; domed nest, made of sticks and twigs and often with a mud or manure base, is lined with mud, grass, rootlets and hair; female incubates 5–13 spotted, greenish-grey eggs for up to 24 days.

Feeding: omnivorous; forages for insects, carrion, human food-waste, nuts, seeds and berries; picks insects and ticks off livestock and deer; occasionally takes the eggs and nestlings of other birds.

Voice: loud, nasal, frequently repeated *yeck-yeck-yeck* or *wah-wah-wah-wah*; also a nasal *maag* or *aag-aag*; many other vocalizations include a repertoire of "soft talk."

Similar Species: none.

Best Sites: widespread; most common at farmsteads, towns and cities; also at roadkills.

103

AMERICAN CROW

Corvus brachyrhynchos

American Crows are wary, intelligent birds that have flourished in spite of considerable efforts, over many generations, to reduce their numbers. One of the reasons for this species' staying power is that it is a generalist, which allows it to adapt and thrive in a variety of environments. • During the breeding season, the density of American Crows varies considerably over its nearly province-wide range. In autumn, when these birds' reproductive duties are complete, they group together in flocks of thousands. These thrilling aggregations (also known as "murders") are merely get-togethers in preparation for evening roosts and preambles for the autumn exodus. • Crows occasionally overwinter in our province, usually in the larger cities. • *Corvus brachyrhynchos* is Latin for "raven with the small nose."

ID: slight purplish iridescence on all-black body; black bill and legs; fan-shaped tail; sleek head and throat. *In flight:* rarely glides.
Size: *L* 43–53 cm; *W* 94 cm.
Status: common in the prairie ecozone and uncommon and local elsewhere from late March to early November; occasional in settled areas from mid-November to mid-March.
Habitat: open woodlands, hedgerows and farm shelterbelts, riparian woodlands, urban parks and shrubby clumps in open areas.
Nesting: in a coniferous or deciduous tree or shrub; medium-sized stick nest is lined with bark, rootlets, fur and soft plant materials; female incubates 4–9 brownish-blotched, blue-green eggs for about 18 days.
Feeding: opportunistic; feeds on carrion, small rodents, reptiles, amphibians, berries, seeds, human food-waste, invertebrates and the eggs and nestlings of other birds.
Voice: distinctive *caw-caw-caw*.
Similar Species: *Common Raven* (p. 105): larger; wedge-shaped tail; shaggy throat; much heavier bill; often glides in flight.
Best Sites: widespread, except in the north where it is restricted to human habitation and other disturbed areas.

COMMON RAVEN

Corvus corax

Whether it is stealing food from a flock of gulls, harassing a Bald Eagle (p. 46) in mid-air or confidently strutting among campers at a park, the raven is worthy of its reputation as a bold and clever bird. Glorified in native cultures throughout the Northern Hemisphere, the Common Raven does not act by instinct alone. From producing complex vocalizations to playfully sliding down snowbanks, this raucous bird exhibits behaviours that many people once thought of as exclusively human. • Common Ravens were permanent residents throughout Saskatchewan during the time of the great bison herds, feeding on bison kills and other carrion. When the herds were exterminated, these birds retreated to northern parts of the province, where they remain common, permanent residents. In recent years, they have reinvaded some of their former haunts to become uncommon winter residents in the prairie ecozone. • Few birds occupy as large a natural range as the Common Raven. Throughout the Northern Hemisphere it is found along coastlines, in deserts, on mountain tops and even on tundra. • The Common Raven is the largest passerine, or perching bird, in the world.

ID: all-black plumage may show a slight, purplish iridescence; heavy, black bill; shaggy throat; rounded wings. *In flight:* often glides; wedge-shaped tail.

Size: *L* 61 cm; *W* 1.3 m.

Status: common in the boreal plain ecozone and northward (and occasionally in the aspen parkland ecoregion) year-round; fairly common and increasing in the aspen parkland ecoregion and the Cypress upland ecoregion from early October to late March.

Habitat: coniferous and mixed forests and woodlands, tundra, townsites, campgrounds and landfills; often forages at dumps and along roadways.

Nesting: on cliffs, ledges, bluffs, tall coniferous trees and utility poles; large stick nest is lined with bark, grass, fur, hair and soft plant materials; female incubates 4–7 brown-blotched, greenish eggs for about 21 days.

Feeding: opportunistic; feeds on carrion, small mammals, reptiles and amphibians, the eggs and nestlings of other birds, berries, invertebrates and human food-waste.

Voice: deep, guttural, far-carrying, repetitive *craww-craww* or *quork quork*; also a croaking *cr-r-ruck* or *prruk* and a metallic *tok*; many other vocalizations.

Similar Species: *American Crow* (p. 104): smaller; fan-shaped tail; throat lacks shaggy feathers; slimmer bill; rarely glides in flight; call is higher-pitched and less variable.

Best Sites: widespread; commonly seen at roadkills and landfills in winter.

105

HORNED LARK

Eremophila alpestris

The tinkling sounds of Horned Larks flying over pastures and fields are a sure sign that another spring season has arrived. Horned Larks are among the earliest arrivals in our province, settling on fields and along roadsides long before the snows are gone. Flying and gliding in circles, displaying males issue their sweet chimes in flight before plummeting towards the ground in dramatic, high-speed dives. • Late winter is also a good time to observe these open-country specialists as they congregate in flocks on farm fields and roadsides, often in the company of Snow Buntings (p. 148). The wintering population includes birds that nest on the southern prairie and those that nest in the Arctic and Subarctic. • Horned Larks belong to the Alaudidae family, a predominantly Old World group that inhabit open, barren landscapes, such as deserts, beaches, grasslands and fields. Most larks are gregarious and many sing beautiful songs when flying over their nesting territories. The Horned Lark is the only member of this family native to North America.

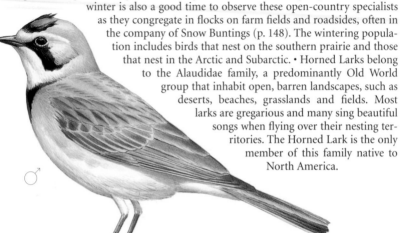

ID: small, black "horns" (not always evident); black line extends from eye to cheek; light yellow to white face; black breast band; dull brown upperparts; dark tail with white outer tail feathers. *Female and Immature:* less distinctive head patterning; duller plumage overall. *In flight:* pale underparts; white outer tail features are obvious.
Size: *L* 18 cm.
Status: common in the boreal plain ecozone and northward from late March to early May and from late September to late October; uncommon at the Athabasca sand dunes from early April to late August; common to abundant in the prairie ecozone from early March to late October; uncommon in settled areas from early November to mid-March.
Habitat: open areas, including pastures, native prairie, cultivated or sparsely vegetated fields, golf courses, airfields and tundra.

Nesting: on the ground; in a shallow scrape among short, sparse vegetation, often beside a rock or dry cow dung; nest is lined with grass, plant fibres and fine roots; female incubates 3–5 pale grey to greenish eggs, blotched and spotted with brown, for about 12 days; often has 2 broods per year.
Feeding: probes the ground for seeds and insects.
Voice: call note is a tinkling *tsee-titi* or *zoot*; flight song (sometimes given from the ground) is a long series of irregular, tinkling chimes *trick trick trick trick trick t-r-r-r-r-r-r-r-r*.
Similar Species: *American Pipit, Sprague's Pipit* (p. 123), *sparrows* and *longspurs:* all lack "horns" and distinctive facial pattern.
Best Sites: *Breeding:* widespread in farmland and ranchland. *In migration* and *Winter:* most common along major roads.

PURPLE MARTIN

Progne subis

At localities scattered throughout parts of Saskatchewan, Purple Martins attempt to hold their ground against pushy European Starlings and House Sparrows (p. 164). Purple Martins once nested in natural tree hollows, but competition with European Starlings for nest sites and the loss of snags through logging has diminished their numbers. Today, they depend mostly on human-made, apartment-style martin complexes or "condos" for nesting sites. To be successful in attracting these large swallows, a martin complex must be placed high on a pole in a large, open area, preferably near water. The complex should have suitably sized cavity openings, and it must be cleaned out each autumn and replaced only after the martins have returned in spring to prevent House Sparrows or European Starlings from moving in. In Moose Mountain Provincial Park this species also nests in the arms of actively pumping oil wells!

ID: large, bluish-black swallow; glossy upperparts; slightly forked tail; pointed wings; small bill. *Male:* the only swallow with dark underparts. *Female* and *Immature:* sooty grey underparts. *In flight:* alternates quick flaps with swooping glides; often spreads its tail.

Size: *L* 18–20 cm.

Status: common in the aspen parkland ecoregion and uncommon and local in the boreal plain ecozone from mid-May to early September; rare in the grasslands in May and August.

Habitat: attracted to martin condos in towns, farmyards and semi-open areas, often near water.

Nesting: colonial; usually in a human-made, apartment-style birdhouse; rarely in tree cavities; nest

materials include feathers, grass, mud and vegetation; female incubates 4–8 unmarked, white eggs for 15–17 days.

Feeding: mostly while in flight; usually eats flies, ants, dragonflies, mosquitoes and other flying insects; may also walk on the ground, taking insects and rarely berries.

Voice: rich, fluty *pew-pew* or *tchew-wew*; gurgling song is often heard in flight.

Similar Species: *European Starling* (p. 122): longer bill (yellow in summer); lacks forked tail. *Barn Swallow* (p. 110): deeply forked tail; buff underparts. *Tree Swallow* (p. 108): smaller; white underparts.

Best Sites: Douglas PP; Greenwater Lake PP; Last Mountain Lake NWA; Moose Mountain PP; Yorkton.

107

TREE SWALLOW

Tachycineta bicolor

Tree Swallows are typically observed perching beside their fencepost nest boxes. When conditions are favourable, these busy birds may return to their nest site to feed their young 10 to 20 times per hour. They are proficient insect-eaters, gracefully catching even the most elusive flying insects in mid-air. • This cavity-nesting swallow is characteristic of treed areas and is a common breeding bird throughout forested regions of Saskatchewan. Tree Swallows prefer to nest in natural tree hollows or woodpecker cavities in standing dead trees, but where cavities are scarce, they readily use nest boxes. • When Tree Swallows leave their nests to forage, they frequently cover their eggs with feathers from their nest. These swallows are so enticed by feathers that nest-building parents will sometimes swoop down to get feathers tossed in the breeze. • In the bright spring sunshine, the back of the Tree Swallow appears blue; prior to autumn migration, the back appears to be green.

ID: iridescent, bluish-black upperparts; white underparts; small bill; long, pointed wings; shallowly forked tail. *Female:* slightly duller. *Autumn adult:* iridescent, green upperparts. *Immature:* dusky brown upperparts; white underparts may show pale brown wash on breast.

Size: *L* 14 cm.

Status: common, except rare and local in the grasslands, from late April to early September.

Habitat: open areas, fencelines with bluebird nest boxes and fringes of open woodlands, especially near water.

Nesting: in a tree cavity or nest box lined with weeds, grass and feathers; female incubates 4–7 pale pink to white eggs for up to 19 days.

Feeding: catches flies, midges, mosquitoes, beetles and ants on the wing; also takes emergent flying insects over water; may eat some berries and seeds.

Voice: alarm call is a metallic, buzzy *klweet* or *chi-veet*; song is a liquid, chattering twitter: *weet, trit, weet.*

Similar Species: *Violet-green Swallow:* green upperparts; white cheek and rump patches, restricted to southwestern Saskatchewan. *Purple Martin* (p. 107): female has sooty grey underparts; male is dark overall. *Bank Swallow* (p. 109): brown upperparts; brown breast band. *Northern Rough-winged Swallow:* brown upperparts; pale brown wash on throat and upper breast. *Barn Swallow* (p. 110): buff underparts; deeply forked tail.

Best Sites: widespread; especially visible at nesting boxes.

BANK SWALLOW

Riparia riparia

A colony of Bank Swallows can be a constant flurry of activity as eager parents pop in and out of their earthen burrows with mouthfuls of insects for their insatiable young. Not surprisingly, all this activity tends to attract attention, but few predators are able to catch these swift and agile birds. • Bank Swallows usually excavate their own nest burrows, initially scraping with their small bills and later digging with their feet. Most nestlings are safe from predators within their nest chamber, which is typically 60 to 90 cm in length. Many burrows are left unfinished, so the numbers of holes in the colony does not necessarily indicate the number of nests. • In pre-settlement days, Bank Swallows were probably much rarer than they are today. These birds once nested in cutbanks along watercourses, but today colonies can also be found in a variety of artificial habitats, such as sand or gravel pits and railway embankments.

ID: brown upperparts; light underparts; brown breast band; long, pointed wings; shallowly forked tail; white throat; dark cheek; small legs.

Size: *L* 13 cm.

Status: common and local in the prairie ecozone and uncommon and local elsewhere from early May to early September.

Habitat: steep banks, lakeshores and open areas.

Nesting: colonial; in a burrow in a steep earthen bank; pair excavates the cavity and incubates 4–5 eggs for up to 16 days.

Feeding: catches flying insects; drinks on the wing.

Voice: twittering chatter: *speed-zeet speed-zeet.*

Similar Species: *Northern Rough-winged Swallow:* lacks dark breast band. *Violet-green Swallow:* green upperparts; white cheek and rump patches; lacks dark breast band. *Tree Swallow* (p.108): lacks dark breast band; greenish upperparts.

Best Sites: *Breeding:* widespread; near cutbanks and gravel pits. *Foraging:* over lakes and rivers.

BARN SWALLOW

Hirundo rustica

Although Barn Swallows do not occur in mass colonies, they are familiar to most of us because they usually build their nests on human-made structures. Barn Swallows once nested on cliffs, but their cup-shaped nests are now often found in barns, picnic shelters, under bridges or in any other structure that provides shelter from predators and inclement weather. Unfortunately, not everyone appreciates their craftsmanship, and many Barn Swallow families have been unceremoniously removed from their nesting sites. Although Barn Swallows are somewhat messy, they are natural pest controllers and should therefore be encouraged to nest. • "Swallow tail" is a term used to describe something that is deeply forked. In Saskatchewan, the Barn Swallow is the only swallow that displays this feature.

ID: long, deeply forked tail; dark, chestnut throat and forehead; buff-coloured underparts; bluish-black upperparts. *Female* and *Immature:* duller underparts; tail is less forked.
Size: *L* 18 cm.
Status: common in the prairie ecozone and uncommon and local elsewhere from late April to early October.
Habitat: open country, including farmyards and townsites, especially where buildings are found near water.
Nesting: singly or in loose colonies; on a building under an overhang, under a bridge or in a culvert; often in an abandoned building; half-cup nest is made of mud and is lined with grass and feathers; pair incubates

4–7 spotted, white eggs for 12–17 days; has 2 or more broods per year.
Feeding: catches flying insects on the wing; rarely eats berries; often drinks and bathes on the wing.
Voice: continuous twittering chatter: *zip-zip-zip*; also *kvick-kvick*.
Similar Species: *Cliff Swallow:* squared tail; buff rump and forehead; light-coloured underparts. *Purple Martin* (p. 107): shallowly forked tail; male is blue-black overall; female has sooty grey underparts. *Tree Swallow* (p. 108): clean white underparts; notched tail.
Best Sites: widespread around rural buildings and bridges but mostly absent from cities.

BLACK-CAPPED CHICKADEE

Poecile atricapilla

Throughout the winter months, Black-capped Chickadees are often found in the company of Golden-crowned Kinglets, nuthatches, and small woodpeckers. At this time of year, chickadees are common visitors to backyard feeders, and they can be enticed to land on an outstretched hand offering sunflower seeds. It is estimated that on a –40° C day, chickadees spend about 20 times longer feeding than on a typical summer day. • Most songbirds, including chickadees, have both songs and calls. The chickadee's *cheese-burger* song is delivered primarily during courtship to attract mates and to defend territories. The *chick-a-dee-dee-dee* call, which can be heard year-round, is used to keep flocks together and to maintain contact within the group. • Saskatchewan is also home to the Boreal Chickadee, a less common relative of the Black-capped Chickadee that resides in the northern boreal forest. It has a grey-brown cap and calls a soft, nasal, whistled *scick-a day day*.

ID: black cap and bib; white cheek; grey back; dark grey wing feathers are edged with white; white underparts; buff sides.
Size: *L* 13–15 cm.
Status: common, except rare or absent from southern grasslands, year-round.
Habitat: deciduous and mixed forests, riparian woodlands, wooded urban parks and wooded backyards with birdfeeders.
Nesting: in a natural cavity, abandoned woodpecker nest or nest box; may also excavate its own cavity; nest is lined with fur, feathers, moss and fine grass; female incubates 6–8 finely dotted, white eggs for up to 13 days.
Feeding: probes vegetation, branches and the ground for small insects, spiders, seeds and berries; frequents seed and suet feeders in winter; also eats conifer seeds and invertebrate larvae and eggs.
Voice: call is a chipper, whistled *chick-a-dee-dee-dee*; song is a simple, whistled *cheese-burger*; as spring approaches its song may change to *spring-is-here*.
Similar Species: *Boreal Chickadee:* grey-brown cap and back; dusky cheeks; rich brown flanks; wing feathers lack white edgings. *Blackpoll Warbler* (p. 131): breeding male has streaked back, 2 white wing bars and dark streaking on flanks.
Best Sites: *Breeding:* widespread in native woodlands. *Winter:* feeders in farmsteads, towns and cities.

RED-BREASTED NUTHATCH

Sitta canadensis

The nasal *yank-yank-yank* call of the Red-breasted Nuthatch is a familiar sound in forested regions of Saskatchewan. Nuthatches stand out from other songbirds because of their striped head, unusual body form, loud nasal calls and habit of moving headfirst down tree trunks. • The Red-breasted Nuthatch smears the entrance of its nesting cavity with sap. This sticky doormat may discourage insects or predators from entering the nest chamber. Invertebrates can be a serious threat to nesting success because they can transmit fungal infections or parasitize nestlings. • This bird visits neighbourhood birdfeeders with regularity, but it darts in like a missile, never lingering longer than it takes to grab a seed and dash off again. • Saskatchewan is also home to the White-breasted Nuthatch. Unlike its red-breasted relative, which typically inhabits mixed and coniferous forests, the White-breasted Nuthatch prefers mature deciduous stands.

ID: rusty underparts; grey-blue upperparts; white eyebrow; black eye line; black cap; straight bill; short tail. *Female:* light rusty wash on underparts; dark grey cap.
Size: *L* 11 cm.
Status: irruptive; fairly common in the boreal shield ecozone from early April to late November; fairly common in the boreal plain ecozone and the Cypress upland ecoregion year-round; fairly common in the prairie ecozone from mid-April to mid-May and from late August to early November, but uncommon and local at other times.
Habitat: *Breeding:* coniferous forests and plantations and coniferous stands in mixed forests (prefers mature forest stands). *Winter:* generally near coniferous stands, especially those with nearby birdfeeders.
Nesting: excavates a cavity in the trunk or branch of a rotting tree or shrub; rarely in an abandoned woodpecker cavity; cavity is lined with bark shreds, fine grass, fur and moss; female incubates 5–7 white eggs, spotted with reddish-brown, for up to 14 days.
Feeding: forages down tree trunks; probes crevices and under loose bark for larval and adult invertebrates; eats pine and spruce seeds during winter; frequents seed and suet feeders.
Voice: sounds like the original toy tin horn; higher, slower and more nasal than the White-breasted Nuthatch's calls: *yank-yank-yank* or *rah-rah-rah-rah*; also a short *tsip*.
Similar Species: *White-breasted Nuthatch:* larger; lacks black eye line; white face and breast.
Best Sites: *Year-round:* Candle Lake PP; Cypress Hills PP; Duck Mountain PP; Meadow Lake PP; Prince Albert NP; Saskatoon. *Winter:* Regina.

BROWN CREEPER

Certhia americana

Brown Creepers are never easy to find. They inhabit mature forests, and their cryptic coloration means they often go unnoticed until a flake of bark suddenly takes the shape of a bird. If a creeper is frightened, it will freeze and flatten against the tree trunk, becoming even more difficult to see. • Intent on feeding, the Brown Creeper spirals up tree trunks, searching for hidden invertebrates with its long, probing bill. When it reaches the upper branches, it floats down to the base of a neighbouring tree to begin its next foraging ascent. Creepers have long, curved claws that enable them to creep about tree trunks and long, stiff tail feathers to prop them up as they hitch their way skyward. • Like the call of the Golden-crowned Kinglet, the thin whistle of the Brown Creeper is so high-pitched that birders often fail to hear it. To further the confusion, the creeper's song often takes on the boisterous warbling quality of a wood-warbler song.

ID: brown back is heavily streaked with greyish white; white eyebrow; white underparts; downcurved bill; long, pointed tail feathers; rusty rump.

Size: *L* 13 cm.

Status: uncommon and local in the boreal plain ecozone year-round; uncommon in the prairie ecozone from late September to early May.

Habitat: mainly coniferous forests, such as spruce, fir and pine.

Nesting: under loose bark; nest is made of grass and conifer needles woven together with spider silk; female incubates 5–6 eggs for 15–17 days.

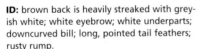

Feeding: creeps up trunks and large limbs, probing loose bark for adult and larval invertebrates.

Voice: faint, high-pitched *trees-trees-trees see the trees.*

Similar Species: *Red-breasted Nuthatch* (p. 112): grey-blue back. *Black-and-white Warbler:* black-and-white plumage; shorter tail. *Woodpeckers:* all lack brown back streaking and have straight bill.

Best Sites: Candle Lake PP; Duck Mountain PP; Meadow Lake PP; Prince Albert NP.

HOUSE WREN

Troglodytes aedon

The House Wren's bubbly song and energetic demeanour make it a welcome addition to any neighbourhood. In the wild, it uses a small cavity in a snag, but in urban areas a nest box is usually all it takes to attract this joyful bird to a backyard. Wrens have adapted well to urban life, and suitable nest sites also include flowerpots, sheds, wood piles and vacant drainpipes, provided there is a local abundance of insect prey. • Like other wrens, male House Wrens are feverish nest builders. The males arrive on their breeding grounds first and build several incomplete nests throughout their territories. Once the females arrive and choose which nest they prefer, the males complete the chosen nest. The other nests scattered throughout the territory are not wasted—they often serve as dormitories later in the season or as dummy nests. In areas where there is a high population of House Wrens, competing males may puncture eggs or kill neighbouring young of their own, or other, species.

ID: brown upperparts; fine, dark barring on wings; "cocked" tail is finely barred with black; sharp, slightly downcurved bill; faint eyebrow stripe; pale eye ring; whitish throat; whitish to buff underparts; faintly barred flanks.
Size: L 12 cm.
Status: common in the prairie ecozone and uncommon and local elsewhere from mid-May to early October.
Habitat: open thickets and shrubby edges of deciduous or mixed woodlands; often in shrubs and thickets in towns and farmyards.
Nesting: in a natural or artificial cavity; commonly uses wren or bluebird nest boxes; nest of twigs and grass is lined with feathers, fur and soft materials; female incubates 6–12 white eggs with heavy reddish-brown spotting for up to 19 days; 2–3 broods per year.

Feeding: probes the ground and vegetation for insects, especially beetles, caterpillars, grasshoppers and spiders.
Voice: bubbly song lasts about 2–3 seconds, rising in a musical burst and falling at the end: *tsi-tsi-tsi-tsi oodle-oodle-oodle-oodle.*
Similar Species: *Winter Wren:* smaller; much darker overall; shorter, stubby tail; prominent dark barring on flanks. *Sedge Wren:* heavily streaked on crown and back; short tail. *Marsh Wren* (p. 115): bold, white eyebrow; black back with white streaks.
Best Sites: Buffalo Pound PP; Duck Mountain PP; Eastend; Estevan; Last Mountain Lake NWA; Pike Lake PP; Moose Mountain PP; Prince Albert NP; Saskatchewan Landing PP; Yorkton.

MARSH WREN

Cistothorus palustris

The energetic and reclusive Marsh Wren is almost always associated with deep-water cattail marshes or dense, wet meadows. This expert hunter can catch flying insects with lightning speed, but don't expect to see it in action—the Marsh Wren is difficult to spot in its dense marshland habitat. Marsh Wrens are compulsive vocalists, however, and they typically sing their distinctive, old-fashioned sewing-machine-like songs atop conspicuous perches. • Marsh Wrens occasionally destroy the nests and eggs of other marsh-nesting songbirds, including other Marsh Wrens and the Red-winged Blackbird (p. 150). The blackbird, however, is prevented from doing the same because the Marsh Wren's globe-shaped nest keeps its eggs well hidden, and several dummy nests scattered around the territory help to conceal the location of the real nest.

ID: white underparts; dusky flanks; brown upperparts; unstreaked, dark crown; distinctive, black triangle on upper back and shoulder is streaked with white; bold, white eyebrow; long, thin, downcurved bill.
Size: *L* 13 cm.
Status: common and local from early May to late September.
Habitat: large cattail and bulrush marshes interspersed with open water; may use tall grass or sedge marshes.
Nesting: among tall emergent vegetation, usually up to 1 m above water; globe-like nest, woven with marsh reeds and grass, is lined with cattail down and feathers; female incubates 4–10 heavily dotted, pale brown eggs for 12–16 days; male

may have more than 1 mate; usually has 2 broods per year.
Feeding: probes vegetation and flycatches for adult aquatic invertebrates, especially dragonflies and damselflies.
Voice: rapid, rattling, warbled *cut-cut-tur-rrrrrr-ur* like an old-fashioned sewing machine or rapid gunfire; call is a harsh *chek* or *tsuck*.
Similar Species: *Sedge Wren:* smaller; streaked crown; buff undertail; song is sweeter and subtler. *House Wren* (p. 114): faint eyebrow; lacks white streaking and black triangle on back.
Best Sites: Buffalo Pound PP; Chaplin Lake/Marsh; Last Mountain Lake NWA; Nicolle Flats; Pike Lake PP; Yorkton.

115

RUBY-CROWNED KINGLET

Regulus calendula

The Ruby-crowned Kinglet is named for its bright but usually concealed crown feathers, and its king-sized song helps merit its surname. In summer, its exuberant song can be heard in coniferous and mixedwood forests in the northern parts of our province. • During courtship, the male kinglet erects his brilliant red crown and sings to impress prospective mates. Throughout most of the year, however, his crown remains hidden among dull feathers and is impossible to see even through binoculars. • While in migration, Ruby-crowned Kinglets are regularly seen flitting about treetops, intermingling with a colourful assortment of warblers and vireos. • The Ruby-crowned Kinglet is sometimes mistaken for a Least Flycatcher (p.95), but its frequent hovering and energetic wing-flicking behaviour sets it apart from similar-looking birds.

ID: bold, broken eye ring; 2 bold, white wing bars; olive green upperparts; dark wings and tail; whitish to yellowish underparts; short tail; flicks its wings. *Male:* small, red crown (usually hidden). *Female:* lacks red crown.
Size: *L* 10 cm.
Status: common in the boreal plain ecozone and northward from late April to late September; common migrant (and local nester) in the prairie ecozone from late April to mid-May and from early September to early October.
Habitat: *Breeding:* mixed and coniferous woodlands and muskegs. *In migration:* any woodland.
Nesting: usually in a spruce tree; hanging nest is made of moss, lichen, twigs and leaves; female incubates 7–9 eggs for up to 16 days.
Feeding: probes and hovers for insects; may eat seeds and berries.

Voice: song is an accelerating and rising *tea-tea-tea-tea-tew-tew-tew look-at-Me, look-at-Me, look-at-Me* or *Mister-WHAT cha-call-EM what-you-DO.*
Similar Species: *Golden-crowned Kinglet:* dark eye line; black-bordered crown; male has orange crown bordered by yellow; female has yellow crown. *Orange-crowned Warbler* (p.126): olive yellow overall; no eye ring or wing bars. Empidonax *flycatchers:* vertical posture; complete eye ring or no eye ring at all; larger bill; longer tail; lack red crown.
Best Sites: *Breeding:* Besnard Lake; Candle Lake PP; Cypress Hills PP; Duck Mountain PP; Hudson Bay; Meadow Lake PP; Prince Albert NP; Tobin Lake. *In migration:* Last Mountain Lake NWA; Regina; Saskatoon.

MOUNTAIN BLUEBIRD

Sialia currucoides

Despite its name, the Mountain Bluebird is a fairly common summer resident in the aspen parkland ecoregion. • Spring and autumn migrations most often consist of small groups of birds, but on occasion, Mountain Bluebirds will migrate in flocks of more than 100 birds. • Natural nest sites, such as woodpecker cavities or holes in sandstone cliffs are in high demand, and aggressive starlings often steal these locations from mild-mannered bluebirds. As a result, bluebirds now frequently use the artificial nest boxes that have been established in some parts of Saskatchewan. Mountain Bluebirds often raise two broods per year. In such cases, fledglings may help to gather food for the second nest. • Although the occasional Mountain Bluebird is recorded on a Christmas bird count, most birds migrate to the western United States for the winter.

ID: black eyes, bill and legs. *Male:* sky blue body; upperparts darker than underparts. *Female:* sky blue wings, tail and rump; blue-grey back and head; grey underparts, sometimes tinged with dull orange.

Size: *L* 18 cm.

Status: common in the prairie ecozone and uncommon and local elsewhere from late March to early October.

Habitat: open forests, forest edges, burned forests, agricultural areas and grasslands.

Nesting: in an abandoned woodpecker cavity, natural cavity or nest box; nest is built of plant stems, grass, conifer needles and twigs and frequently lined with a few feathers; female incubates 5–6 pale blue eggs for 13 days.

Feeding: swoops from a perch for flying and terrestrial insects; also forages on the ground for a variety of invertebrates, such as beetles, ants and bugs.

Voice: call is a low *turr turr*. *Male:* song is a short warble of *chur* notes.

Similar Species: *Eastern Bluebird:* male has extensive orange below; female is duller, with pale orange extending to neck and flanks; uncommon in southeastern Saskatchewan. *Blue Jay* (p. 102): prominent crest. *Townsend's Solitaire:* peach-coloured patches on wings and tail; white outer tail feathers; rare to uncommon in Saskatchewan.

Best Sites: local in areas with sandy soils and nestboxes; Buffalo Pound PP; Cypress Hills PP; eastern Qu'Appelle Valley; Pike Lake PP.

SWAINSON'S THRUSH

Catharus ustulatus

On its breeding grounds, the Swainson's Thrush is rarely seen but often heard singing its ethereal and flute-like song. In migration, it skulks on the ground under shrubs and tangles and often finds itself in backyards and neighbourhood parks. • Most thrushes feed on the ground, but the Swainson's Thrush is also adept at collecting invertebrates from the tree canopy, sometimes briefly hovering to forage like a warbler or vireo. A wary bird, it is most often seen as it flushes from the ground to a low perch. If you can spot where it has landed you may be able to watch it long enough to distinguish it from other thrushes, such as the Veery, Gray-cheeked Thrush or Hermit Thrush. All four species occur as migrants in the southern part of the province but choose different areas of Saskatchewan to breed: the Gray-cheeked Thrush nests in the far north, the Hermit and Swainson's thrushes share the boreal forest, and the Veery is found mainly in the aspen parkland ecoregion and southern woodlands.

ID: grey-brown upperparts; noticeable, buff eye ring; buff wash on cheek and upper breast; triangular spots arranged in streaks on throat and breast; white belly and undertail coverts; brownish-grey flanks.
Size: *L* 18 cm.
Status: common in the boreal plain ecozone and northward from mid-May to mid-September; common in the prairie ecozone from early to late May and from mid-August to mid-September.
Habitat: *Breeding:* dense understorey in coniferous and mixedwood boreal forest; prefers moist areas with spruce and fir. *In migration:* moist riparian areas and shrubby parks and gardens.
Nesting: usually in a shrub or small tree; cup nest of weeds, grass, leaves, roots and lichen is lined with fur and soft fibres; female incubates 3–5 spotted, pale blue eggs for 12–13 days.

Feeding: skims vegetation and forages on the ground for invertebrates; may hover while foraging; also eats berries.
Voice: song is a slow, rolling, rising spiral: *Oh, Aurelia will-ya, will-ya will-yeee;* call is a sharp *wick.*
Similar Species: *Gray-cheeked Thrush:* lacks conspicuous eye ring; greyish cheeks; less or no buff wash on breast; uncommon in Saskatchewan. *Hermit Thrush:* reddish tail and rump contrast against greyish-brown back; darker breast spotting on whiter breast. *Veery:* lacks bold eye ring; more reddish upperparts; faint breast streaking.
Best Sites: *Breeding:* Besnard Lake; Candle Lake PP; Cypress Hills PP; Duck Mountain PP; Meadow Lake PP; Nisbet PF; Prince Albert NP. *In migration:* Last Mountain Lake NWA; Regina; Saskatoon.

AMERICAN ROBIN

Turdus migratorius

American Robins are widespread and abundant in many of Saskatchewan's natural habitats, but they are familiar to most of us because they commonly inhabit residential lawns, gardens and parks. Of the birds adapted to urban life, the American Robin is the best known. Its cheery songs, spotted young and vulnerability to house cats are familiar throughout Saskatchewan. • These birds are widely recognized as harbingers of spring, and when March rolls around we look forward to their arrival in our province. However, Robins are not necessarily absent in winter, they are only less abundant. Most winter records are from open springs and cities. • When hunting, robins may appear to be listening for prey beneath a lawn, but they are in fact looking for movements in the soil—they tilt their heads because their eyes are placed so far to the sides. • Robins usually raise two broods per year. While the male cares for fledglings from the first brood, the female incubates the second clutch of eggs. Young robins are easily distinguished from their parents by their dishevelled appearance and heavily spotted undersides.

ID: grey-brown back; dark head, tail and wings; white throat is streaked with black; white undertail coverts; incomplete, white eye ring; yellow, black-tipped bill.
Male: deep brick red breast; darker head.
Female: dark grey head; light brick red breast. *Immature:* heavily spotted, rusty breast.
Size: *L* 25 cm.
Status: common in the boreal plain ecozone and northward and fairly common elsewhere from late March to early November; uncommon and local in the settled south from mid-November to mid-March.
Habitat: *Breeding:* residential lawns, gardens, urban parks, woodlot edges and openings, burned areas, clear-cuts, bogs and fens. *Winter:* near fruit-bearing trees and springs.

Nesting: often in a coniferous tree or shrub; sometimes on a protected building ledge; well-built cup nest of grass, moss and loose bark is cemented with mud and grass; female incubates 4 light blue eggs for 11–16 days; usually has 2 broods per year.
Feeding: forages on the ground for larval and adult insects, earthworms, other invertebrates and berries.
Voice: song is a prolonged series of rising and falling phrases: *cheerily cheer-up cheerio*; call is a rapid *tut-tut-tut* or *tyeep*.
Similar Species: *Varied Thrush:* orange eye stripe and wing bars; dark breast band; rare in Saskatchewan.
Best Sites: widespread but restricted mainly to farmsteads, towns and cities in the south. *Winter:* mainly at springs in towns and cities.

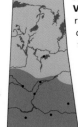

119

GRAY CATBIRD

Dumetella carolinensis

True to its name, the Gray Catbird has a call that sounds much like the mewing of a house cat. This secretive bird is often far easier to hear than to see—whether it's feeding or nesting, it typically remains hidden among dense deciduous shrubs, thorny fenceline thickets and streamside brambles. Catbirds are typically shy birds, but their curiosity will occasionally draw them close to a patient, motionless observer. • The Gray Catbird's courtship activities involve an unusual "mooning" display in which the male raises his long, slender tail to show off his red undertail coverts. As if proud of his red posterior, the male often looks back over his shoulder in mid-performance. • Gray Catbirds vigorously defend their nesting territories. They are so thorough in chasing away intruders that the nesting success of neighbouring warblers and sparrows increases as a result of the catbird's vigilance. • Female catbirds spend most of their time on their nests, so they are less susceptible to parasitism by Brown-headed Cowbirds (p. 155). Even if a cowbird sneaks past the watchful female to deposit an egg in the nest, the foreign egg is often quickly recognized and ejected.

ID: dark grey overall; black cap; long tail may be dark grey to black; chestnut undertail coverts; black eyes, bill and legs.
Size: *L* 20–23.5 cm.
Status: common from mid-May to mid-September.
Habitat: dense thickets, brambles, shrubby or brushy areas and hedgerows, often near water; also along forest edges, but not in deep forest.
Nesting: low in a dense shrub; bulky cup nest of twigs, leaves and grass is lined with fine materials; female incubates 2–6 greenish-blue eggs for up to 15 days; often has 2 broods per year.

Feeding: probes the ground and vegetation for ants, beetles, grasshoppers, caterpillars, moths and spiders; also eats berries and visits feeders.
Voice: calls include a cat-like *meow* and a harsh *check-check*; song is a variety of warbles, squeaks and mimicked phrases issued only once and often interspersed with a *mew* call.
Similar Species: *Gray Jay* (p. 101): lacks black cap and chestnut undertail coverts.
Best Sites: eastern Qu'Appelle Valley; Estevan; Last Mountain Lake NWA; Leader; Nicolle Flats; Pike Lake PP; Saskatchewan Landing PP; Yorkton.

BROWN THRASHER

Toxostoma rufum

Brown Thrashers have the most extensive vocal repertoire of any North American bird—biologists have estimated that a male thrasher is capable of producing up to 3000 distinctive song phrases. He adds new phrases to his songs by reproducing sounds made by other male thrashers and neighbouring birds. This thrasher's complex song of repeated phrases distinguishes it from other mimic thrushes (members of the Mimidae family), such as the Gray Catbird (p. 120), which rarely repeats each phrase, and the Northern Mockingbird, which tends to issue each phrase three times.
• The Brown Thrasher frequently feeds in the open but is rarely found far from cover. At the slightest sign of danger, it scurries towards safety—a typical thrasher sighting consists of nothing more than a flash of rufous as the bird zips beneath a shrubby tangle.
• The Brown Thrasher is a common breeding bird throughout southern parts of our province. In the grasslands, it frequents riparian brush and shrubbery, while in the aspen parkland ecoregion it uses the edges of aspen groves.

ID: reddish-brown upperparts; light-coloured underparts with heavy, brown spotting and streaking; long, downcurved bill; orange-yellow eyes; long, rufous tail; 2 white wing bars. *Immatures:* grey eyes.

Size: L 27–30 cm.

Status: common from early May to late September.

Habitat: dense shrubs and thickets along woodland edges, shelterbelts, and farmsteads; rarely nests in urban areas.

Nesting: low in a shrub; rarely on the ground; cup nest of grass, twigs, leaves and bark is lined with rootlets and fine vegetation; pair incubates 3–6 reddish-brown dotted, pale blue eggs for up to 14 days; often has 2 broods per year.

Feeding: probes the ground and digs among debris for larval and adult invertebrates; also eats seeds and berries.

Voice: sings a variety of phrases similar to the catbird's song, but each phrase is usually repeated twice: *dig-it dig-it, hoe-it hoe-it, pull-it-up, pull-it-up;* calls include a harsh *shuck,* a soft *churr* or a whistled 3-note *pit-cher-ee.*

Similar Species: *Hermit Thrush:* shorter tail; grey-brown back and crown; dark brown eyes; much shorter bill; lacks wing bars. *Sage Thrasher:* grey back; shorter tail and bill; rare in southwestern Saskatchewan.

Best Sites: eastern Qu'Appelle Valley; Estevan; Last Mountain Lake NWA; Leader; Pike Lake PP; Saskatchewan Landing PP; Yorkton.

EUROPEAN STARLING

Sturnus vulgaris

The European Starling was introduced to North America from Europe around 1890. About 60 birds were released in New York City's Central Park as part of a local Acclimatization Society's plan to introduce to the city all the birds mentioned in Shakespeare's writings. The starling then spread to almost every corner of the continent—reaching Saskatchewan around 1940—usurping nesting sites from native, cavity-nesting birds. Despite concerted efforts to control or even eradicate the European Starling, the species continues to thrive. Its rapid spread across North America and its effect on native birds is a classic example of the hazards of introducing exotic species into an environment that is too complex for us to fully understand. • During the breeding season, starlings prefer open habitats, such as farmland and urban areas. Their nests are found in a variety of locations, including barns, grain elevators, nest boxes and woodpecker holes.

breeding

ID: short, squared tail; dark eyes. *Breeding:* blackish, iridescent plumage; yellow bill. *Non-breeding:* dark plumage is heavily speckled; white on head, neck and underparts; dark bill. *In flight:* pointed, triangular wings; swift flight. *Immature:* grey-brown plumage; dark bill.
Size: *L* 22 cm.
Status: common in the prairie ecozone and uncommon and local in the boreal plain ecozone from late March to late November; uncommon and local at farmsteads and in cities from early December to mid-March.
Habitat: *Breeding:* cities, towns, residential areas, farmyards, woodland fringes and clearings. *Winter:* near feedlots and pastures.
Nesting: in a natural or artificial cavity; nest is made of grass, twigs, feathers and straw; mostly the

female incubates 4–6 bluish to greenish eggs for 12–14 days; has 2–3 broods per year.
Feeding: very diverse diet includes invertebrates, berries, seeds and human food-waste.
Voice: variety of whistles, squeaks and gurgles, including a harsh *tseeeer* and a whistled *whooee*; often imitates other birds, including Killdeers (p. 66), hawks and jays.
Similar Species: *Rusty Blackbird:* longer tail; black bill; lacks spotting; yellow eyes; rust-tinged upperparts in autumn. *Brewer's Blackbird* (p. 153): longer tail; black bill; lacks spotting; male has yellow eyes; female is brown overall. *Brown-headed Cowbird* (p. 155): lacks spotting; dark, stout bill; longer tail; adult male has brown head; juvenile has streaked underparts.
   Best Sites: widespread in farmsteads, towns and cities; sometimes around chimneys in winter.

SPRAGUE'S PIPIT

Anthus spragueii

This prairie vocalist delivers an uplifting melody from high above the ground, its song carrying across the open landscape. As he sings, the male often flies in a continuous circle, sometimes for an hour or more at a time. The Sprague's Pipit has few musical rivals. Its plumage, on the other hand, is quite ordinary. It wears a pattern common to many prairie passerines: camouflaged browns with white outer tail feathers that are only visible in flight. • This threatened bird has adapted poorly to the cultivation of agricultural crops in the prairies because it requires extensive native grassland areas. • Isaac Sprague was a talented illustrator who accompanied famed artist John J. Audubon across the northern Great Plains. He later became one of America's foremost botanical artists.

ID: white outer tail feathers; thin bill; light-coloured legs; greyish-brown upperparts streaked with buff; lighter underparts; faint breast streaks.

Size: *L* 16–17 cm.

Status: fairly common and local in the prairie ecozone from early May to early September.

Habitat: native short-grass prairie, preferably ungrazed or lightly grazed.

Nesting: in a depression on the ground; well-built cup nest is made of woven grass; female incubates 4–5 heavily spotted, white eggs.

Feeding: walks along the ground foraging for grasshoppers, beetles, moths and other invertebrates; may also eat seeds.

Voice: swirling and descending, bell-like *choodly choodly choodly chooodly*.

Similar Species: *American Pipit:* darker plumage; darker legs; wags its tail. *Vesper Sparrow* (p. 141): heavier bill; chestnut shoulder patch. *Baird's Sparrow:* lacks white outer tail feathers.

Best Sites: Grasslands NP; Last Mountain Lake NWA; Leader; Maple Creek; Saskatchewan Landing PP.

BOHEMIAN WAXWING

Bombycilla garrulus

There is indeed a redeeming feature of prairie winters. Large flocks of elegant Bohemian Waxwings descend upon our cities to feast on the fruit of mountain ash and other ornamental trees. Waxwings have a remarkable ability to digest a wide variety of berries, some of which are inedible or even poisonous to humans. They will gorge on berries for hours with seemingly insatiable appetites, but they must be careful because an overindulgence of fermenting berries in the spring can lead to accidents related to drinking and flying! In rural areas, where ornamentals are scarce and where wild berry crops are unpredictable, waxwing flocks are more modest in size. • Some of the birds that are found here in winter nest in the open coniferous forests of northern Saskatchewan, but many raise their young in the mountains of the West. • Waxwings get their name from the waxy tips on the inner flight feathers of most birds. The significance of this trait is unknown, but males and older birds of both sexes have more waxy tips than younger birds.

ID: cinnamon crest; black mask; black throat; soft grey-brown body; yellow terminal tail band; red undertail coverts; white, red and yellow spots on wings. *Immature:* brown-grey above; streaked underparts; light throat; no mask; white wing patches.
Size: *L* 18 cm.
Status: fairly common in the taiga shield and boreal shield ecozones from early March to late November; uncommon in the western portion of the boreal plain ecozone year-round; uncommon to abundant in the prairie ecozone from late October to early April.
Habitat: *Breeding:* forest edges, second-growth, riparian and open deciduous woodlands. *Winter:* farm shelterbelts and wooded residential parks and gardens, especially near fruit trees and springs.

Nesting: often in a coniferous tree; cup nest made of twigs, grass, moss and lichen is often lined with fine grass and seed fluff; female incubates 3–5 spotted, pale bluish-grey eggs for 12–16 days.
Feeding: catches flying insects on the wing; also eats large amounts of berries and wild fruit.

Voice: faint, high-pitched, trilled whistle: *tseee-tseee-tseee.*
Similar Species: *Cedar Waxwing:* smaller; slight yellow wash on belly; lacks red undertail coverts and white in wings, calls are much softer.
Best Sites: *Breeding:* widespread in burns and open forest in the far north. *Winter:* widespread in wooded areas; especially common in larger cities.

TENNESSEE WARBLER

Vermivora peregrina

Tennessee Warblers lack the bold, brilliant colours of other Saskatchewan warblers. Even so, they are difficult birds to miss because they have a loud staccato song and are relatively common in our province. • In spring, migrating Tennessee Warblers are difficult to see as they sing their tunes and forage for insects in the high upper canopy of trees. In August and early September, our river valleys and woodlots are bustling with these small migrants. • Spruce budworm outbreaks are welcomed by Tennessee Warblers, which generally produce larger clutches with higher survival rates during such events. • Alexander Wilson discovered this species along the Cumberland River in Tennessee and named it after that state. Its name is misleading, however, because it is found there only in migration and breeds almost exclusively in Canada. This misnomer is not an isolated incident: the Cape May, Nashville and Connecticut warblers all bear names that misrepresent their breeding distributions.

breeding

ID: *Breeding male:* grey cap; olive green back, wings and tail; white eyebrow stripe; grey to black eye line; clean, white underparts; thin bill. *Breeding female:* duller, yellow wash on breast and eyebrow; olive grey upperparts (including crown). *Non-breeding:* olive yellow upperparts; yellow eyebrow; yellow underparts, except for white undertail coverts; males may have white belly.
Size: *L* 12 cm.
Status: common in the boreal plain ecozone and northward from mid-May to mid-September; fairly common in the prairie ecozone from mid- to late May and from late July to mid-September.
Habitat: *Breeding:* mature deciduous or mixedwood forests; spruce bogs and swamps. *In migration:* a variety of wooded habitats including farmsteads, parks and gardens.
Nesting: on the ground; often on a raised hummock in a swampy area; small cup nest of grass, moss and rootlets is lined with hair; female incubates 4–7 white eggs, marked with brown or purple, for 12 days.

Feeding: probes foliage and buds for small insects, caterpillars and other invertebrates; may also eat berries.
Voice: *Male:* accelerating, loud, 3-part song: *ticka ticka ticka ticka swit-swit-swit chew-chew-chew-chew-chew;* call is a sweet *chip.*
Similar Species: *Warbling Vireo:* stouter overall; thicker bill; greyer upperparts. *Philadelphia Vireo:* stouter; thicker bill; yellow breast and sides. *Orange-crowned Warbler* (p. 126): more grey-green overall, with dull breast streaking and yellowish undertail coverts; adults lack white eyebrow and blue-grey head.
Best Sites: *Breeding:* Besnard Lake; Candle Lake PP; Duck Mountain PP; Greenwater Lake PP; Hudson Bay; Meadow Lake PP; Nisbet PF; Prince Albert NP; Tobin Lake. *In migration:* Last Mountain Lake NWA; Regina; Saskatoon.

125

ORANGE-CROWNED WARBLER

Vermivora celata

Don't bother to look for the Orange-crowned Warbler's hidden orange crown, because this warbler's most distinguishing characteristic is its lack of obvious field marks—wing bars, eye rings and colour patches are all conspicuously absent. • Orange-crowned Warblers are fairly common summer residents in much of Saskatchewan. In the north, they inhabit regenerating burns and clearcuts, while in the south, they appear along coulees and aspen-covered hillsides. Orange-crowned Warblers are frequently encountered, whether in migration or on their breeding grounds, as a blurred olive yellow bundle flitting nervously while picking insects from leaves, buds and branches. • Wood-warblers are strictly confined to the New World. All 109 species (56 of which occur in North America) originated in South America, which boasts the highest diversity of wood-warblers.

ID: olive grey body; lighter undertail coverts; dark eye line; yellowish eyebrow; faintly streaked underparts; thin bill; faint, orange crown patch.
Size: *L* 13 cm.
Status: fairly common in the boreal plain ecozone and northward from early May to late September; common migrant (and local nester) in the prairie ecozone from late April to mid-May and from late August to early October.
Habitat: *Breeding:* deciduous or mixed forests, shrubby slopes, woodlands and riparian thickets. *In migration:* a wide variety of wooded habitats including farmsteads, parks and gardens.

Nesting: on the ground or in a low shrub; well-hidden, small cup nest is made of coarse grass; incubates 4–5 eggs for 12–14 days.
Feeding: probes foliage for invertebrates, berries, nectar and sap.
Voice: *Male:* faint trill that breaks downward halfway through.
Similar Species: *Tennessee Warbler* (p. 125): blue-grey head; olive back; dark eye line; whitish undertail coverts. *Ruby-crowned Kinglet* (p. 116): broken eye ring; wing bars. *Wilson's Warbler:* female has no eyebrow, yellower underparts and light-coloured legs.
Best Sites: *Breeding:* Besnard Lake; Cypress Hills PP; Douglas PP; Nisbet PF. *In migration:* Last Mountain Lake NWA; Regina; Saskatoon.

YELLOW WARBLER

Dendroica petechia

The Yellow Warbler is the only warbler present as a summer resident in many areas of the southern part of the province. It is often mistakenly called a "wild canary" because of its bright yellow plumage, but an observant eye and a discriminating ear will quickly decipher this bird's unique character. • Unlike other wood-warblers, Yellow Warblers routinely nest in human-influenced habitats, such as hedgerows, farm shelterbelts and urban parks and gardens. They are among the most frequent victims of Brown-headed Cowbird (p. 155) parasitism, but they are able to recognize the foreign cowbird egg and will abandon their nests or build a new nest on top of the old eggs. • Many different species of warblers can inhabit the same area because they each focus their foraging efforts on different parts of the habitat. This habitat partitioning is also evident within the Yellow Warbler species: males take advantage of exposed singing perches in the tree canopy while females remain in the dense understorey foliage where their nests are concealed. • The Yellow Warbler is the most widespread of all the wood-warblers: its breeding range covers most of North America.

ID: bright yellow underparts; black bill and eyes; grey to olive yellow upperparts with bright yellow highlights. *Male:* red streaks on breast, sides and flanks. *Female:* red streaks are faint or absent; olive yellow upperparts. *Immature:* duller than adults of the corresponding sexes.
Size: *L* 13 cm.
Status: common in the prairie eco-zone and uncommon elsewhere from early May to mid-September.
Habitat: habitat generalist; moist, open woodlands, dense scrub, shrubby meadows, second-growth woodlands, riparian woods and urban parks and gardens.
Nesting: in the fork of a deciduous tree or shrub; compact cup nest of grass, weeds and shredded bark is lined with fine grass, seed fluff and

hair; female incubates 4–6 speckled, greenish-white eggs for 11–12 days.
Feeding: probes foliage and vegetation for caterpillars, inchworms, beetles, aphids and cankerworms; will also hover.
Voice: song is a fast, variable *sweet-sweet-sweet summer sweet.*
Similar Species: *Orange-crowned Warbler* (p. 126): duller, yellow underparts (under-tail coverts are brightest); lacks reddish breast streaks of male; darker olive upperparts; dark eye line. *American Goldfinch* (p.162): black wings and tail. *Wilson's Warbler:* bright yellow eye-brow; male has black crown; female has dark crown. *Common Yellowthroat* (p. 136): black-masked male is obviously different; female lacks bright yellow edgings on wing and tail feathers.
Best Sites: widespread.

127

MAGNOLIA WARBLER

Dendroica magnolia

The male Magnolia Warbler is striking, especially when its bright colours flash among green forest foliage. It has a white stripe above its eye and white patches on its tail and wings that distinguish it from the somewhat similar-looking Canada Warbler. • Magnolia Warblers typically inhabit open coniferous stands, where they are often seen feeding and singing at eye level. When they migrate with large, mixed-species flocks, Magnolia Warblers are often seen foraging away from the pack, usually along the lower branches of trees and shrubs. • Magnolia Warblers travel long distances between their nesting grounds, which are mostly in Canada, and their wintering grounds in Central America and the West Indies. Warblers typically migrate at night, which is unfortunate, because many are killed each year when they collide with buildings, telecommunication towers and tall smokestacks. It is only in migration that the Magnolia Warbler is seen anywhere near magnolia trees.

breeding

ID: *Breeding male:* yellow underparts with bold, black streaks; black mask; white eyebrow stripe; blue-grey crown; dark upperparts; white wing bars often blend into wing patch. *Breeding female* and *Non-breeding male:* duller overall; 2 distinct white wing bars; streaked, olive back. *In flight:* yellow rump; dark tail has 2 white patches.
Size: *L* 12–13 cm.
Status: common in the boreal plain ecozone and northward from mid-May to mid-September; fairly common in the prairie ecozone from mid- to late May and from late August to late September.
Habitat: *Breeding:* open coniferous and mixed forests, mostly in natural openings and along edges, often near water; young balsam fir and white spruce stands are favoured. *In migration:* a wide variety of wooded habitats, including farmsteads, parks and gardens.
Nesting: on a horizontal limb in a conifer; loose cup nest of grass,

twigs and weeds is lined with rootlets; female incubates 3–5 white eggs, marked with brown and grey, for 11–13 days.
Feeding: probes vegetation and buds and also flycatches for beetles, flies, wasps, caterpillars and other insects; may also eat some berries.
Voice: song is weak and variable, but always ends with a 2-note phrase that rises at the end: *pretty pretty lady, swee swee swee witsy* or *wheata wheata wheet-zu; clank* call.
Similar Species: *Yellow-rumped Warbler* (p. 129): mostly white underparts; yellow patches on rump, crown and shoulders. *Cape May Warbler:* olive green upperparts; chestnut cheek patch; lacks white tail patches. *Canada Warbler:* lacks yellow rump and white patches on wing and tail.
Best Sites: *Breeding:* Besnard Lake; Candle Lake PP; Meadow Lake PP; Prince Albert NP. *In migration:* Last Mountain Lake NWA; Regina; Saskatoon.

YELLOW-RUMPED WARBLER

Dendroica coronata

Yellow-rumped Warblers are the first warblers to arrive in our province, appearing in late April or early May. • This bird has one of the most extensive nesting ranges of all the North American warblers—it is very adaptable, and in Saskatchewan it is common in a wide variety of forest habitats. • These birds coexist with other wood-warblers by partitioning foraging and nesting niches and feeding strategies. By foraging and nesting on different parts of the same trees, employing different feeding styles and nesting at slightly different times, competition for food sources is reduced and the exhaustion of particular resources is avoided. • There are two races of the Yellow-rumped Warbler: the "Myrtle Warbler," which has a white throat, and the "Audubon's Warbler," which has a yellow throat. The Cypress Hills is the summer home of the Audubon's subspecies, but the Myrtle is the dominant race in the rest of the province.

"Myrtle Warbler"
breeding

ID: yellow crown, foreshoulder patches and rump; white underparts; dark cheek; white wing bars. *Breeding male:* blue-grey upperparts with black streaking; black cheek; black breast patches; black streaking along sides and flanks. *Breeding female:* grey-brown cheek and upperparts; dark streaking on breast, sides and flanks. *Non-breeding* and *Immature:* similar to female, but duller and with fainter streaking on breast and sides.
Size: *L* 13–15 cm.
Status: common in the boreal plain ecozone and northward from early May to late September; common to abundant migrant (and local nester) in the prairie ecozone from late April to late May and from early August to early October.
Habitat: *Breeding:* open coniferous and mixed forests; rarely in pure deciduous woodlands. *In migration:* a wide variety of habitats including woodlands, farmsteads, parks and gardens, even areas with little or no woody cover.

Nesting: on a horizontal limb or in the crotch of a conifer; compact cup nest of twigs, grass, bark strips, moss, lichen and spider silk is lined with hair and feathers; female incubates 4–5 white eggs, splotched with brown and grey, for up to 13 days; may have 2 broods per year.
Feeding: hawks, hovers or skims vegetation for insects; may also eat some berries.
Voice: song is 6–8 repetitions of the same note followed by a rising or falling trill: *seet-seet-seet-seet-seet-seet-seet trrrrrr*; call is a distinctive *chip.*
Similar Species: *Magnolia Warbler* (p. 128): yellow underparts, including throat; lacks yellow crown and shoulder patches. *Cape May Warbler:* lacks yellow crown and shoulder patches; yellow underparts with fine, dark streaks.
Best Sites: *Breeding:* Besnard Lake; Candle Lake PP; Cypress Hills PP (Audubon's race); Duck Mountain PP; Meadow Lake PP; Prince Albert NP. *In migration:* almost anywhere, even areas devoid of trees.

PALM WARBLER

Dendroica palmarum

Contrary to its common name, the Palm Warbler has little to do with palm trees, even on its southern wintering grounds. This bird's summer range lies exclusively in Canada, and it could just as easily have been named the "Bog Warbler" because of its preference for northern bogs of tamarack and black spruce. • In spring, the Palm Warbler is among the earliest arrivals to our province. It often travels with large flocks of Yellow-rumped Warblers, and it is easily recognized by its incessant tail-wagging—its tail pumps whether the bird is hopping on the ground or perched momentarily on an elevated limb. Even in autumn migration, when its distinctive chestnut crown has faded to olive brown, its tail wagging is its most prominent field mark. • In migration, the Palm Warbler is a common transient in the prairie ecozone, where it is seen in a variety of habitats, including woodlands, shrubbery and weedy fields. In summer, it is a common nester in open or semi-open bogs in northern parts of the province.

breeding

ID: *Breeding:* chestnut cap; yellowish eyebrow; yellow throat, breast and undertail coverts; dark streaking on breast and sides; unstreaked, white belly; olive brown upperparts; yellowish-green rump; 2 faint wing bars; frequently bobs its tail. *Non-breeding* and *Immature:* greyish-brown cap and upperparts; buff underparts; buff line over each eye; throat, breast and sides have hint of yellow and faint streaking.

Size: *L* 11–14 cm.

Status: common in the boreal plain ecozone and northward from mid-May to mid-September; fairly common in the prairie ecozone from early to late May and from late August to early October.

Habitat: *Breeding:* mature *Sphagnum* bogs with scattered black spruce; also in cutline openings in spruce-tamarack forests and young jack pine stands. *In migration:* riparian woodlands, woodland edges, shrubby field margins, farmsteads, parks and gardens.

Nesting: on the ground, in a low shrub or on a stunted spruce; cup nest of grass, weeds and bark is lined with feathers; mostly the female incubates 4–5 brown-marked, creamy white eggs for 12 days.

Feeding: insects are picked from the ground and vegetation; also hovers and flycatches; eats some berries and seeds.

Voice: weak notes repeated 6–7 times: *zhe-zhe-zhe-zhe-zhe-zhe;* call is a sharp *sup* or *check.*

Similar Species: *Yellow-rumped Warbler* (p. 129): female has bright yellow rump, crown and shoulder; white wing bars, throat and undertail coverts. *Chipping Sparrow* (p. 139) and *American Tree Sparrow:* stouter bills and bodies; lack yellow plumage.

Best Sites: *Breeding:* most nesting areas are remote but try Hudson Bay area and Meadow Lake PP. *In migration:* Last Mountain Lake NWA; Saskatoon; Regina.

BLACKPOLL WARBLER

Dendroica striata

In spring, Blackpoll Warblers follow the unfolding aspen leaves northward through our province. They pass through quietly—often singly or in pairs—with a business-like determination to reach their breeding grounds in the stunted forests of northern Saskatchewan. Once there, they build their well-concealed nests in spruce trees. • The low numbers of summer records for the Blackpoll Warbler in Saskatchewan are most likely because their breeding grounds in the the extreme north of the province are relatively inaccessible and because their high-pitched song is beyond the hearing range of many people. Where this species has been noted, however, it has been described as an uncommon summer resident of spruce bogs and regenerating burns. • The Blackpoll Warbler has the longest migration route of all the warblers. Migrants reaching the Eastern Seaboard of the United States fly south over the Atlantic to the coast of Venezuela, not touching land or resting again until they get there.

breeding

ID: 2 white wing bars; light-coloured legs.
Breeding male: black cap and upperparts;
white cheek; black-streaked underparts.
Breeding female: streaked, greenish upperparts; black-streaked or white underparts;
dirty cheek. *Nonbreeding and Immature:*
similar to breeding female but greener and
often less prominently striped.
Size: *L* 14 cm.
Status: common in the taiga shield
and boreal shield ecozones and
uncommon and local in the boreal
plain ecozone from mid-May to early
September; common in the prairie
ecozone from early to late May and
from late August to mid-September.
Habitat: *Breeding:* black spruce
forests, muskegs, burns and occasionally mixed forests. *In migration:* any
wooded habitat including farmsteads,
parks and gardens.

Nesting: well concealed in a stunted spruce
tree; nest is made of twigs, bark shreds, grass,
lichen and fur; female incubates 4–5 eggs for
about 12 days.
Feeding: probes buds, leaves and branches
for larval insects, aphids and scale insects;
also flycatches for insects.
Voice: high-pitched, uniform *tsit tsit tsit.*
Similar Species: *Black-and-white
Warbler:* dark legs; striped, black-and-
white crown. *Bay-breasted Warbler:*
dark legs; non-breeding males often
have rufous on flanks.
Best Sites: *Breeding:* most nesting
areas are in the remote north but try
the Hudson Bay area. *In migration:*
Last Mountain Lake NWA; Saskatoon;
Regina.

131

AMERICAN REDSTART

Setophaga ruticilla

Behaving more like a butterfly than a bird, the American Redstart flits from branch to branch in dizzying pursuit of prey. Even when perched, its tail flicks open and closed, revealing colourful orange (male) or yellow (female) tail patches. The American Redstart is consistently listed as a favourite among birders for its contrasting plumage, approachability and amusing behaviour. Perhaps it is for these reasons that it is affectionately known as "candelita" (the little candle) in parts of its Central American wintering grounds. • The American Redstart is equipped with flycatcher-like bristles around its mouth, which help it to sense when prey is close enough to trap it in its ready bill. Its genus name *Setophaga* comes from the Greek for "insect-eater." • In parts of its range, the redstart competes with the male Least Flycatcher (p. 95) for food and nesting sites. In some cases, an aerial chase will result, usually with the flycatcher in pursuit. • You may be surprised to hear a courtship song coming from the mouth of a female redstart, but what you are seeing is most likely a second-year male that has not yet acquired his striking black-and-orange adult plumage.

ID: *Male:* black overall; bright orange shoulder, wing and tail patches; white belly and undertail coverts. *Female:* olive brown upperparts; olive grey head; yellow shoulder, wing and tail patches; clean, white underparts. *Immature male:* resembles female, but has dark blotching on breast and patches are dull orange-yellow.
Size: *L* 13 cm.
Status: common in the boreal plain ecozone and uncommon and local in the boreal shield ecozone from mid-May to early September; fairly common migrant (and local nester) in the prairie ecozone from mid-May to early June and from mid-August to mid-September.
Habitat: *Breeding:* shrubby woodland edges, second-growth woodlands and open or semi-open deciduous or mixed forests; often near water. *In migration:* any wooded habitat, including farmsteads, parks and gardens.

Nesting: in the fork of a shrub or sapling; rarely on the ground; open cup nest of plant fibres, bark shreds, grass and rootlets is lined with hair and feathers; female incubates 3–5 brown-marked, white eggs for 12 days.
Feeding: actively probes foliage and hovers or hawks for insects and spiders; rarely eats seeds and berries.
Voice: *Male:* highly variable series of high notes, including *tsee tsee tsee tsee tsee-o* (with the last note dropping), *zee zee zee zee zwee* (with a high last note) and *teetsa-teetsa-teetsa-teet*; call is a sharp, sweet *chip.*
Similar Species: none.
Best Sites: *Breeding:* Candle Lake PP; Douglas PP; Duck Mountain PP; Estevan; Moose Mountain PP; Prince Albert NP. *In migration:* Last Mountain Lake NWA; Regina; Saskatoon; Yorkton.

OVENBIRD

Seiurus aurocapillus

The Ovenbird's loud and joyous ode to "teachers" is unwittingly familiar to many of us, even though the bird itself is not a familiar sight. An Ovenbird will rarely expose itself to the open forest, and it usually stops calling as soon as an intruder enters its territory. • The Ovenbird's name originates from its unusual, oven-shaped ground nest. An incubating female nestled within her woven dome is usually confident enough in her nest that, unless closely approached, she will choose to sit tight rather than flee approaching danger. In years when food is plentiful, such as during spruce budworm outbreaks, Ovenbirds usually lay more eggs, are successful in raising most of their young and are able to produce two broods in a single summer. • Ovenbirds (and most warblers) are most easily observed in migration, when they may be present just about anywhere. Their spring and autumn movements carry them through suburban neighbourhoods, where almost any of our Saskatchewan warblers might suddenly appear outside a kitchen window.

ID: olive brown upperparts; heavy, dark streaking on white breast, sides and flanks; white eye ring; orange crown bordered by black; pink legs.

Size: *L* 15 cm.

Status: common in the boreal plain ecozone and uncommon and local in the boreal shield ecozone from mid-May to early September; fairly common migrant (and local nester) in the prairie ecozone from mid-May to early June and from late July to mid-September.

Habitat: *Breeding:* undisturbed mature deciduous forest or poplar stands in mixed forest; usually under a closed canopy with little understorey. *In migration:* woodlands, especially those with dense shrubbery; also farmsteads, parks and gardens.

Nesting: on the ground; domed nest of grass, bark, twigs and dead leaves is lined with rootlets and hair; female incubates 4–6 darkly spotted, white eggs for 11–13 days.

Feeding: probes the ground and leaf litter for worms, snails and insects; also eats some seeds.

Voice: loud, distinctive *tea-cher tea-cher Tea-CHER Tea-CHER* or *teach teach Teach Teach TEACH TEACH*, repeated up to 12 times and increasing in speed and volume; night song is an elaborate series of bubbly, warbled notes, often ending in *teacher-teacher*; call is a brisk *chip*, *cheep* or *chock*.

Similar Species: *Northern Water-thrush* (p. 134): bold, yellowish or white eyebrow stripe; lacks rufous crown. *Thrushes:* larger; lack rufous crown bordered by black.

Best Sites: *Breeding:* Besnard Lake; Candle Lake PP; Cypress Hills PP; Douglas PP; Duck Mountain PP; Hudson Bay; Meadow Lake PP; Moose Mountain PP; Prince Albert NP. *In migration:* Last Mountain Lake NWA; Regina; Saskatoon.

NORTHERN WATERTHRUSH

Seiurus noveboracensis

Birders who are not satisfied with simply hearing a Northern Waterthrush in its nesting territory must literally get their feet wet if they want much hope of seeing one—this bird spends much of its time along the shores of deciduous swamps or coniferous bogs, searching along logs, shrubby tangles and soggy ground for insects and worms. The easiest time to look for this waterthrush is during relatively bug-free months in spring or autumn migration, when it typically appears in more accessible habitats, such as drier, upland forests or along lofty park trails. • Like the Ovenbird, the waterthrush is a walker, not a hopper. Moreover, like other birds that tend to forage in damp areas, the Northern Waterthrush walks with a bit of a teetering motion, not unlike that of the Spotted Sandpiper (p. 70). • The male waterthrush sings on its nesting grounds and also in migration. Its sweet song, which is exceptionally loud for such a small bird, may be delivered from atop a small tree in a bog or while walking along a fallen log.

ID: pale yellow eyebrow; streaked breast; spotted throat; olive brown upperparts; pinkish legs; often teeters.

Size: L 13–15 cm.

Status: common in the boreal plain ecozone and northward from mid-May to early September; fairly common in the prairie ecozone from mid-May to early June and from late July to mid-September.

Habitat: *Breeding:* deciduous, riparian thickets, forests and streams. *In migration:* any wooded area, especially near water.

Nesting: often on the ground, on a mossy mound or low on a broken stump or branch; usually near water; small, well-hidden cup nest is made

of moss, leaves and fine bark shreds; female incubates 4–5 eggs for 13 days.

Feeding: probes foliage and the ground for invertebrates, frequently tosses aside vegetation with its bill; also dips into shallow water for aquatic invertebrates and very occasionally for small fish.

Voice: loud, penetrating *chew chew chew chew where-where-where-where-where.*

Similar Species: *Ovenbird* (p. 133): russet crown; lacks pale eyebrow.

Best Sites: *Breeding:* Besnard Lake; Candle Lake PP; Duck Mountain PP; Meadow Lake PP; Prince Albert NP. *In migration:* Last Mountain Lake NWA; Regina; Saskatoon; Yorkton.

MOURNING WARBLER

Oporornis philadelphia

Mourning Warblers seldom leave the protection of their often impenetrable habitat, which is typically dense, shrubby thickets and nettle patches. Although these birds can be quite common in some areas, they are seen less frequently than we might expect. They rarely travel in large numbers and usually sing only on their nesting territories. • Riparian areas, regenerating cut-blocks and patches of forest that have been recently cleared by fire provide the low shrubs and sapling trees that this warbler relies on for nesting and foraging. • The Mourning Warbler is named for its sombre dark hood, which reminded Alexander Wilson, who first recorded this bird in his early 19th century series *American Ornithology*, of someone in mourning. This warbler's bright yellow underparts and cheery song belie its name.

ID: grey hood; yellow underparts; olive green upperparts; short tail; pinkish legs. *Male:* no eye ring; black upper breast patch. *Female:* hood is light grey; may have thin eye ring. *Immature:* pale grey to yellow "chin" and throat; buffy breast; thin, incomplete eye ring.
Size: *L* 13–14 cm.
Status: uncommon and local in the boreal shield ecozone and common in the boreal plain ecozone from late May to mid-September; fairly common in the prairie ecozone from mid-May to early June and from mid-August to mid-September.
Habitat: *Breeding:* dense shrubs in open deciduous woods or along the edges of bogs and marshes; also found in deciduous second growth. *In migration:* any wooded area, especially with thick undergrowth.
Nesting: on or near the ground, often at the base of a shrub; bulky nest of leaves, weeds and grass is

lined with fur and fine grass; female incubates 3–5 brown-spotted or blotched, creamy white eggs for about 12 days.
Feeding: forages in dense, low shrubs for caterpillars, beetles, spiders and other invertebrates.
Voice: husky, 2-part song is variable but often descends at the end: *blee blee blee blee-blee choochoo*; call is a loud, low *check*.
Similar Species: *MacGillivray's Warbler:* bold but broken eye ring; occurs only in extreme southwestern Saskatchewan. *Connecticut Warbler:* bold, complete eye ring; lacks black breast patch; long undertail coverts make tail look very short; immature has light grey throat. *Nashville Warbler:* bright yellow throat; dark legs.
Best Sites: *Breeding:* Candle Lake PP; Duck Mountain PP; Hudson Bay; Meadow Lake PP; Moose Mountain PP. *In migration:* Last Mountain Lake NWA; Regina.

135

COMMON YELLOWTHROAT

Geothlypis trichas

The Common Yellowthroat favours habitats shunned by most other wood-warblers. In Saskatchewan, its favoured haunts are brushy coulees and riparian thickets in the grasslands and the Cypress Hills, cattails and bulrushes in the aspen parkland ecoregion, and shrubby fringes of muskegs and watercourses in the boreal plain ecozone and northward. • In May and June, male yellowthroats issue their distinctive songs while perched atop tall cattails or shrubs. An extended look at the male in action will reveal the location of his favourite singing perches, which he visits regularly, in rotation. These strategic outposts mark the boundary of his territory, and they are fiercely guarded from intrusions by other males. • Common Yellowthroats maintain their plumage by "bathing"—they immerse themselves or roll in water and shake off the excess water by flicking or flapping their wings. Other birds with limited access to water will bathe themselves in dust. • Common Yellowthroats are often parasitized by Brown-headed Cowbirds (p. 155), which are primarily open-country birds and usually target nests in less-forested habitats.

ID: yellow throat and breast; white belly; olive green upperparts. *Breeding male:* broad, black mask with white upper border. *Female* and *Immature:* no mask; may show faint, white eye ring; tan-coloured sides; immature male may show faint signs of a mask.
Size: *L* 11–14 cm.
Status: common in the prairie ecozone and uncommon elsewhere from early May to early October.
Habitat: dense thickets in coulees, open marshes with scattered shrubs, riparian willow and alder clumps, sedge wetlands and bogs.
Nesting: on or near the ground; in aquatic vegetation or in a shrub; bulky, open cup nest of grass, sedges and shredded bark is lined with hair and soft plant fibres; female incubates 3–6 brown-specked, creamy white eggs for 12 days; usually has 2 broods per year.

Feeding: hovers and probes vegetation for insects and beetles; may eat some seeds.
Voice: clear, oscillating song: *witchety witchety witchety-witch*; call is a sharp *tcheck* or *tchet*.
Similar Species: male is distinctive. *Yellow Warbler* (p. 127): yellow highlights on wings; all-yellow underparts. *Wilson's Warbler:* yellow forehead, eyebrow and cheek; all-yellow underparts; male has dark crown. *Orange-crowned Warbler* (p. 126): dull, greenish-yellow underparts (undertail coverts are brightest); faint, dark grey breast streaks. *Mourning* (p. 135), *MacGillivray's* and *Connecticut warblers:* lack yellow throat.
Best Sites: Besnard Lake; Candle Lake PP; Douglas PP; Duck Mountain PP; Estevan; Leader; Nicolle Flats; Pike Lake PP; Saskatchewan Landing PP; Yorkton.

WESTERN TANAGER

Piranga ludoviciana

No other bird in Saskatchewan can match the splendour of a male Western Tanager. His golden body and red head, accentuated by his black wings and tail, express his true character. Western Tanagers live in the tropics for most of the year—they fly to Saskatchewan for only a few short months to raise a new generation on the abundance of food available in our forests in summer. Their exotic colours remind us of the ecological ties between our boreal forests and the Latin American rainforest where this family of birds reaches its maximum diversity. "Tanager" is derived from *tangara*, the Tupi Indian name for this group of birds in the Amazon basin. • The song of the male tanager can be difficult to learn, because it closely resembles the song of the American Robin (p. 119). The tanager's song tends to sound hoarser, however, as if the bird has a sore throat. Fortunately, the tanager's hiccup-like *pit-a-tik* call is distinctive. • From a Saskatchewan perspective, the Western Tanager's name is particularly appropriate, because its distribution is generally restricted to the western half of the province.

ID: yellow underparts, wing bars and rump; black back, wings and tail; has variable amount of red on head; light-coloured bill. *Breeding female:* olive green overall; lighter underparts; darker upperparts; faint wing bars.
Size: *L* 18 cm.
Status: uncommon in the boreal pain and boreal shield ecozones and fairly common in the Cypress upland ecoregion from late May to early September; rare to uncommon in the prairie ecozone from mid-May to early June and from mid-August to mid-September.
Habitat: *Breeding:* mature coniferous or mixedwood forests and aspen woodlands. *In migration:* any wooded area.

Nesting: on a horizontal branch or fork in a conifer; well out from the trunk; cup nest is loosely built of twigs, grass and other plant materials and lined with fine vegetation; female incubates 4 eggs for 13–14 days.
Feeding: probes vegetation and catches flying insects on the wing; eats wasps, beetles, flies and other insects, including caterpillars; also eats fruit.
Voice: call is a hiccup-like *pit-a-tik*. *Male:* song is hoarse and robin-like: *hurry, scurry, scurry, hurry.*
Similar Species: male is distinctive. *Baltimore Oriole* (p. 156): female has thinner bill and darker olive plumage.
Best Sites: Candle Lake PP; Cypress Hills PP; Meadow Lake PP; Prince Albert NP.

137

SPOTTED TOWHEE

Pipilo maculatus

Spotted Towhees are most likely to be encountered where dried leaves have accumulated on the ground under shrubs. Towhees are cheeky birds that typically rustle about in dense undergrowth, craftily scraping back layers of dry leaves to expose the seeds, berries, earthworms and insects hidden beneath. Sometimes these birds rustle leaves so noisily that you expect an animal of deer-sized proportions to be the source of all the ruckus. They rarely leave their sub-arboreal world, but on occasion they can be enticed into view by "squeaking" or "pishing," immitating the noises that birds often make to alert other birds of an intrusion. • Until recently, the Spotted Towhee and the Eastern Towhee (a spotless, eastern bird) were considered a single species, known as the Rufous-sided Towhee. • Although you wouldn't guess it, this colourful bird is a member of the American Sparrow family—a group that is usually drab in colour.

ID: dark hood, wings and upperparts; white spots on wings; rufous sides and flanks; white outer tail corners; white lower breast and belly; buff undertail coverts; red eyes; dark bill. *Male:* black hood and upperparts. *Female:* black is replaced by dark grey-brown.
Size: *L* 18–21 cm.
Status: common from early May to late September.
Habitat: dense shrubs with leaf litter, woodland openings and forest edges.
Nesting: on the ground or in a dense, low shrub; cup nest is made of twigs, bark strips, grass, weeds, rootlets and animal hair; mostly the male incubates 3–6 spotted, creamy white to pale grey eggs for 10–12 days; usually has 2 broods per year.
Feeding: scratches at leaf litter for insects, seeds and berries.
Voice: song is 1–8 hurried notes followed by a buzzy trill: *che che che che che zheeee*; call is a harsh rising *zhreeee!*
Similar Species: *Eastern Towhee:* lacks spotting on back; fairly common in southeastern Saskatchewan. *Dark-eyed Junco* (p. 146): much smaller; pale bill; black eyes; outer tail feathers are completely white.
Best Sites: Buffalo Pound PP; Douglas PP; Eastend; Estevan; Grasslands NP; Leader; Nicolle Flats; Pike Lake PP; Saskatchewan Landing PP.

CHIPPING SPARROW

Spizella passerina

The Chipping Sparrow is easily distinguished from other Saskatchewan sparrows by its rufous crown and wide, white eyebrow. Its song, however, is remarkably similar to the Dark-eyed Junco's (p. 146), and even experienced birders can have difficulty distinguishing between the two. Listen for the Chipping Sparrow's rapid trill, which is slightly faster, drier and less musical. • Chipping Sparrows are found throughout most of Saskatchewan from early May to late September. In southern parts of the province, they are generally restricted to cities, towns and farmsteads, and are particularly drawn to conifers. • Approximately 5 percent of all male Chipping Sparrows are polygynous. A polygynous male will nest with a second female while his first mate incubates his first brood.

breeding

ID: *Breeding male:* prominent, rufous cap; white eyebrow; black eye line; grey cheek; light grey underparts; mottled brown upperparts, except for grey rump; dark bill; 2 faint wing bars; light-coloured legs. *Breeding female:* generally duller; may have dark streaks through crown. *Non-breeding:* pale brown crown with dark streaks; brown eye line; tan grey cheek; grey rump; pale lower mandible. *Immature:* brown-grey overall with dark brown streaking through crown, back, breast and sides; grey rump; pale lower mandible; dark lores.
Size: *L* 13–15 cm.
Status: common in the boreal plain ecozone and northward and fairly common elsewhere from early May to late September.
Habitat: *Breeding:* open coniferous or mixed forests and woodland fringes; often in yards and gardens with tree and shrub borders.
Nesting: at mid-level in a small tree or shrub (often coniferous); compact cup nest is woven with grass and

rootlets and lined with hair or fur; female incubates 3–5 pale blue eggs, lightly spotted with brown, for 11–14 days; usually has 2 broods per year.
Feeding: probes the ground and vegetation for small seeds and invertebrates; may also visit feeding stations.
Voice: a chipping rattle, given at a constant pitch (faster and less metallic than the Dark-eyed Junco's call); call note is a high-pitched *chip*.
Similar Species: *American Tree Sparrow:* dark, central breast spot; lacks bold, white eyebrow; red eye line. *Field Sparrow:* lacks eye stripe; has white eye ring; pink bill; rare in extreme southeastern Saskatchewan. *Swamp Sparrow:* lacks white eyebrow, black eye line and white wing bars. *Clay-colored Sparrow* (p. 140): immature has brownish rump and light lores.
Best Sites: ubiquitous in the north but local in the south; usually near conifers (native or planted).

139

CLAY-COLORED SPARROW

Spizella pallida

The smell of silverberry and the cicada-like buzz of the Clay-colored Sparrow are sure signs that summer has arrived on the prairies. This bird is often overlooked because its plumage, habits and voice all contribute to a cryptic lifestyle, but keen eyes and ears will quickly lead you to shrubby woodland clearings, forest edges or brushy pastures, where these sparrows are common inhabitants. Clay-colored Sparrows are particularly partial to patches of silverberry, and they favour snowberry shrubs as nesting sites. • Clay-colored Sparrows are common hosts of Brown-headed Cowbird (p. 155) eggs. They often recognize the foreign eggs and many will either abandon their nest or build another in a new territory. • Clay-colored Sparrows benefited from the forest-clearing practices of the late 1800s and early 1900s, flourishing along the margins of agricultural fields and wherever brushy patches grew in forest clearcuts. However, recent breeding bird surveys have revealed that their numbers are in significant decline throughout North America.

ID: unstreaked, white underparts; buff breast and flanks; grey nape; light brown rump; sharply outlined, pale brown "ear" patch; brown crown with dark streaks and 1 pale central stripe; buff-white eyebrow; white "jaw" stripe bordered by brown; white throat; mostly pale bill. *Immature:* buffier breast, sides and flanks.
Size: *L* 13–14 cm.
Status: common in the prairie eco-zone and fairly common elsewhere from early May to late September.
Habitat: brushy open areas, woodland edges and openings, abandoned fields and riparian thickets.
Nesting: low in a grass tuft or shrub; open cup nest made of twigs, grass and weeds is lined with rootlets, fine grass and fur; pair incubates 3–5 pale blue eggs, speckled with brown, for

10–12 days; often has 2 broods per year.
Feeding: forages on the ground and in low vegetation for seeds and insects.
Voice: song is generally 3–4 unmusical, insect-like buzzes; call is a soft *chip*.
Similar Species: *Chipping Sparrow* (p. 139): prominent rufous cap; grey cheek; greyish-white underparts; all-dark bill; immature has grey rump and dark lores; lacks grey nape and buff sides. *Brewer's Sparrow:* paler, crown is solid and lacks light median stripe. *Le Conte's Sparrow* and *Nelson's Sharp-tailed Sparrow:* buff-orange face; buff breast and sides with fine, dark streaks. *Grasshopper Sparrow:* top of head is flatter; buff cheek; lacks grey nape.
Best Sites: widespread; especially common in pastures with abundant silverberry or snowberry.

VESPER SPARROW

Pooecetes gramineus

For birders who live on the prairies, with multitudes of confusing little brown sparrows, the Vesper Sparrow offers welcome relief—white outer tail feathers and a chestnut shoulder patch announce its identity whether it is perched or in flight. The Vesper Sparrow is also distinguished by its bold and easily recognizable song. Its sweet melody, which is typically issued from the top of an elevated perch, is a common summer sound in the southern half of our province. It is this lovely song, reminiscent of vesper worship services given at dusk, that inspired this sparrow's name. • Vesper Sparrows spend most of their time on the ground, and they are commonly seen along roadsides, their white tail feathers flashing as they flit about. When the business of nesting begins, they will scour their neighbourhood for a potential nesting site. Inevitably, they will settle in almost any open dry habitat as long as there are trees, shrubs or even fenceposts nearby to serve as song perches. • Recent surveys have revealed that Vesper Sparrow numbers are declining throughout North America.

ID: streaky, brown upperparts; chestnut shoulder patch (often hidden); white outer tail feathers; weak breast and flank streaking; white eye ring; dark "ear" patch bordered by white "moustache."

Size: L 14–17 cm.

Status: common in the prairie ecozone and uncommon and local in the north from late April to early October.

Habitat: open fields and grasslands bordered by or interspersed with shrubs, shrubby woodland fringes and clearings.

Nesting: in a scrape on the ground, often under a canopy of grass or at the base of a shrub; loosely woven grass cup nest is lined with rootlets, fine grass and hair; mostly the female incubates 3–6 whitish eggs, speckled with brown, for 11–13 days; has 2 broods per year.

Feeding: probes the ground for grasshoppers, beetles, cutworms, other invertebrates and small seeds.

Voice: 2 pairs of preliminary notes, with the 2nd pair higher in pitch: *here-here there-there*, followed by a bubbly trill.

Similar Species: *Lark Sparrow:* white-tipped tail; white outer tail feathers; striking facial pattern. *American Pipit* and *Sprague's Pipit* (p. 123): thinner bills; lack chestnut shoulder patch; bob their tails when feeding. *Lapland Longspur* (p. 147): non-breeding plumage shows broad, pale eyebrow, reddish edgings on wing feathers and buff wash on upper breast. *McCown's Longspur:* also has chestnut shoulder patch but has more white on face and tail. *Other sparrows:* lack white outer tail feathers and chestnut shoulder patch.

Best Sites: widespread; especially common in areas where roads, fencelines and grasslands meet.

LARK BUNTING

Calamospiza melanocorys

Wherever there are grasslands or hayfields in southwestern Saskatchewan, you will have a good chance of seeing the spectacular courtship flight of the male Lark Bunting. As he rises into the air, the male flutters about in circles above the prairie, beating his wings slowly and deeply. His bell-like, tinkling song spreads over the landscape until he decides to fold his wings and float to the ground like a falling leaf. • The numbers and breeding range of the Lark Bunting vary markedly from year to year. In drought years, it breeds further north than usual and becomes one of the most conspicuous and abundant birds in southern Saskatchewan. It breeds in native prairie and hayfields, as well as in roadside ditches. • Because the Lark Bunting's courtship behaviour evolved before the arrival of fenceposts and power poles on which to perch in the prairie, it developed the habit of delivering its song on the wing.

breeding

ID: dark, conical bill; large, white wing patch. *Breeding male:* all-black plumage; white patch at tip of tail. *Female:* mottled brown upperparts; lightly streaked underparts; pale eyebrow.
Size: *L* 18 cm.
Status: varies from uncommon to abundant in the grasslands from mid-May to early August.
Habitat: short-grass prairie, sagebrush, hayfields and grassy ditches.
Nesting: on the ground; sheltered by a canopy of grass or by a small bush; cup nest is loosely built with grass, roots and other plant material and lined with plant down and fur;

mostly the female incubates 4–5 pale blue eggs for 11–12 days.
Feeding: walks or hops along the ground collecting insects, including grasshoppers, beetles and ants, seeds and waste grain.
Voice: rich and warbling, with clear notes.
Similar Species: *Other sparrows:* all lack white wing patch. *Bobolink:* male has creamy nape, white rump and back patches.
Best Sites: Grasslands NP; Maple Creek; erratic and unpredictable to the north and east.

SAVANNAH SPARROW

Passerculus sandwichensis

In spring and summer, the male Savannah Sparrow belts out his distinctive, buzzy tunes, usually while perched atop a prominent shrub, blade of grass or fencepost. This sparrow is one of Saskatchewan's most common open-country birds, and most of us have probably seen or heard it at one time or another. In the settled south, the Savannah Sparrow is a common summer resident of lightly grazed pastures, wet meadows, hayfields and roadsides, but in the north it is only fairly common and restricts itself to open bogs and other openings in generally closed forests. • Like most sparrows, the Savannah Sparrow maintains a cryptic lifestyle. Much of the time it scurries along the ground, hidden under the cover of concealing grass. It takes flight only as a last resort, fluttering only a short distance before touching the ground again. • The Savannah Sparrow was not named for the savannah habitat type, but for the place where it was discovered: Savannah, Georgia.

ID: brown streaking on breast, sides and flanks; mottled brown upperparts; whitish underparts; pale stripe through crown; prominent, yellowish eyebrow stripe; short, notched tail. *Immature:* buffier upperparts and underparts, lacks yellowish eyebrow.
Size: *L* 11–16 cm.
Status: common in the prairie ecozone and uncommon elsewhere from late April to early October.
Habitat: grasslands, hayfields, weedy fields, marsh edges, tundra, open bogs, roadside ditches and overgrown fencelines.
Nesting: on the ground; shallow scrape is well concealed by overhanging vegetation; open, grassy cup nest is lined with fine grass and hair; mostly the female incubates 3–6 greenish-blue eggs, speckled with brown, for 12–13 days.
Feeding: probes the ground for insects and small seeds.

Voice: song is a buzzy *tsip-tsip-tsip-tsooreeeeeeeyoo* or *tea tea tea teeeeea today* (rising on 2nd-last note and dropping at end); call is a high *tsit*.
Similar Species: *Vesper Sparrow* (p. 141): white outer tail feathers; chestnut shoulder patches. *Lincoln's Sparrow:* buff "jaw" line; buff wash and fine, black streaks across breast; broad, grey eyebrow. *Baird's Sparrow:* face and crown stripe are washed with buff-orange; lacks yellow lores. *Grasshopper Sparrow:* unstreaked breast. *Le Conte's Sparrow* and *Nelson's Sharp-tailed Sparrow:* ochre on head; streaking is mainly on flanks. *Song Sparrow* (p. 144): lacks yellow eyebrow stripe; bold "moustache" stripes.
Best Sites: widespread; especially common in longer grasses, such as around wetlands, in ditches and along fencelines.

SONG SPARROW

Melospiza melodia

The Song Sparrow is an early arrival to our province, heralded by its cheerful song, which is heard wherever shrubs and thickets border water. The Song Sparrow's heavily streaked, low-key plumage doesn't prepare you for its springtime rhapsody, which is among the most impressive of Saskatchewan's songsters. • Many young male songbirds learn to sing by listening to their fathers or rival males. By the time a male Song Sparrow is a few months old, he has already formed the basis for his own courtship tune, which he will test the following spring. Few males are able to attract a mate or secure a territory in their first year, however. • The Song Sparrow is one of North America's most variable songbirds, with 31 recognized subspecies. • The Song Sparrow and the Yellow Warbler (p. 127) are the most frequent hosts of Brown-headed Cowbird (p. 155) eggs.

ID: whitish underparts with heavy, brown streaking that converges into 1 central breast spot; greyish face; brown eye line; white "jaw" line bordered by dark whisker and "moustache" stripes; dark crown with pale, central stripe; mottled brown upperparts; rounded tail tip; often pumps its tail in flight. *Immature:* buffier with less grey.
Size: *L* 14–18 cm.

Status: common from early April to early October; occasional in the prairie ecozone from mid-October to mid-April.
Habitat: shrubby areas, usually near water, including willow shrublands, riparian thickets, forest openings, fence-lines and lakeshores; also the brushy edges of gardens, fields and roads.
Nesting: on the ground or low in a shrub; open cup nest of grass, weeds, leaves and bark is lined with fine materials; female incubates 3–6 pale

bluish-green eggs, blotched with brown, for 12–14 days; has 2–3 broods per year.
Feeding: probes and scratches the ground litter for seeds, cutworms, beetles, ants and other invertebrates.
Voice: musical, buzzy melody usually starts with 3–4 introductory notes: *Hip Hip Hip Hooray Boys, the spring is here again* or *Sweet, Sweet, Sweet Tea in your tea kettle kettle tea;* calls include a short *tsip* and a nasal *tchep.*
Similar Species: *Fox Sparrow:* larger; much heavier spots and streaks on underparts; head is mostly dark; rusty, unstreaked upperparts. *Lincoln's Sparrow:* lightly streaked breast with buff breast band; buff "jaw" line. *Savannah Sparrow* (p. 143): yellow eyebrow; lacks dark "moustache"; notched tail. *Vesper Sparrow* (p. 141): white outer tail feathers; chestnut shoulder patch.
Best Sites: widespread in most wooded areas near water.

WHITE-THROATED SPARROW

Zonotrichia albicollis

This patriot of Canada's northern forests arrives in our province each spring singing its familiar song from the top branches of shrubs or small trees. Many of us might not recognize a White-throated Sparrow if we saw one. Its clear, sweet song, however, rings memorably in the ears of all who have visited the northern woods in summer. • During the nesting season, the White-throated Sparrow shuns large tracts of forest in favour of second-growth woodlands and forest edges. In migration, it commonly inhabits small shrubs or thickets, where it often intermingles with other sparrows. • This handsome sparrow is easily identified by its bold, white throat, yellow lores and striped crown. Two colour morphs are common throughout Saskatchewan: one has black-and-white stripes on its head; the other has brown-and-tan stripes. • Like many "snowbirds," most White-throated Sparrows move to warmer climates in autumn and early winter.

white-striped morph

ID: black-and-white (or brown-and-tan) striped head; well-defined white throat; grey cheek; yellow lores; grey, unstreaked breast; lighter belly; rusty upperparts with black streaks; greyish bill. *Immature:* brown and greyish buff head stripes; breast has dusky streaks.

Size: *L* 17–18 cm.

Status: common in the boreal plain ecozone and northward from late April to early October; common to abundant in the prairie ecozone from late April to mid-May and from early September to mid-October; occasional, especially at feeders, from late October to mid-April.

Habitat: *Breeding:* semi-open deciduous, coniferous and mixed forests, regenerating clearings and shrubby forest edges. *In migration* and *Winter:* brushy edges of gardens, fields and roads, often near feeders.

Nesting: on or near the ground; open cup nest of moss, grass, twigs and conifer needles is lined with rootlets, fine grass and hair; female incubates 4–6 speckled, bluish-white eggs for 11–14 days.

Feeding: scratches the ground for invertebrates, seeds and berries; collects insects from vegetation and while in flight.

Voice: variable song is a clear and distinct whistled *dear sweet Canada Canada Canada*; call is a sharp *chink* or slurred *tseet*.

Similar Species: *White-crowned Sparrow:* lacks well-defined, white throat and yellow lores; upperparts are not as rusty; pinkish bill; grey collar.

Best Sites: *Breeding:* Besnard Lake; Candle Lake PP; Duck Mountain PP; Meadow Lake PP; Moose Mountain PP; Tobin Lake. *In migration:* widespread in almost any wooded or brushy area.

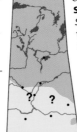

DARK-EYED JUNCO

Junco hyemalis

The Dark-eyed Junco passes through virtually every moderately sized woodlot in Saskatchewan at some point in the year, and it is one of our most familiar forest species. Juncos spend most of their time on the ground, and they are readily flushed from wooded trails and feeders, their distinctive, white outer tail feathers flashing as they fly away. These birds are trusting by nature, sometimes picking up grain and seeds at the feet of a silent observer. • Juncos are uncommon winter residents in southern parts of our province, where they make regular visits to backyard feeders. If a seed supply is maintained, a flock might remain in the area throughout the winter. • North America boasts a great diversity of junco subspecies. Our province is typically home to the subspecies known as the "Slate-colored Junco"; the "Oregon Junco" breeds in the Cypress Hills. Birds of these subspecies frequently interbreed, producing many confusing variations.

"Slate-colored Junco"

ID: white outer tail feathers are obvious in flight; pinkish bill. *Male:* dark slate grey overall, except for white lower breast, belly and undertail coverts. *Female:* brownish-grey rather than dark grey. *Immature:* like female, but streaked with darker brown.
Size: *L* 14–17 cm.
Status: common in the boreal plain ecozone and northward from early April to late October; common to abundant in the prairie ecozone from early April to early May and from mid-September to late October; rare to uncommon, mainly at feeders, from early November to late March.
Habitat: *Breeding:* open coniferous and mixed forests, bogs, burned-over areas and shrubby regenerating clearings. *In migration* and *Winter:* any brushy or wooded habitat; near granaries, spilled grain or feeders.
Nesting: on the ground, often against a vertical bank; rarely in a

tree, shrub or building; cup nest of twigs, bark shreds, grass and moss is lined with fine grass, moss and hair; female incubates 3–6 speckled, pale bluish eggs for 12–13 days; usually has 2 broods per year.
Feeding: scratches the ground for invertebrates; also eats berries and seeds.
Voice: song is a long, dry trill very similar to, but slower and more musical than, the song of the Chipping Sparrow (p. 139); distinctive "smacking" alarm note can be imitated by smacking the tongue from the roof of the mouth.
Similar Species: *Spotted Towhee* (p. 138): much larger; black bill; red eyes; only outer tail corners are white.
Best Sites: *Breeding:* Besnard Lake; Candle Lake PP; Cypress Hills PP; Duck Mountain PP; Meadow Lake PP; Tobin Lake. *In migration:* almost anywhere that there is woody cover. *Winter:* feeders, especially in urban areas.

LAPLAND LONGSPUR

Calcarius lapponicus

In late autumn and early spring, huge flocks of Lapland Longspurs and other arctic-nesting songbirds pass through Saskatchewan, making brief stop-overs in fallow fields and along roadsides. The flocks can be surprisingly inconspicuous until they are closely approached—anyone attempting a closer look will be awed by the sight of the birds suddenly erupting into the skies, flashing their white outer tail feathers. • In autumn, these birds arrive from their breeding grounds looking like mottled brownish sparrows, and they retain their drab plumage throughout the winter months. By the time farmers work their fields in spring, however, male Lapland Longspurs have moulted into their bold breeding plumage. • The male Lapland Longspur's courtship displays include a conspicuous tinkling flight song issued as he rises into the air and then floats downward with outstretched wings and a spread tail.

non-breeding

ID: white outer tail feathers; pale yellowish bill. *Breeding male:* black crown, face and bib outlined with white; chestnut collar. *Breeding female* and *Non-breeding male:* rusty nape; often has rufous in wings; mottled brown-and-black upperparts; finely streaked breast and sides on otherwise light underparts. *Non-breeding female:* mottled brown with black streaks on upperparts; narrow, lightly streaked buff breast band. *Immature:* greyish nape; broader, buff-brown breast band.
Size: *L* 16 cm.
Status: common to abundant from mid-March to late May and from late September to late November; uncommon in the extreme south of the prairie ecozone from early December to early March.
Habitat: *In migration* and *Winter:* open areas, pastures, meadows, roadsides and weedy fields.

Nesting: does not nest in Saskatchewan.
Feeding: probes the ground for insects and some small seeds; eats mostly seeds and waste grain in winter.
Voice: flight song is a rapid, slurred warble; various musical calls; flight calls include *tickt-tick-tew* and a descending *teew.*
Similar Species: *Snow Bunting* (p. 148): winter adults have an unstreaked, tan head and mostly white wings with black tips. *Smith's Longspur:* completely buff to buff-orange underparts; uncommon in Saskatchewan. *Chestnut-collared Longspur:* breeding male has all-black underparts (except throat and lower belly), black crown, black eye line and rusty nape. *Vesper Sparrow* (p. 141): bold, white eye ring; chestnut shoulder patch.
Best Sites: *In migration:* Besnard Lake; Buffer Lake; Last Mountain Lake NWA. *Winter:* Grasslands NP.

SNOW BUNTING

Plectrophenax nivalis

In early winter, flocks of Snow Buntings descend on fields and roadsides in open areas of Saskatchewan, their startling, black-and-white wings flashing in contrast with the snow-covered landscape. Through the winter, they congregate in open fields where food is available, spending almost all of their time on the ground, scratching and pecking at exposed seeds and grains. • It may seem strange that Snow Buntings are whiter in summer than in winter, but the darker winter plumage may help these birds absorb heat on the coldest, clear winter days. • Unlike most of our songbirds, Snow Buntings arrive in our province after the breeding season. They spend their summers north of our province, often nesting in arctic communities. Snow Buntings have beautiful, clear courtship songs, but during the Saskatchewan winter we only hear the twittering of large flocks as they sweep across the province.

non-breeding

ID: black-and-white wings and tail; white underparts. *Breeding male:* black back; all-white head and rump; black bill. *Breeding female:* unstreaked, tan head; streaked, brown back; white rump; dark bill. *Non-breeding:* yellowish bill; unstreaked, golden-brown crown and rump.
Size: *L* 15–18 cm.
Status: common in the taiga shield ecozone from early October to early November and from late March to early May; fairly common to abundant in the rest of the province from late October to early May.

Habitat: cultivated or stubble fields, pastures, grassy meadows, lakeshores, roadsides and railways.
Nesting: does not nest in Saskatchewan.
Feeding: probes the ground and vegetation for seeds and waste grain.
Voice: song is a musical, high-pitched *chi-chi-churee*; call is a whistled *teer* or *tew*; also a rough, purring *brrrt*.
Similar Species: *Lapland Longspur* (p. 147): lacks black-and-white wing pattern; streaked head pattern in winter plumage.
Best Sites: widespread; often abundant in open country.

ROSE-BREASTED GROSBEAK

Pheucticus ludovicianus

The vibrant, spirited song and distinctive sharp *tick* call note of the Rose-breasted Grosbeak are commonly heard among Saskatchewan's mixed woodlands in spring and summer. Its song is quite similar to that of the American Robin but is richer and has rapid phrases that run together without pausing. Although the female lacks the magnificent colours of the male, she shares his vocal flair. • These birds are not meticulous nest-builders—sometimes their nests are so loosely built that you can see right through them. Many songbirds quietly incubate their eggs, but male Rose-breasted Grosbeaks often sing while they are on the nest. • Grosbeaks often raise two broods per year. In such cases, the male will care for the fledged young from the first brood while the female builds a second nest.

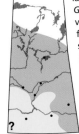

ID: pale, stout bill; dark wings with large, white wing bars and bold, white patches (obvious in flight); dark tail. *Male:* black head, throat and back; red breast and underwings; white rump and belly. *1st-spring male:* may show brown instead of black. *1st-autumn male:* like female, but breast and sides are streaked orangish; reddish wing linings. *Female:* bold, whitish eyebrow and thin crown stripe; brown upperparts; light buff underparts with dark brown streaking; yellow underwings.
Size: *L* 18–21 cm.
Status: fairly common in the boreal plain ecozone from late May to mid-August; fairly common in the prairie ecozone from mid-May to early June and from early August to early September.
Habitat: *Breeding:* riparian woodlands, woodlots and deciduous and mixed boreal forest with tall, sparse undergrowth. *In migration:* any wooded area.
Nesting: fairly low in a tree or shrub, often near water; flimsy cup nest of twigs, bark strips, grass and leaves is lined with rootlets and hair; pair incubates 3–5 spotted, pale bluish-green eggs for 9–12 days.

Feeding: probes tree foliage for insects, seeds, buds, blossoms, berries and some fruit; may visit feeding stations.
Voice: song is a long, melodious series of whistled notes, much like a fast and more varied version of an American Robin's (p. 119) song; call is a distinctive metallic *kik*.
Similar Species: male is distinctive. *Purple Finch* (p. 158): female is much smaller, has darker bill, heavier streaking on underparts and lacks yellow underwings. *Black-headed Grosbeak:* female and immatures are very similar but are buffier below, with faint flank streaking; uncommon in southwestern Saskatchewan.
Best Sites: *Breeding:* Candle Lake PP; Duck Mountain PP; eastern Qu'Appelle Valley; Hudson Bay; Meadow Lake PP; Moose Mountain PP; Nisbet PF; Prince Albert NP; Tobin Lake. *In migration:* Last Mountain Lake NWA; Regina; Saskatoon.

RED-WINGED BLACKBIRD

Agelaius phoeniceus

The Red-winged Blackbird is one of our most abundant summer birds and is possibly the most conspicuous. Arriving in Saskatchewan a week or so before the females, male Red-winged Blackbirds get an early start on the spring to stake out territories. At this time of year, few wetlands and cattail marshes are free from the classic calls of these bossy, aggressive birds. Swaying atop cattail stalks, males display their bright red shoulder patches while singing their loud *konk-a-ree or ogle-reeeee* calls. A male's shoulder patches, or "epaulettes," and song are his most important tools in the often intricate strategy he employs to defend his territory from rivals. A flashy and richly voiced male that has managed to establish a large territory can attract several mates to his cattail kingdom. In field experiments, males whose red shoulders were painted black soon lost their territories to rivals they had previously defeated. • In autumn, Red-winged Blackbirds roost and feed together in mixed-species flocks that include female Red-winged Blackbirds, grackles, Rusty Blackbirds, starlings and cowbirds.

ID: *Male:* all black, except for large, red shoulder patch outlined in yellow (occasionally concealed). *Female:* heavily streaked underparts; mottled brown upperparts; may have pinkish tinge on throat; light eyebrow stripe. *Immature male:* mottled blackish-brown plumage; faint red shoulder patch.
Size: *L* 18–24 cm.
Status: common to abundant from early April to late October.
Habitat: cattail marshes, wet meadows and ditches, shoreline shrubbery and upland shrubs; ranges widely to feed in croplands and in open country.
Nesting: colonial and polygynous; in emergent vegetation near or over water; rarely in shoreline shrubs; bulky open cup nest composed of dried cattail leaves, grass, reeds and rootlets is lined with fine grass; female incubates 3–6 bluish-white

eggs, marked with purple and black, for 10–12 days; has 2–3 broods per year.
Feeding: probes the ground or vegetation for seeds, insects, other invertebrates, grain and berries; also catches insects in flight; attracted to some crops in migration and to feedlots or spilled grain in winter.
Voice: song is a loud, raspy *konk-a-ree* or *ogle-reeeee*; calls include a harsh *check* and a high *tseert*; female may give a loud *che-che-che chee chee chee*.
Similar Species: male is distinctive (when shoulder patch is visible). *Brewer's Blackbird* (p. 153) and *Rusty Blackbird:* females have unstreaked underparts. *Brown-headed Cowbird* (p. 155): smaller; stubbier bill.
Best Sites: *Breeding:* widespread in and near any wetland with emergent vegetation. *Winter:* occasionally frequents feedlots.

WESTERN MEADOWLARK

Sturnella neglecta

This open-country bird is common in southern parts of our province. It typically inhabits agricultural areas and can be seen perched on fenceposts and powerlines wherever grassy meadows and pastures are found. Many people think of it as the true harbinger of spring because it arrives early in the season, usually in late March. Its rich and varied song (males have up to 12 song types) is recognized as one of the most beautiful voices of the prairies. • The meadowlark has distinguishing features that include a black, V-shaped "necklace," bright yellow underparts and a short tail with white outer feathers, which are often flicked open and closed. It is shaped much like a starling, thus the scientific name *Sturnella*, or "little starling." It also flies in a similar style, alternating several quick wingbeats with a short glide. • The Western Meadowlark has adapted fairly well to human settlement on the prairies, nesting in considerable abundance in healthy grasslands, haylands and grassy ditches. However, because this bird requires some residual cover for nesting, abuse of lands through overgrazing and intensive cultivation has rendered it uncommon and declining in many areas.

breeding

ID: *Male:* yellow underparts, including throat; dark streaks on white sides; broad, black breast band; mottled brown upperparts; short tail with white outer tail feathers; long, pinkish legs; yellow lores; long, light median crown stripe; long, sharp bill. *Female:* slightly smaller; paler yellow; black "V" on breast is less defined.
Size: *L* 23–24 cm.
Status: common in the prairie ecozone and uncommon and local elsewhere from early April to late October.
Habitat: grassy meadows, native prairie, pastures, hayfields and grassy road allowances.
Nesting: in a depression or scrape on the ground; domed grass nest with a side entrance is woven into

and concealed by surrounding vegetation; female incubates 3–7 white eggs, spotted with brown and purple, for 13–15 days; usually has 2 broods per year.
Feeding: probes the ground for grasshoppers, crickets, beetles, other insects and spiders; also eats some seeds and digs up grubs and worms.

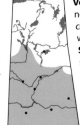

Voice: song is a melodic series of fluty notes; calls include a low, loud *chuck* or *chup*, a rattling flight call or a few clear, whistled notes: *who-who are you?*
Similar Species: *Dickcissel:* much smaller; conical bill; chestnut shoulder; rare in southeastern Saskatchewan.
Best Sites: widespread; most common in extensive areas of open pasture.

YELLOW-HEADED BLACKBIRD

Xanthocephalus xanthocephalus

You might expect that the Yellow-headed Blackbird would have a brilliant song to match its splendid gold-and-black plumage. Unfortunately, a trip to a nearby marsh will quickly reveal the shocking truth: when the male arches his golden head backward, he struggles to produce a painful, discordant, grinding noise. In fact, this bird's song is regarded by many birders as the worst in North America. • Where Yellow-headed Blackbirds occur with Red-winged Blackbirds (p. 150), the larger Yellow-heads dominate, commandeering the centre of the wetland and pushing their red-winged competitors to the periphery. • Yellow-headed Blackbirds routinely leave their marsh habitat to forage for seeds and insects in upland fields and pastures. Unlike other blackbirds, however, their nests are never found away from deep water. • According to surveys, Yellow-headed Blackbird numbers are increasing at a dramatic rate across North America.

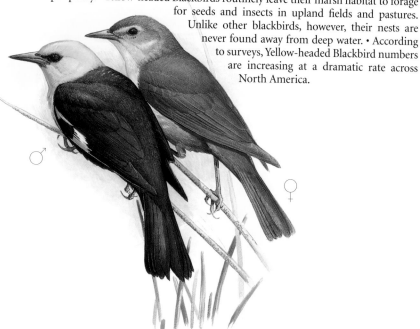

ID: *Male:* yellow head and breast; black body; white wing patches; black lores and bill. *Female:* dusky-brown overall; yellow wash on breast, throat and eyebrow; some yellow on face; white lower breast.
Size: *L* 20–28 cm.
Status: common in the prairie ecozone and uncommon and local elsewhere from late April to late September.
Habitat: permanent marshes, sloughs and river impoundments where cattails or dense stands of emergent vegetation dominate; will forage on upland fields, pastures and grasslands.
Nesting: in loose colonies; bulky, deep basket nest made of wet aquatic vegetation is bound to emergent vegetation over water and lined with dry grass; female incubates 3–5 brown-blotched, greenish-white eggs for 11–13 days.
Feeding: probes the ground and vegetation for seeds, beetles, snails, waterbugs and dragonflies; young are fed by regurgitation.
Voice: low, hoarse, grating song; call is a deep *kack* or *kruck*.
Similar Species: male is distinctive. *Other female blackbirds:* lack yellow throat and face.
Best Sites: widespread; Chaplin Lake/Marsh; Last Mountain Lake NWA; Nicolle Flats; Quill Lakes.

BREWER'S BLACKBIRD

Euphagus cyanocephalus

The Brewer's Blackbird is a common summer resident in open country through-out southern Saskatchewan, where it is commonly seen along roadsides searching for road-killed insects and squabbling with Rock Doves (p. 80) and European Starlings. As it walks, the Brewer's Blackbird jerks its head back and forth like a chicken, which helps to distinguish it from other blackbirds. • Unlike the more solitary Rusty Blackbird of northern bogs and wetlands, this gregarious bird almost always nests in colonies, where birds can team together if a Northern Harrier (p. 47) comes looking for a meal. As autumn approaches, these colonies join with other family groups to form large, migrating flocks. • John J. Audubon, the famous wildlife artist, named this bird after his friend and prominent oologist (student of eggs) Thomas Mayo Brewer.

ID: *Male:* pale yellow eyes; iridescent, green body and purplish head often look black; autumn males may show faint rusty feather edgings. *Female:* brownish-grey plumage; darker back, wings and tail; brown eyes.
Size: *L* 20–25 cm.
Status: common in the prairie ecozone and uncommon and local elsewhere from late April to early October.
Habitat: *Breeding:* open country with scattered brush, field edges, shelter-belts and roadsides. *Winter:* may overwinter in feedlots.
Nesting: in loose colonies; on the ground or low in a shrub or tree, often near water; bulky open nest of twigs, grass, mud and forbs is lined with rootlets, fine grass and hair; female incubates 3–7 brown-spotted, pale grey eggs for 12–14 days.
Feeding: probes the ground for

invertebrates and seeds while walking along shorelines and open areas; may eat some fruit and berries.
Voice: song is a creaking *k-shee*; call is a metallic *chick* or *check*.
Similar Species: *Rusty Blackbird:* more slen-der bill; rusty wash overall in non-breeding plumage; breeding male has subtler, green-and-blue gloss in plumage; female has yellow eyes. *Common Grackle* (p. 154): much longer, keeled tail; larger body and bill. *Brown-headed Cowbird* (p. 155): shorter tail; stubbier, thicker bill; male has dark eyes and brown head; female has paler, streaked underparts and pale throat. *European Starling* (p. 122): bill is yel-low in summer; speckled appearance; dark eyes.
Best Sites: widespread; most abun-dant in pastures; forms large flocks with other blackbirds in autumn.

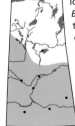

COMMON GRACKLE

Quiscalus quiscula

The Common Grackle is a poor but spirited singer. Often from a perch in a shrub, a male grackle will puff out his plumage, close his eyes and give a loud, strained *tssh-schleek*. Despite his lack of musical talent, he remains smug and proud, with his bill held high. • The Common Grackle is easily distinguished from other glossy blackbirds by its relatively large size, its heavy bill and its long, "keeled" or wedge-shaped tail. In flight, the grackle's tail trails behind it like a hatchet blade. • In late autumn and early winter, most grackles migrate to the U.S., but each year a few remain in our province, usually in the larger cities. • Grackles are widespread and abundant in North America east of the Rockies, but their numbers are declining. They are widespread in our province, although their numbers vary considerably by region.

ID: *Male:* iridescent plumage (purplish-blue head and breast, bronze back and sides and purple wings and tail) often looks black; long, keeled tail; yellow eyes; long, heavy bill. *Female:* smaller and less iridescent. *Immature:* dull brown overall; dark eyes.
Size: *L* 28–34 cm.
Status: common in the boreal plain ecozone and uncommon and local elsewhere from early April to early October.
Habitat: hedgerows, open forests, riparian woodlands, shrubby urban and suburban parks and gardens, partly open areas with scattered trees and edges of coniferous forests.
Nesting: in dense tree or shrub or emergent vegetation, often near water; sometimes in a conifer; bulky cup nest of twigs, grass and mud is lined with fine grass or feathers;

female incubates 3–6 brown-blotched, pale blue eggs for 12–14 days.
Feeding: probes the ground for insects, earthworms, seeds, grain, aquatic invertebrates and fruit; may eat some bird eggs and nestlings.
Voice: song is a split, rasping *tssh-schleek* or *gri-de-leeek*; call is a loud *graack* or *swaaaack*.
Similar Species: *Rusty Blackbird* and *Brewer's Blackbird* (p. 153): smaller overall; lack heavy bill and keeled tail. *Red-winged Blackbird* (p. 150): shorter, unkeeled tail; male has red shoulder patch and dark eyes. *European Starling* (p. 122): short tail; long, thin bill (yellow in summer); speckled overall; dark eyes.
Best Sites: Besnard Lake; Candle Lake PP; Duck Mountain PP; Meadow Lake PP; Regina; Saskatoon; Yorkton.

BROWN-HEADED COWBIRD

Molothrus ater

The Brown-headed Cowbird's song, a bubbling, liquidy *glug-ahl-whee*, might translate to other birds as "here comes trouble!" Historically, Brown-headed Cowbirds followed bison herds across the plains and prairies, and their nomadic lifestyle made it impossible for them to construct and tend a nest. Instead, cowbirds engage in "brood parasitism," laying their eggs in the nests of other songbirds. Many songbirds do not recognize cowbird eggs as different and raise the young cowbirds as their own. Cowbird chicks typically hatch first and develop much more quickly than their nestmates, which are often pushed out of the nest or out-competed for food. • The expansion of agriculture and forestry and the growing network of transportation corridors has significantly increased the cowbird's range. It now parasitizes more than 140 bird species in North America, including many that probably had no contact with it prior to widespread human settlement.

ID: short, stubby bill; squared tail; dark eyes. *Male:* blackish body may show slight blue iridescence; brown head. *Female:* grey-brown overall; paler underparts with faint streaking; pale throat. *Immature:* paler buff-grey with soft breast streaking.
Size: *L* 15–20 cm.
Status: common in the prairie ecozone and fairly common and local elsewhere from mid-May to early September.
Habitat: woodland fringes, forest openings, shrubby grasslands and areas near cattle (pastures, feedlots and stockyards); also around campgrounds and picnic areas.
Nesting: does not build a nest; females lay up to 40 eggs per year in the nests of other birds (usually 1 egg per nest); whitish eggs, marked with grey and brown, hatch after 10–13 days.

Feeding: probes the ground for seeds, waste grain and invertebrates, especially grasshoppers, beetles and true bugs.
Voice: song is a high, liquidy *gurgle glug-ahl-whee* or *glug-glug-gleee*; call is a whistled *seep* or *weee-titi*, often given in flight; also a fast, chipping *ch-ch-ch-ch-ch-ch*.
Similar Species: *Blackbirds:* larger; lack contrasting brown head and darker body; slimmer, longer bills; longer tails; all have yellow eyes, except for female Brewer's Blackbird (p. 153). *Common Grackle* (p. 154): much larger overall; longer, heavier bill; longer, keeled tail. *European Starling* (p. 122): longer bill; shorter tail.
Best Sites: widespread; especially common near cattle and in the company of other blackbirds.

155

BALTIMORE ORIOLE

Icterus galbula

Baltimore Orioles are fairly common in central and southern parts of our province, but they are often difficult to find because they inhabit the forest canopy. The striking males are visible when they sing their musical, flute-like song from perches, but the females typically remain near their nest, which is hidden in the upper canopy of a large shade tree. • Baltimore Orioles prefer small stands of mature deciduous trees over extensive forest. In urban areas, such requirements are met by shade trees; in the grasslands by riparian woodlands and wooded coulees; and in the parklands by aspen groves. • Baltimore Orioles are some of the last birds to move into our province each spring, and they are among the first to leave in autumn.

ID: *Male:* black head, throat, back, wings and central tail feathers; bright orange underparts, shoulder stripe, rump and outer tail feathers; white wing bar and flight feather edgings. *Female:* olive-brown upperparts (darkest on head); dull yellowish-orange underparts and rump; 2 white wing bars. *Immature:* resembles adult female, but male has brighter underparts, female duller upperparts.
Size: *L* 18–20 cm.
Status: common in the prairie ecozone and fairly common and local elsewhere from mid-May to early September.
Habitat: parkland and open, mixed coniferous forests, mature riparian woodlands, forest fringes and openings, orchards and yards with scattered shade trees.
Nesting: high in a deciduous tree; deep, hanging-pouch nest of grass, shredded bark, string, hair and plant fibres is lined with fine grass, rootlets and fur; female incubates 4–6 greyish-white eggs, marked with black, for 12–14 days.

Feeding: probes canopy vegetation and shrubs for caterpillars, beetles, wasps and other invertebrates; eats some fruit and nectar; may visit hummingbird feeders.
Voice: 2- or 3-note phrases are strung together into a delightfully robust song: *peter peter here here peter;* other calls include a 2-note *tea-too,* a rapid chatter *ch-ch-ch-ch-ch* and a low, whistled *hewli* note.
Similar Species: *Bullock's Oriole:* male has large, white wing patch, black throat patch and orange face with black eye line; female has greyer back and white belly; uncommon and local in southwestern Saskatchewan. *Orchard Oriole:* smaller; male has darker chestnut plumage; female and immature are olive and yellow and lack orange overtones; uncommon in southeastern Saskatchewan. *Scarlet Tanager:* females have thicker, paler bill and lack wing bars and orange underparts; rare in Saskatchewan.
Best Sites: Eastend; Last Mountain Lake NWA; Maple Creek; Moose Mountain PP; Yorkton.

PINE GROSBEAK

Pinicola enucleator

Pine Grosbeaks are colourful nomads of the boreal forest. Much of their survival depends on the availability of conifer seeds, from pine and spruce trees in particular, so they are always in search of a good crop. Although these birds breed locally in northern Saskatchewan, they are best known as winter visitors to southern parts of our province. Pine Grosbeaks do not regularly migrate from their nesting range, and their winter visits are erratic—it is a great moment in a typical winter when the Pine Grosbeaks emerge from the wilds to settle on your backyard feeder. The invasions are not completely understood, but it is thought that widespread cone crop failures or even changes to forest ecology caused by logging, forest fires or climatic factors may force these hungry birds southward in search of food. • During the nesting season, adults develop throat pouches for transporting seeds.

ID: stubby, dark bill; 2 white wing bars; black wings and tail. *Male:* crimson-red head, rump and breast; streaked back; grey sides, flanks, belly and undertail coverts. *Female* and *Immature:* grey overall; males have yellow or orangy-crimson wash on head and rump. *In flight:* deeply undulating flight style.
Size: *L* 20–25 cm.
Status: irruptive; uncommon in the taiga shield ecozone from early April to late October; rare to common in the rest of the province from late October to late March.
Habitat: *Breeding:* open spruce-fir coniferous forests and forest fringes. *In migration* and *Winter:* conifer plantations and urban and rural yards with feeders and fruiting mountain ash and crabapple trees.
Nesting: in a conifer or tall shrub; bulky cup nest, loosely made of twigs, grass, forbs and rootlets, is lined with lichen, rootlets and fine grass; female incubates 3–5 speckled, pale greenish-blue eggs for 13–15 days.
Feeding: eats buds, berries and seeds from coniferous and deciduous trees; may use feeders in winter.
Voice: typical flight call is a whistled *tew-tew-tew*; alarm call is a musical *chee-vli*.
Similar Species: *White-winged Crossbill* (p. 159): much smaller; lacks stubby bill; larger, white wing bars. *Red Crossbill:* much smaller; lacks stubby bill and white wing bars. *Evening Grosbeak* (p. 163): female has yellow bill, tan underparts and bold, white wing patches.
Best Sites: *Breeding:* only in the far north. *Winter:* widespread; especially common where ash trees are present.

PURPLE FINCH

Carpodacus purpureus

The Purple Finch's gentle nature, rich song and lovely plumage make it a welcome guest in any backyard. Its presence near an ornamental shrub or feeder is certain to brighten a drab winter's day. Platform feeding stations with nearby tree cover may attract Purple Finches in spring or autumn migrations • Purple Finches prefer to nest in shrubs and coniferous trees but while in migration and in winter they feed in deciduous trees and from feeders. • The courtship of Purple Finches is a gentle and appealing ritual. Upon the arrival of an interested female, the colourful male dances lightly around her, vocalizing and beating his wings until he lifts softly into the air. • Purple is an overstated description of this bird's delicate colour. The eminent ornithologist Roger Tory Peterson said it best when he described the Purple Finch as "a sparrow dipped in raspberry juice."

ID: *Male:* crimson-red head, throat, breast and rump; brownish-red cheek patch, sides and streaked back; dark, notched tail; light, unstreaked belly and undertail. *Female and Immature:* dark brown cheek and "jaw" line; white eyebrow and lower cheek stripes; dark brown upperparts; heavily streaked underparts; lighter, unstreaked belly and undertail.
Size: *L* 13–15 cm.
Status: fairly common in the boreal plain ecozone from mid-April to late October; fairly common in the prairie ecozone from early April to late May and from late August to late October; occasional in winter in the prairie ecozone.
Habitat: *Breeding:* open coniferous and mixed forests, forest fringes and conifers in cities and towns. *In migration:* open coniferous, mixed or parkland forests. *Winter:* feeders or fruit trees.

Nesting: on a conifer branch; cup nest, woven with twigs, grass and rootlets, is lined with fine grass, moss and hair; female incubates 3–6 pale greenish-blue eggs, marked with black and brown, for 13 days.
Feeding: probes the ground and vegetation for seeds, buds, blossoms, berries and insects; also visits table-style feeders.
Voice: song is a fast, lively warble similar to the Warbling Vireo's song but richer and more sustained; call is a metallic *tick* or *weet*.
Similar Species: *House Finch:* male has distinct, brown cap and cheek patch; plain-faced female lacks white eyebrow and dark cheek patch and "chin" stripes. *Red Crossbill:* bill has crossed tips; male is richer red overall and has darker wings.
Best Sites: *Breeding:* Candle Lake PP; Duck Mountain PP; Hudson Bay; Nisbet PF; Prince Albert NP; Tobin Lake. *In migration:* Last Mountain Lake NWA; Regina; Saskatoon; Yorkton.

WHITE-WINGED CROSSBILL

Loxia leucoptera

Crossbills are the gypsies of the bird world, wandering far and wide in search of ripe conifer cones. There is no telling when or where they will find the next bumper crop, and they may breed regardless of the season. White-winged Crossbills favour spruce and tamarack seeds, and the crossed tips of their bills are perfectly designed to pry open cones. Crossbills are so efficient at extracting seeds that a flock foraging high in a spruce tree can create an unforgettable shower of cone scales and discarded cones. • When not foraging in spruce spires, White-winged Crossbills often drop to ground level, where they drink water from shallow forest pools or lick salt from winter roads. Unfortunately, their habit of licking salt from roadsides often results in crossbill fatalities. • Saskatchewan is also home to the Red Crossbill. This bird is also nomadic, but it wanders through forests in search of pine, not spruce, seeds.

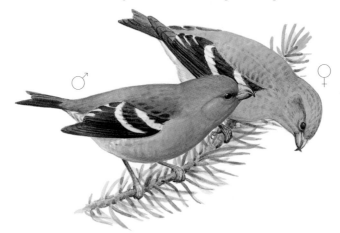

ID: bill has crossed tips; 2 bold, white wing bars; dark wings and tail. *Male:* pinkish-red overall, pink is replaced with orange and yellow on immature male. *Female:* streaked olive yellow upperparts; dusky yellow underparts, slightly streaked with brown. *Immature:* streaky olive brown overall.
Size: *L* 15–17 cm.
Status: irruptive; uncommon to common in the boreal plain ecozone and northward year-round; rare to fairly common in the prairie ecozone from early October to early May.
Habitat: coniferous forests (primarily spruce, fir and tamarack); may appear in conifers in townsites and may also forage in poplars in mixed stands or in sunflower fields.
Nesting: on the outer branch of a conifer; open cup nest of twigs, grass, bark shreds and forbs is lined with moss, lichen, rootlets, hair, feathers and plant down; female incubates

2–5 pale bluish-green eggs, spotted with brown and lavender, for 12–14 days.
Feeding: prefers spruce and tamarack seeds; also eats deciduous tree seeds, buds, berries and some insects; often licks salt and minerals from roads; young are fed by regurgitation.
Voice: song is a mingling of warbles, trills and pure, clear notes; call note is a liquid *cheat* and a dry *chif-chif*, often given in flight.
Similar Species: *Red Crossbill:* lacks white wing bars; male is deeper red. *Pine Siskin* (p. 161): similar to juvenile, but lacks crossed bill, is smaller, has lighter coloured underparts and yellow highlights in wing. *Pine Grosbeak* (p. 157): much larger, stubby bill; thinner wing bars; female is greyer. *Purple Finch* (p. 158) and *House Finch:* stubby bills; less red overall; lack wing bars.
Best Sites: *Breeding:* Candle Lake PP; Meadow Lake PP; Nisbet PF. *Winter:* Saskatoon; Regina.

COMMON REDPOLL

Carduelis flammea

Common Redpolls are renowned for their effective winter adaptations. They have a very large surface area relative to their internal volume, so they lose heat quickly and are in constant danger of running out of fuel and dying from hypothermia. Hence, redpolls must eat almost constantly during winter, and most of their time is spent gleaning waste grain from fields or stocking up on seed at winter feeders. Because they focus so completely on food, wintering redpolls are remarkably fearless of humans, provided the observer moves slowly and quietly. • Common Redpolls and Hoary Redpolls can be confusing to differentiate because they look alike, share similar ranges and have similar calls. The Hoary Redpoll is almost always seen with flocks of Common Redpolls, and it is generally paler and less streaked. Both redpolls are remote northern nesters and "predictably unpredictable" winter visitors to our province—like many finches, they can be abundant one year and nearly absent the next.

non-breeding

ID: red forecrown; black "chin" patch; yellowish bill; streaky, brown upperparts; lightly streaked rump, sides, flanks and undertail coverts; notched tail. *Male:* pinkish-red breast is brightest in breeding plumage. *Female:* whitish to pale grey breast.
Size: *L* 13 cm.
Status: fairly common in the taiga shield ecozone year-round; irruptive and uncommon to abundant in the boreal shield ecozone and southward from late October to early April.
Habitat: *Breeding:* scattered shrubs within tundra and boreal taiga. *In migration* and *Winter:* weedy fields (especially sunflower fields), roadsides, railways, farmyards with spilled grain and backyards with feeders.
Nesting: in a low shrub, dwarf spruce or crevice among rocks; open cup nest of fine twigs, grass, plant stems, lichen and moss is lined with feathers,

hair and seed fluff; female incubates 4–7 blue eggs, spotted with purple, for 10–11 days.
Feeding: probes the ground and weed patches in large flocks for seeds in winter; often visits feeding stations; may also eat suet; small seeds and insects are taken in summer.
Voice: song is a high-pitched melody, usually followed by rattling *chit* notes; twitters constantly in flight, interspersed by long, 2-note *sssssss-eeeet* calls.
Similar Species: *Hoary Redpoll:* shorter bill; unstreaked or lightly streaked rump; usually has faint streaking or no streaking on sides, flanks and undertail; generally paler and more plump overall. *Pine Siskin* (p. 161): heavily streaked overall; yellow highlights in wings and tail; lacks red cap.
Best Sites: *Breeding:* only in the far north. *Winter:* widespread; usually common in winters beginning in even-numbered years; uncommon to rare in odd-numbered years.

PINE SISKIN

Carduelis pinus

Birders in pursuit of these active birds are often met with frustration, aching feet and a sore, crimped neck. The easiest way to see these birds is to set up a finch feeder filled with niger seed or millet in your backyard and wait for them to appear. Pine Siskins will visit feeders at just about any time of year, but they often disappear just as suddenly as they appeared. • Siskins are frequently heard before they are seen. When in flight, flocks twitter incessantly and deliver frequent rising *zzzreeeee* calls. They are highly gregarious birds, often nesting in loose colonies and feeding in mixed-species flocks that include goldfinches, juncos and crossbills. • Although its name implies an association with pine forests, the Pine Siskin nests in a variety of forest types. Like most finches, it is highly nomadic and rarely occupies the same nesting territory in successive years. • Pine Siskins are rare winter visitors to our province, but recent surveys suggest they are becoming more frequent with the increase in birdfeeders.

ID: heavily streaked underparts; yellow highlights at base of tail feathers and in wings (easily seen in flight); dull wing bars; darker brown, heavily streaked upperparts; deeply forked tail; striped facial pattern; pointed bill. *Immature:* dull white in wings and tail.
Size: *L* 11–13 cm.
Status: irruptive; generally fairly common in the boreal plain ecozone and northward and rare to fairly common elsewhere from early April to late October; rare to uncommon at feeders from early November to late March.
Habitat: *Breeding:* coniferous and mixed forests, urban parks, rural ornamental trees and shade trees. *Winter:* often near feeders, weedy areas and sunflower fields.
Nesting: usually in loose colonies; on the outer branch of a conifer; loose cup nest of twigs, grass and rootlets is lined with feathers, hair, rootlets and seed fluff; female incubates 3–6 lightly spotted, pale blue eggs for 13 days.

Feeding: coniferous and deciduous tree seeds, thistle seeds, buds, sap and some insects; attracted to road salts and birdfeeders.
Voice: song is similar to the American Goldfinch's (p. 162) but is coarser and wheezy, sometimes resembling a jerky laugh; call is a buzzy, rising *zzzreeeee*; also *tit-i-tit* and a loud *chlee-ip*.
Similar Species: *Common Redpoll* (p. 160) and *Hoary Redpoll:* red forecrown; much shorter bill; lack yellow in wings and tail; underparts are not streaked throughout. *Purple Finch* (p. 158) and *House Finch:* no yellow in wings or tail; darker head and upperparts; females have thicker bill. *Sparrows:* all lack yellow in wings and tail; underparts are not streaked throughout.
Best Sites: *Breeding:* Candle Lake PP; Cypress Hills PP; Duck Mountain PP; Hudson Bay; Meadow Lake PP; Nisbet PF; Prince Albert NP. *Winter:* erratic; look for it at feeders.

AMERICAN GOLDFINCH

Carduelis tristis

The American Goldfinch seems perpetually cheerful as it flies about in flocks issuing jubilant *po-ta-to-chip* calls. This songbird is commonly seen in weedy fields, along roadsides and among backyard shrubs. It seems to delight in perching upon late-summer thistle heads as it searches for seeds, and in migration it will eat niger seed or millet at finch feeders • Goldfinches are readily identified by their bright yellow plumage, deeply undulating flight and distinctive calls. The male's black cap and wings set him apart from the other yellow birds that are also mistakenly called "wild canaries." • In Saskatchewan, goldfinches nest in loose colonies in open and semi-open areas, especially where disturbances such as cultivation, logging and burns have encouraged the growth of thistles. They are among the province's latest nesters, usually delaying their reproductive duties until late June to ensure there is a dependable source of seeds to feed their young.

breeding

ID: *Breeding male:* black cap (extends onto forehead), wings and tail; bright yellow body; white wing bars and undertail; orangy bill and legs. *Breeding female:* dull yellow-green upperparts; black wings with 2 bold, white wing bars; dark tail. *Non-breeding:* similar to summer female but is greyish-brown overall; some yellow on throat, face and wings; pale rump.

Size: *L* 11–14 cm.

Status: common in the prairie eco-zone and fairly common and local elsewhere from mid-May to early October.

Habitat: weedy fields, meadows and gardens, deciduous woodland fringes, shrubby riparian areas and open parks.

Nesting: in a deciduous shrub or tree; compact cup nest, woven with plant fibres, grass and spider silk, is lined with seed fluff and hair; female incubates 4–7 pale blue eggs for 10–12 days.

Feeding: primarily eats insects, berries and thistle, birch and alder seeds; commonly visits feeding stations; young are fed by regurgitation.

Voice: song is a canary-like series of trills, twitters and warbles; calls include *po-ta-to-chip* or *per-chic-or-ee* (often delivered in flight) and a whistled *dear-me, see-me.*

Similar Species: *Evening Grosbeak* (p. 163): much larger; massive bill; lacks black forehead. *Wilson's Warbler:* olive upperparts; greenish wings without wing bars; thin, dark bill; black cap does not extend onto forehead.

Best Sites: widespread; look for it in thistle patches in late summer.

EVENING GROSBEAK

Coccothraustes vespertinus

Evening Grosbeaks often descend unannounced upon backyard feeders in southern Saskatchewan. These stunning gold-and-black birds are enjoyable to watch, and they may return to your feeder day after day. Like most finches, Evening Grosbeaks are highly irruptive, meaning that large numbers are generally encountered every other year. Recently, however, dependable supplies of seed at backyard feeders has caused these birds to be less irruptive than they have been in the past. As April approaches, grosbeak numbers dwindle in southern parts of the province as the birds depart for their boreal nesting sites. • It was once thought that the Evening Grosbeak sang only in the evening, a fact that is reflected in both its common and scientific names (*vespertinus* is Latin for "of the evening").

ID: massive, light-coloured bill; black wings and tail; broad, white wing patches. *Male:* dark crown; bright yellow eyebrow and forehead band; dark brown head gradually fades into golden-yellow belly and lower back. *Female:* grey head and upper back; yellow-tinged underparts; white undertail coverts.
Size: *L* 18–22 cm.
Status: fairly common in the boreal plain ecozone year-round; uncommon in the prairie ecozone from late September to mid-May.
Habitat: *Breeding:* coniferous and mixed forests; also in second-growth woodlands and parks. *In migration* and *Winter:* parks, towns and farms and coniferous, mixed and deciduous forests.
Nesting: on the outer limb of a conifer; flimsy cup nest of twigs and roots is lined with rootlets, fine

grass, plant fibres, moss and pine needles; female incubates 3–5 pale greenish-blue eggs, speckled with brown and grey, for 11–14 days.
Feeding: eats tree and shrub seeds, buds and berries; also eats insects and licks mineral-rich soil; favours feeders with sunflower seeds.
Voice: song is a wandering, halting warble; call is a loud, sharp *clee-ip* or a clear *thew.*
Similar Species: *American Goldfinch* (p. 162): much smaller; small bill; smaller wing bars; male has black cap. *Pine Grosbeak* (p. 157): female has smaller black bill, smaller wing bars and is grey overall.
Best Sites: *Year-round:* Candle Lake PP; Duck Mountain PP; Hudson Bay area; Nisbet PF; Prince Albert NP. *Winter:* Pike Lake PP.

163

HOUSE SPARROW

Passer domesticus

The House Sparrow was introduced into North America in the 1850s near New York City as part of a plan to control insect infestations that were damaging grain and cereal crops. However, the House Sparrow is largely vegetarian, so its impact on crop pests proved to be minimal. Since then, it has managed to colonize most human-altered environments on the continent. • House Sparrows were released in eastern Canada during the mid-1800s, and they were first noted in our province in 1899. Their spread was rapid after their arrival here, and within 20 years House Sparrows were found throughout the settled south. Their attempts to establish themselves in northern parts of the province, however, have been unsuccessful. • House Sparrows are not closely related to other North American sparrows; they belong to the Weaver Finch family and are native to Eurasia and North Africa. • People who prefer to have Purple Martins (p. 107), Tree Swallows (p. 108) or bluebirds rather than House Sparrows in their nest boxes should plug the entrances in the autumn and open them just before these birds return in the spring.

breeding

ID: *Breeding male:* grey crown and cheek; black lores; chestnut brown eyebrows wrap around to nape; white neck; black bib and bill; white wing bar; mottled brown upperparts; grey rump and underparts. *Non-breeding male:* smaller black bib; light-coloured bill. *Female:* brown upperparts; rusty-brown streaked wings and shoulders; greyish-brown underparts; buff eyebrow; lighter bill.
Size: *L* 14–17 cm.
Status: abundant in the prairie ecozone and uncommon and local elsewhere year-round.
Habitat: townsites, urban and suburban areas, farmyards, agricultural areas and other developed sites.
Nesting: often communal; in buildings, nest boxes, trees (especially conifers), shrubs or natural cavities; large, dome-shaped nest of grass, plant fibres and litter is lined with feathers; mostly female incubates 4–7 thickly speckled, dull white eggs for 10–13 days.
Feeding: seeds, insects and fruit; frequently visits feeding stations for seeds.
Voice: song is a plain, monotone *cheap-cheap-cheap-cheap*; call is a short *chill-up*.
Similar Species: *Harris's Sparrow:* grey face; black cap; pink-orange bill. *White-crowned Sparrow:* immature is similar to female House Sparrow, but has pink bill and stripe through crown.
Best Site: widespread in farmsteads, towns and cities throughout the settled south.

GLOSSARY

accipiter: a forest hawk (genus *Accipiter*); characterized by a long tail and short, rounded wings; feeds mostly on birds.

bog: a peat-covered wetland characterized by *Sphagnum* mosses, heath shrubs and sometimes trees (most often black spruce).

brood: *n.* a family of young from one hatching; *v.* to sit on eggs so as to hatch them.

buteo: a high-soaring hawk (genus *Buteo*); characterized by broad wings and a short, wide tail; feeds mostly on small mammals and other land animals.

crop: an enlargement of the esophagus; serves as a storage structure and (in pigeons) has glands that produce secretions.

dabbling: a foraging technique used by ducks, in which the head and neck are submerged but the body and tail remain on the water's surface; dabbling ducks can usually walk easily on land, can take off without running and have brightly coloured speculums.

diurnal: active during the day.

eclipse: the dull, female-like plumage that male ducks briefly acquire after moulting from their breeding plumage.

endangered: a species facing imminent extirpation or extinction.

extinct: a species that no longer exists.

extirpated: a species that no longer exists in a part of its former range (Saskatchewan, for example) but still exists elsewhere in the world.

fen: a peat-covered wetland characterized by brown aquatic mosses, sedges, willows and tamarack.

fledgling: a young bird that has left the nest but is dependent upon its parents.

flushing: a behaviour where frightened birds explode into flight in response to a disturbance.

flycatching: a feeding behaviour where the bird leaves a perch, snatches an insect in mid-air and returns to the same perch.

hawking: attempting to catch insects through aerial pursuit.

irruptive: when a bird is abundant in some years and almost absent in others.

keeled tail: wedge-shaped tail.

leading edge: the front edge of the wing as viewed from below.

mantle: feathers of the back and upperside of folded wings.

marsh: a wetland with little peat characterized by reeds, rushes, grasses or sedges.

median: in the centre; along the length of the body.

moulting: the periodic replacement of worn out feathers (often twice per year).

muskeg: a complex mosaic of boreal fens, bogs, swamps and scrubby forest; increasingly common to the north.

nape: the back of the neck.

niche: an ecological role filled by a species.

nocturnal: active during the night.

parasitism: a relationship between two species where one benefits at the expense of the other.

plucking post: a perch habitually used by raptors to remove feathers and fur from prey.

polyandry: a mating strategy in which one female breeds with several males.

polygyny: a mating strategy in which one male breeds with several females.

primaries: the outermost flight feathers.

raptor: a carnivorous (meat-eating) bird; includes eagles, hawks, falcons and owls.

rufous: rusty red in colour.

snag: a standing dead tree.

special concern: status given to a species that may become threatened in the future because it is particularly sensitive to human activities or natural events, owing to low population numbers, loss of habitat or other factors.

speculum: a brightly coloured patch in the wings of many dabbling ducks.

threatened: a species likely to become endangered if limiting factors are not reversed.

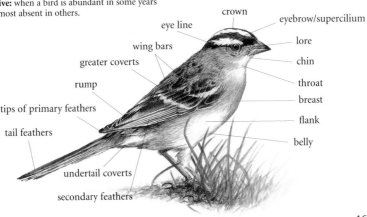

SELECT REFERENCES

Acton, D.F., G.A. Padbury and C.T. Stushnoff. 1998. *The Ecoregions of Saskatchewan.* Canadian Plains Research Centre, University of Regina, Regina.

American Ornithologists' Union. 1998. *Check-list of North American Birds.* 7th ed. (and its supplements). American Ornithologists' Union, Washington, D.C.

Choate, E.A. 1985. *The Dictionary of American Bird Names.* Rev. ed. Harvard Common Press, Cambridge, Mass.

Ehrlich, P.R., D.S. Dobkin and D. Wheye. 1988. *The Birder's Handbook: A Field Guide to the Natural History of North American Birds.* Simon & Schuster Inc., New York.

Farrand, J., ed. 1983. *The Audubon Society Master Guide to Birding.* Vols. 1–3. Alfred A. Knopf, New York.

Godfrey, W.E. 1986. *The Birds of Canada.* Rev. ed. National Museum of Natural Sciences, Ottawa.

Kaufman, K. 1996. *Lives of North American Birds.* Houghton Mifflin Co., Boston.

Kaufman, K. 2000. *Birds of North America.* Houghton Mifflin Co., New York.

Mearns, B. and R. Mearns. 1992. *Audubon to Xantus: The Lives of Those Commemorated in North American Bird Names.* Academic Press Ltd., London, England.

National Geographic Society. 1999. *Field Guide to the Birds of North America.* 3rd ed. National Geographic Society, Washington, D.C.

Peterson, R.T. 1990. *A Field Guide to the Western Birds.* 3rd ed. Houghton Mifflin Co., Boston.

Salt, W.R. and J.R. Salt. 1976. *The Birds of Alberta.* Hurtig Publishers, Edmonton.

Sibley, D.A. 2000. *National Audubon Society The Sibley Guide to Birds.* Alfred A. Knopf, New York.

Smith, A.R. 1996. *Atlas of Saskatchewan Birds.* Saskatchewan Natural History Society (Nature Saskatchewan), Regina.

Stokes, D. and L. Stokes. 1996. *Stokes Field Guide to Birds: Western Region.* Little, Brown and Co., Boston.

Terres, J.K. 1995. *The Audubon Society Encyclopedia of North American Birds.* Wings Books, New York.

CHECKLIST

The following checklist contains 427 species of birds that have been recorded in Saskatchewan. Species are grouped by family and listed in taxonomic order in accordance with the A.O.U. *Check-list of North American Birds* (7th ed.) and its supplements.

Hypothetical species, whose presence in Saskatchewan is based on unconfirmed reports, are identified by (^). Accidental species, which are known on the basis of 25 or fewer records and are not believed to occur in Saskatchewan on an annual basis, are listed in italics. An asterisk (*) identifies species that nest or have nested in the province. A plus (+) identifies introduced species. In addition, the following COSEWIC (Committee on the Status of Endangered Wildlife in Canada) risk categories are also noted: extinct or extirpated (ex), endangered (en), threatened (th) and special concern (sc).

Loons (Gaviidae)
- ❏ Red-throated Loon*
- ❏ Pacific Loon
- ❏ Common Loon*
- ❏ *Yellow-billed Loon*

Grebes (Podicipedidae)
- ❏ Pied-billed Grebe*
- ❏ Horned Grebe*
- ❏ Red-necked Grebe*
- ❏ Eared Grebe*
- ❏ Western Grebe*
- ❏ Clark's Grebe*

Pelicans (Pelicanidae)
- ❏ American White Pelican*

Cormorants (Phalacrocoracidae)
- ❏ Neotropic Cormorant^
- ❏ Double-crested Cormorant*

Herons (Ardeidae)
- ❏ American Bittern*
- ❏ *Least Bittern*
- ❏ Great Blue Heron*
- ❏ Great Egret*
- ❏ Snowy Egret*
- ❏ *Little Blue Heron*
- ❏ Tricolored Heron^
- ❏ Cattle Egret*
- ❏ *Green Heron*
- ❏ Black-crowned Night-Heron*
- ❏ *Yellow-crowned Night-Heron*

Ibises & Spoonbills (Threskiornithidae)
- ❏ Glossy Ibis^
- ❏ *White-faced Ibis*

Vultures (Cathartidae)
- ❏ Black Vulture^
- ❏ Turkey Vulture*

Waterfowl (Anatidae)
- ❏ Greater White-fronted Goose
- ❏ Snow Goose
- ❏ Ross's Goose
- ❏ Canada Goose*
- ❏ Brant
- ❏ Barnacle Goose^
- ❏ Trumpeter Swan*
- ❏ Tundra Swan*
- ❏ Wood Duck*
- ❏ Gadwall*
- ❏ *Eurasian Wigeon*
- ❏ American Wigeon*
- ❏ American Black Duck*
- ❏ Mallard*
- ❏ Blue-winged Teal*
- ❏ Cinnamon Teal*
- ❏ Northern Shoveler*
- ❏ Northern Pintail*
- ❏ *Garganey*^
- ❏ Green-winged Teal*
- ❏ Canvasback*
- ❏ Redhead*
- ❏ Common Pochard^
- ❏ Ring-necked Duck*
- ❏ *Tufted Duck*^
- ❏ Greater Scaup

(continued)
- ❏ Lesser Scaup*
- ❏ *King Eider*
- ❏ *Common Eider*
- ❏ Harlequin Duck
- ❏ Surf Scoter*
- ❏ White-winged Scoter*
- ❏ Black Scoter
- ❏ Long-tailed Duck
- ❏ Bufflehead*
- ❏ Common Goldeneye*
- ❏ Barrow's Goldeneye
- ❏ Hooded Merganser*
- ❏ Common Merganser*
- ❏ Red-breasted Merganser*
- ❏ Ruddy Duck*

Kites, Hawks & Eagles (Accipitridae)
- ❏ Osprey*
- ❏ Swallow-tailed Kite^
- ❏ *Mississippi Kite*
- ❏ Bald Eagle*
- ❏ Northern Harrier*
- ❏ Sharp-shinned Hawk*
- ❏ Cooper's Hawk*
- ❏ Northern Goshawk*
- ❏ Red-shouldered Hawk^
- ❏ Broad-winged Hawk*
- ❏ Swainson's Hawk*
- ❏ Red-tailed Hawk*
- ❏ Ferruginous Hawk* (sc)
- ❏ Rough-legged Hawk
- ❏ Golden Eagle*

Falcons & Caracaras (Falconidae)
- ❑ American Kestrel*
- ❑ Merlin*
- ❑ Gyrfalcon
- ❑ Peregrine Falcon* (th)
- ❑ Prairie Falcon*

Grouse & Allies (Phasianidae)
- ❑ Gray Partridge*+
- ❑ Ring-necked Pheasant*+
- ❑ Ruffed Grouse*
- ❑ Greater Sage-Grouse* (en)
- ❑ Spruce Grouse*
- ❑ Willow Ptarmigan
- ❑ *Rock Ptarmigan*
- ❑ Sharp-tailed Grouse*
- ❑ Greater Prairie-Chicken (ex*)
- ❑ Wild Turkey*+

Rails & Coots (Rallidae)
- ❑ Yellow Rail* (sc)
- ❑ Virginia Rail*
- ❑ Sora*
- ❑ American Coot*

Cranes (Gruidae)
- ❑ Sandhill Crane*
- ❑ Common Crane^
- ❑ Whooping Crane*

Plovers (Charadriidae)
- ❑ Black-bellied Plover
- ❑ American Golden-Plover
- ❑ Pacific Golden-Plover^
- ❑ *Snowy Plover* *
- ❑ Semipalmated Plover*
- ❑ Piping Plover* (en)
- ❑ Killdeer*
- ❑ Mountain Plover^* (en)

Stilts & Avocets (Recurvirostridae)
- ❑ *Black-necked Stilt* *
- ❑ American Avocet*

Sandpipers & Allies (Scolopacidae)
- ❑ Greater Yellowlegs*
- ❑ Lesser Yellowlegs*
- ❑ *Spotted Redshank*
- ❑ Solitary Sandpiper*
- ❑ Willet*
- ❑ Spotted Sandpiper*
- ❑ Upland Sandpiper*
- ❑ Eskimo Curlew^ (en)
- ❑ Whimbrel
- ❑ Long-billed Curlew* (sc)
- ❑ Black-tailed Godwit^
- ❑ Hudsonian Godwit
- ❑ Bar-tailed Godwit^
- ❑ Marbled Godwit*
- ❑ Ruddy Turnstone
- ❑ Surfbird^
- ❑ Red Knot
- ❑ Sanderling
- ❑ Semipalmated Sandpiper
- ❑ *Western Sandpiper*
- ❑ Red-necked Stint^
- ❑ Least Sandpiper*
- ❑ White-rumped Sandpiper
- ❑ Baird's Sandpiper
- ❑ Pectoral Sandpiper
- ❑ Sharp-tailed Sandpiper^
- ❑ Rock Sandpiper^
- ❑ Dunlin
- ❑ Curlew Sandpiper^
- ❑ Stilt Sandpiper
- ❑ Buff-breasted Sandpiper
- ❑ *Ruff*
- ❑ Short-billed Dowitcher*
- ❑ Long-billed Dowitcher
- ❑ Common Snipe*
- ❑ American Woodcock^
- ❑ Wilson's Phalarope*
- ❑ Red-necked Phalarope*
- ❑ *Red Phalarope*

Gulls & Allies (Laridae)
- ❑ *Pomarine Jaeger*
- ❑ Parasitic Jaeger
- ❑ *Long-tailed Jaeger*
- ❑ Laughing Gull^
- ❑ Franklin's Gull*
- ❑ *Little Gull*
- ❑ Bonaparte's Gull*
- ❑ Mew Gull*
- ❑ Ring-billed Gull*
- ❑ California Gull*
- ❑ Herring Gull*
- ❑ Thayer's Gull*
- ❑ Iceland Gull^
- ❑ *Lesser Black-backed Gull*
- ❑ *Slaty-backed Gull*
- ❑ Glaucous-winged Gull^
- ❑ Glaucous Gull

- ❑ Great Black-backed Gull^
- ❑ *Sabine's Gull*
- ❑ *Black-legged Kittiwake*
- ❑ Ross's Gull^
- ❑ Ivory Gull^
- ❑ Caspian Tern*
- ❑ Common Tern*
- ❑ Arctic Tern*
- ❑ Forster's Tern*
- ❑ *Least Tern*
- ❑ Black Tern*

Alcids (Alcidae)
- ❑ *Black Guillemot*
- ❑ Pigeon Guillemot^
- ❑ Long-billed Murrelet^
- ❑ Ancient Murrelet^

Pigeons & Doves (Columbidae)
- ❑ Rock Dove*+
- ❑ *Band-tailed Pigeon*
- ❑ *Eurasian Collared-Dove*
- ❑ Mourning Dove*
- ❑ Passenger Pigeon (ex*)

Cuckoos (Cuculidae)
- ❑ Black-billed Cuckoo*
- ❑ Yellow-billed Cuckoo^

Owls (Strigidae)
- ❑ *Barn Owl*
- ❑ Flammulated Owl^
- ❑ Western Screech-Owl^
- ❑ Eastern Screech-Owl*
- ❑ Great Horned Owl*
- ❑ Snowy Owl
- ❑ Northern Hawk Owl*
- ❑ Burrowing Owl* (en)
- ❑ Barred Owl*
- ❑ Great Gray Owl*
- ❑ Long-eared Owl*
- ❑ Short-eared Owl* (sc)
- ❑ Boreal Owl*
- ❑ Northern Saw-whet Owl*

Nightjars (Caprimulgidae)
- ❑ Common Nighthawk*
- ❑ Common Poorwill*
- ❑ Whip-poor-will*

Swifts (Apodidae)
- ❑ Black Swift^
- ❑ Chimney Swift*

Hummingbirds (Trochilidae)
- ❑ Ruby-throated Hummingbird*
- ❑ Black-chinned Hummingbird^
- ❑ *Anna's Hummingbird*
- ❑ *Calliope Hummingbird*
- ❑ *Rufous Hummingbird*

Kingfishers (Alcedinidae)
- ❑ Belted Kingfisher*

Woodpeckers (Picidae)
- ❑ Lewis's Woodpecker
- ❑ Red-headed Woodpecker* (sc)
- ❑ *Red-bellied Woodpecker*
- ❑ *Williamson's Sapsucker*
- ❑ Yellow-bellied Sapsucker*
- ❑ Red-naped Sapsucker*
- ❑ Downy Woodpecker*
- ❑ Hairy Woodpecker*
- ❑ Three-toed Woodpecker*
- ❑ Black-backed Woodpecker*
- ❑ Northern Flicker*
- ❑ Pileated Woodpecker*

Flycatchers (Tyrannidae)
- ❑ Olive-sided Flycatcher*
- ❑ Western Wood-Pewee*
- ❑ Eastern Wood-Pewee
- ❑ Yellow-bellied Flycatcher*
- ❑ Acadian Flycatcher^
- ❑ Alder Flycatcher*
- ❑ Willow Flycatcher*
- ❑ Least Flycatcher*
- ❑ Gray Flycatcher^
- ❑ Dusky Flycatcher
- ❑ Eastern Phoebe*
- ❑ Say's Phoebe*
- ❑ Great Crested Flycatcher*
- ❑ Great Kiskadee^
- ❑ Western Kingbird*
- ❑ Eastern Kingbird*
- ❑ *Scissor-tailed Flycatcher*
- ❑ Fork-tailed Flycatcher^

Shrikes (Laniidae)
- ❑ Loggerhead Shrike* (th)
- ❑ Northern Shrike*

Vireos (Vireonidae)
- ❑ *White-eyed Vireo*
- ❑ Yellow-throated Vireo*
- ❑ Blue-headed Vireo*
- ❑ Plumbeous Vireo^
- ❑ Warbling Vireo*
- ❑ Philadelphia Vireo*
- ❑ Red-eyed Vireo*

Crows, Jays & Magpies (Corvidae)
- ❑ Gray Jay*
- ❑ *Steller's Jay*
- ❑ Blue Jay*
- ❑ Pinyon Jay^
- ❑ *Clark's Nutcracker*
- ❑ Black-billed Magpie*
- ❑ American Crow*
- ❑ Common Raven*

Larks (Alaudidae)
- ❑ Horned Lark*

Swallows (Hirundinidae)
- ❑ Purple Martin*
- ❑ Tree Swallow*
- ❑ Violet-green Swallow*
- ❑ Northern Rough-winged Swallow*
- ❑ Bank Swallow*
- ❑ Cliff Swallow*
- ❑ Barn Swallow*

Chickadees & Titmice (Paridae)
- ❑ Black-capped Chickadee*
- ❑ *Mountain Chickadee*
- ❑ Boreal Chickadee*
- ❑ Bridled Titmouse^
- ❑ Tufted Titmouse^

Nuthatches (Sittidae)
- ❑ Red-breasted Nuthatch*
- ❑ White-breasted Nuthatch*
- ❑ Pygmy Nuthatch^

Creepers (Certhiidae)
- ❑ Brown Creeper*

Wrens (Troglodytidae)
- ❑ Cactus Wren^
- ❑ Rock Wren*
- ❑ Canyon Wren^
- ❑ Carolina Wren^
- ❑ House Wren*
- ❑ Winter Wren*
- ❑ Sedge Wren*
- ❑ Marsh Wren*

Dippers (Cinclidae)
- ❑ *American Dipper*

Kinglets (Regulidae)
- ❑ Golden-crowned Kinglet*
- ❑ Ruby-crowned Kinglet*

Gnatcatchers (Sylviidae)
- ❑ Blue-gray Gnatcatcher^

Thrushes (Turdidae)
- ❑ Northern Wheatear^
- ❑ Eastern Bluebird*
- ❑ Western Bluebird^
- ❑ Mountain Bluebird*
- ❑ Townsend's Solitaire*
- ❑ Veery*
- ❑ Gray-cheeked Thrush*
- ❑ Swainson's Thrush*
- ❑ Hermit Thrush*
- ❑ *Wood Thrush*
- ❑ American Robin*
- ❑ Varied Thrush

Mockingbirds & Thrashers (Mimidae)
- ❑ Gray Catbird*
- ❑ Northern Mockingbird*
- ❑ Sage Thrasher* (en)
- ❑ Brown Thrasher*
- ❑ Bendire's Thrasher^
- ❑ Curve-billed Thrasher^

Starlings (Sturnidae)
- ❑ European Starling*+

Pipits (Motacillidae)
- ❑ American Pipit
- ❑ Sprague's Pipit* (th)

Waxwings (Bombycillidae)
- ❑ Bohemian Waxwing*
- ❑ Cedar Waxwing*

Wood-Warblers (Parulidae)
- ❏ *Blue-winged Warbler*
- ❏ *Golden-winged Warbler*
- ❏ Tennessee Warbler*
- ❏ Orange-crowned Warbler*
- ❏ Nashville Warbler*
- ❏ *Northern Parula*
- ❏ Yellow Warbler*
- ❏ Chestnut-sided Warbler*
- ❏ Magnolia Warbler*
- ❏ Cape May Warbler*
- ❏ Black-throated Blue Warbler*
- ❏ Yellow-rumped Warbler*
- ❏ *Black-throated Gray Warbler*
- ❏ Black-throated Green Warbler*
- ❏ *Townsend's Warbler* *
- ❏ Blackburnian Warbler*
- ❏ Yellow-throated Warbler^
- ❏ Pine Warbler
- ❏ Prairie Warbler^
- ❏ Palm Warbler*
- ❏ Bay-breasted Warbler*
- ❏ Blackpoll Warbler*
- ❏ Black-and-white Warbler*
- ❏ American Redstart*
- ❏ *Prothonotary Warbler*
- ❏ Worm-eating Warbler^
- ❏ Ovenbird*
- ❏ Northern Waterthrush*
- ❏ Kentucky Warbler^
- ❏ Connecticut Warbler*
- ❏ Mourning Warbler*
- ❏ MacGillivray's Warbler*
- ❏ Common Yellowthroat*
- ❏ *Hooded Warbler*
- ❏ Wilson's Warbler*
- ❏ Canada Warbler*
- ❏ Yellow-breasted Chat*

Tanagers (Thraupidae)
- ❏ *Summer Tanager*
- ❏ Scarlet Tanager*
- ❏ Western Tanager*

Sparrows & Allies (Emberizidae)
- ❏ *Green-tailed Towhee*
- ❏ Spotted Towhee*
- ❏ Eastern Towhee*
- ❏ American Tree Sparrow*
- ❏ Chipping Sparrow*
- ❏ Clay-colored Sparrow*
- ❏ Brewer's Sparrow*
- ❏ Field Sparrow
- ❏ Vesper Sparrow*
- ❏ Lark Sparrow*
- ❏ *Black-throated Sparrow*
- ❏ Lark Bunting*
- ❏ Savannah Sparrow*
- ❏ Grasshopper Sparrow*
- ❏ Baird's Sparrow*
- ❏ Le Conte's Sparrow*
- ❏ Nelson's Sharp-tailed Sparrow*
- ❏ Fox Sparrow*
- ❏ Song Sparrow*
- ❏ Lincoln's Sparrow*
- ❏ Swamp Sparrow*
- ❏ White-throated Sparrow*
- ❏ Harris's Sparrow*
- ❏ White-crowned Sparrow*
- ❏ *Golden-crowned Sparrow*
- ❏ Dark-eyed Junco*
- ❏ McCown's Longspur*
- ❏ Lapland Longspur
- ❏ Smith's Longspur
- ❏ Chestnut-collared Longspur*
- ❏ Snow Bunting
- ❏ McKay's Bunting^

Grosbeaks & Buntings (Cardinalidae)
- ❏ *Northern Cardinal*
- ❏ Rose-breasted Grosbeak*
- ❏ Black-headed Grosbeak*
- ❏ Blue Grosbeak^
- ❏ Lazuli Bunting*
- ❏ Indigo Bunting*
- ❏ Painted Bunting^
- ❏ *Dickcissel* *

Blackbirds & Allies (Icteridae)
- ❏ Bobolink*
- ❏ Red-winged Blackbird*
- ❏ Western Meadowlark*
- ❏ Yellow-headed Blackbird*
- ❏ Rusty Blackbird*
- ❏ Brewer's Blackbird*
- ❏ Common Grackle*
- ❏ Great-tailed Grackle^
- ❏ Brown-headed Cowbird*
- ❏ Orchard Oriole*
- ❏ Baltimore Oriole*
- ❏ Bullock's Oriole*

Finches (Fringillidae)
- ❏ *Brambling*
- ❏ Gray-crowned Rosy-Finch
- ❏ Black Rosy-Finch^
- ❏ Pine Grosbeak*
- ❏ Purple Finch*
- ❏ Cassin's Finch^
- ❏ House Finch*+
- ❏ Red Crossbill*
- ❏ White-winged Crossbill*
- ❏ Common Redpoll*
- ❏ Hoary Redpoll
- ❏ Pine Siskin*
- ❏ Lesser Goldfinch^
- ❏ American Goldfinch*
- ❏ Oriental Greenfinch^
- ❏ Evening Grosbeak*

Old World Sparrows (Passeridae)
- ❏ House Sparrow*+

INDEX OF SCIENTIFIC NAMES

This index references only the primary species accounts.

INDEX OF COMMON NAMES

Page numbers in boldface refer to primary, illustrated species accounts.

ABOUT THE AUTHOR

An exacting scientist, inspired wildlife artist and all-around outdoor enthusiast, Alan Smith has travelled Saskatchewan extensively seeking the records of fellow birders and in search of new bird sightings. He is author of *Atlas of Saskatchewan Birds*, a comprehensive guide chronicling bird sightings in Saskatchewan, and has worked for the Canadian Wildlife Service for close to 30 years. This career has taken him all over Saskatchewan as well as to such faraway places as the High Arctic to study seabirds and Costa Rica to study North American songbirds. Most recently, he has been involved in the establishment and operation of the Last Mountain Bird Observatory on the north shore of Last Mountain Lake.

ABOUT THE CONTRIBUTORS

Eloise Pulos has a B.Sc. and is a keen naturalist who has spent many field seasons studying woodpeckers in Alberta and British Columbia. She was recently part of a wildlife field study in southern Africa. Eloise has edited or contributed to a number of Lone Pine bird guides.

Chris Fisher is a wildlife biologist who researched endangered species management and wildlife interpretation as part of a graduate degree. He enjoys sharing his enthusiasm for nature and is author or coauthor of a number of Lone Pine field guides.

Andy Bezener has a degree in conservation biology and has done fieldwork for the Canadian Wildlife Service. His concern and admiration for wilderness and wildlife have inspired him to coauthor a number of Lone Pine field guides.